MATTER AND MIND

MATTER AND MIND
TWO ESSAYS IN EPISTEMOLOGY

İlham Dilman

BOOKS
10 East 53d St. New York 10022
(a division of Harper & Row Publishers, Inc.)

© İlham Dilman 1975

First published 1975 by
THE MACMILLAN PRESS LTD
London and Basingstoke

Published in the U.S.A. 1975 by
HARPER & ROW PUBLISHERS, INC.
BARNES & NOBLE IMPORT DIVISION

ISBN 0-06-491689-8
0333188330
Printed in Great Britain

Contents

Preface

It is a central contention of this book that it makes no sense to doubt the existence of the material world and the existence of 'other minds'. This is not to say that we cannot be said to *know* such things as that the car park is full or that a friend is angry, pleased or distressed. *Can* we know such things? If so, *how* do we know them? The book is an investigation of these questions.

In Part One questions about the existence of material things and our knowledge of it are seen to emerge largely from a tendency to rarefy the basis of our claims to knowledge in this sphere. It is rarefied into the philosopher's 'sense-data propositions' from which it becomes impossible to find our way back to the claims in question. The central difficulty is sometimes expressed in the following way:

> 'Whenever anything is perceived, it is always and necessarily sense-data that are perceived.'

I argue that this is an illusion. In Part Two I push this difficulty further:

> 'Whenever anything is really seen, it is always I who see it.'

Thus while in Part One our attention centres largely, but not wholly, on the tendency to make the philosopher's 'sense-data' either into a barrier to our knowledge of the material world or into the very material of it, in Part Two it is the philosopher's 'I', in this place, which becomes the centre of our attention – at least in Chapters Three to Seven. Solipsism emerges as one of the centres towards which the discussion gravitates.

vii

Part One Moore had claimed that his premise that here is a hand
entails his conclusion that there are material things and that by
asserting the former he could prove the existence of material
things. It was this that led me to note (Chapter Two) the distinction between formal concepts and ordinary concepts. A
consideration of this distinction made us notice that whereas a
person may know what e.g. a unicorn is without knowing
whether or not there are unicorns, he cannot likewise know
what a material thing is without knowing that there are such
things as sticks and stones. There is no distinction between
'possessing the concept of a material thing' and 'knowing that
there are such things as sticks and stones'. Possessing that concept is being familiar with the overall role in language of a
whole host of words; and that means being familiar with a
whole set of interrelated practices, being able to take part in
them. This overall role which Wittgenstein calls 'grammar'
guarantees the *possibility* of saying many true things with these
words. That is why you can say of a formal concept that its
essence implies its existence.

I argue that what Moore thought he had proved cannot be
proved, or even stated, nor can it be doubted or denied. But
philosophers seem to have doubted or denied it. The question
is: *What* were they doubting or denying? My answer may be
summarised as follows:

A. (a) 'Matter doesn't exist' →   (b) 'Matter is nothing over
   and above our sense impressions'
   The arrow is meant to signify a transition effected by
   philosophical argument. We cannot substitute the equivalence sign ($\equiv$) in place of the arrow without qualification.
B. How far is (b) like and how far unlike (c) 'The average
   man doesn't exist'? I argue (Chapter Seven) that while
   we may characterise (c) as a *logical* claim, we may characterise (b) as a *conceptual* one – though again not without
   qualification.

To appreciate what a philosopher who says 'Matter doesn't
exist' wants to deny we have to consider his words in their
philosophical setting – and this involves taking account of the
difficulties he is trying to meet or surmount. If we do so we shall

see that whatever may be wrong with denying the existence of matter one cannot oppose it in the way Moore does – one cannot prove it wrong. It calls for a different kind of work.

In a nutshell, in the first half of Part One I consider (A) Moore's conclusion and (B) the philosophical assertion he tried to refute. This involves considering the relation between Moore's premise and his conclusion (Does P entail C?) and the relation between Moore's conclusion and the assertion he tried to prove wrong (Are they contradictory?). The questions at the centre of these considerations are:

(A) Can one directly state or prove what Moore wanted to assert?
    Can one affirm or support what belongs to *grammar*?
(B) Can one disprove what Berkeley or McTaggart had asserted?
    Can one refute a *philosophical* claim in the way Moore tried to refute it?
(a) If not, how is one to bring out what is wrong with it? Might there not also be something right about it?
(b) If Moore's proof does not show Berkeley or McTaggart to be wrong, does it not still achieve something important?

You cannot meet the question 'Do material things exist?' head on as Moore did – it is not an *empirical* question. Neither can you meet the transformed question 'Are material things anything over and above our sense impressions?' head on – it is not a *logical* question like 'Is the average man anyone over and above individual men?' (i) It is these questions themselves we need to scrutinize and the terms in which they are asked – e.g. the concept of a sense-datum or sense impression, the 'assumption' that whenever we make a claim about a stick or stone we necessarily base our claims on our sense impressions. (ii) We must also make clear what the 'externality', the 'continued and independent existence' of material things amounts to:

If there is a grammatical difference between an after-image and a physical object does it follow that we can at best have inductive reasons for our claims about physical objects?

This is one question I discuss in the second half of Part One.

There I turn to Moore's premise. I ask:

(C) Why can one not prove P? Why can one not doubt it?

Moore had said 'I know P' and part of his reason was 'I cannot doubt P'. He said 'I know things that I cannot prove', but was undecided over whether *as a philosopher* he ought to be able to prove P. He was divided in his response because he, himself, shared some of the assumptions made by the sceptic who wants a proof of P. On the other hand, behind his qualms there is some recognition that something further needs to be done if scepticism is to be met. I ask:

(D) Where exactly does the philosophical sceptic demand a proof in connection with Moore's premise? What does he want proved before he concedes that we can and do know it?

I point out three difficulties with which the sceptic is impressed in connection with Moore's premise, three difficulties which he finds insurmountable:

(i) If material things have a continued and independent existence then we can at best know them indirectly. In that case, if we know them, it must be possible to show that the step from our sense impressions to the claims we make about physical objects is justified.

(ii) If material things have a continued and independent existence so that propositions about material things are predictive in character, then on no occasion can we do enough by way of making sure that such a proposition as Moore's premise will not turn out to be false.

(iii) When it seems to me that I see a hand I may be dreaming. Therefore unless I know that I am not dreaming I cannot know that there is a hand before me.

So the sceptic's claim 'We cannot know P' is a way of saying that these difficulties cannot be surmounted. His demand for a proof is a demand that he should be shown a way to surmount these difficulties. What he asks for may be expressed as follows: 'Show me or prove that the step from our sense impressions to the claims we make about physical objects is justified. Show me or prove that there are circumstances in which we can claim a physical object proposition to be true come what *further* may. Prove that I can know that I am not dreaming now, or at least that I cannot intelligibly ask whether I might be dreaming now.' What needs to be shown in connection with (i) is not that the step is justified but that in the normal case there is no step. In other words, Moore's premise is not based on evidence even if we know it to be true because we can see Moore lifting his hands, and would not know it to be true in the same way were we blind. We can have direct knowledge of physical objects (Chapter Ten). In connection with (iii), which I do not discuss here, what needs to be shown is that the suggestion that I may be dreaming now is senseless, that I cannot entertain such a thought with regard to myself. I discuss (ii) in Chapter Eleven.

When we recognise the sceptic's difficulties we see that what provides an obstacle to the knowledge he doubts we have are features of the *grammar* in which we talk about physical things. He sees them as obstacles because of unexamined assumptions he makes which embody conceptual confusion.

Still his search for what is indubitable is of great importance in philosophy, even if his failure to find it in this area of talk and thought comes from confusion. What is important to see is the sense in which some propositions are beyond doubt and proof or justification (Chapter Twelve).

Part Two Some of the same themes reemerge. We see in Chapter Two that the philosophical affirmation that the soul exists, or that men have souls, like Moore's affirmation of the existence of matter, is an attempt to bring into focus a whole dimension of our life and speech. There are interesting parallels – for instance, how the many claims we make in both spheres of discourse seem to go beyond what they are ultimately based on, so that what knowledge we can have in both cases appears as at best necessarily indirect. In both parts of the book I argue that we *can* have direct knowledge – direct knowledge of what stands before our eyes and direct knowledge of other people's thoughts, intentions, feelings and desires:

(i) What we perceive is not always a sense-datum. Only in *special* cases is this so – e.g. when we see an hallucination.

(ii) What we are faced with in our contacts with other people is not always a barrier or façade. Only in *special* cases is this so – e.g. when people are insincere, mistrust us, are afraid of us, are interested in getting something out of us and so have ulterior motives, when they are self-deceived, etc.

A discussion of this question involves making use of Wittgenstein's distinction between symptoms and criteria. I introduce and discuss this distinction in Part One, Chapter Ten, and return to it in Part Two, Chapter Eight.

More interesting, however, are the differences between the grammatical categories brought into focus – the differences between things and persons. In fact, one thing that begins to emerge out of our epistemological inquiries in Part Two is the grammatical silhouette of a human being. We see, for instance, the profound difference which speaking a language makes to the kind of beings we are. The very possibility of thought and reasoning, and much that we feel and do, is bound up with this – including the possibility of lying about ourselves and hiding our feelings and intentions from other people. We get an inkling of the kind of interdependence there is between the unity of a person's life and the unity of the language he speaks and the culture from which he derives sustenance. A man's identity as a human being is rooted in the life and culture he shares with other people. Hence from the outset (Part Two, Chapter Two) we are led to suspect that there is something wrong with the inner-outer dichotomy, as made by philosophers, which introduces a gulf between people which cannot be bridged.

Two conceptual splits are responsible for this gulf:

(i) Between the meanings of words and the kind of life in the weave of which they are used. Hence: 'I cannot tell you what I *mean*.'
(ii) Between people's states of mind and the circumstances in which they find expression, as well as the expressions themselves. Hence: 'I cannot show you what I *feel*.'

Hence I approach this supposed gulf from two angles:

(i) The possibility of a language which only I can

understand (Chapter Four).

(ii) The possibility that I might be the only sentient and intelligent being in existence (Chapter Five).

Both these turn out to be philosophical illusions on examination. Considerations which show us that the actions and reactions into which our words enter are not external to the forms of communication we carry on with each other by means of these words also bring out the kind of conceptual tie there is between our mental life and behaviour. Hence Chapters Four and Eight are closely connected.

In Chapters Four and Five I consider the tendency to think:

(A) 'I cannot understand what you mean by "red" and "pain".' (This is the reverse of 'I cannot tell you or get you to understand what I mean by "red" and "pain".')

In Chapter Six I consider the tendency to think:

(B) 'I cannot feel your sensations; I cannot have numerically the same sensation that you have.'

This leads us to consider two further problems:

(a) Whether our sensations are objects of acquaintance – the idea of introspection as a species of perception.

(b) In what sense I 'own' my sensations and other mental states. How sensations are individuated at all.

The latter questions lead us to examine what is distinctive about the use of the personal pronoun in connection with mental states and how this enters into the logic of psychological discourse (Chapter Seven).

Earlier I had quoted Wittgenstein's words: 'If one sees the behaviour of a living thing one sees its soul' (*Inv.* sec. 357). Part of what Wittgenstein means is that the *possibility* of joy and sorrow, love, grief, hope and despair depends on the life and behaviour of those who are capable of these things, so that the reality of the soul can be seen in human behaviour. This was the topic of Chapter Two. Another part of what Wittgenstein means is that we can see what state of soul a man is in, whether for instance he is joyful or depressed, in his behaviour. This is the topic of Chapter Eight. In Chapter Nine I try to pull together the different strands of the argument in Part Two and to bring into relief how Wittgenstein cuts through the opposition between Behaviourism and Cartesianism in the philosophy of mind. (This parallels the way he cut through the opposition between Conventionalism and Realism in the philosophy of logic and mathematics.)

Let me say at once that none of the points I make in this book are original. They come largely from Wittgenstein. Those who are familiar with Professor John Wisdom's work will know how much indebted I am to him in my treatment of them. It is their arrangement that is my own, the way I have connected them together in a continuous argument. I hope that this provides a fresh perspective on them or, at least, an appreciation which is lost if one takes them in isolation – as it is easy to do if one gets bogged down in detail. The detail is, of course, important and in working through it at the different stages of the argument I have aimed at clarity. If I have succeeded in these two aims I hope that this book will contribute to a better understanding of Wittgenstein and help the student of epistemology.

I am grateful to Professor Godfrey Vesey for allowing me to use here Part I of my paper 'Wittgenstein on the Soul' which appeared in the seventh volume of the Royal Institute of Philosophy Lectures, *Understanding Wittgenstein*, of which he was the editor.

Works referred to by initials in the text are identified in the Bibliography.

March 1975   İlham Dilman

Part One

Moore's 'Proof of an External World'

1 Moore's Proof

Moore's proof was directed against such philosophers as McTaggart who denied the existence of the material world, and not against the sceptic who denies our knowledge of its existence.

Moore thought it quite preposterous that anyone should deny the existence of material things, 'things outside of us', 'independent of our minds' as he goes on to explain at length in his British Academy Lecture. He thought that we all *believe* that there are material things and that we are right to do so. He further thought that it was a task of philosophy to show or demonstrate that we are right. He would have said that the generality and fundamental character of this belief makes its defence a task for the philosopher.

In 'A Defence of Common Sense' he gives examples of philosophical assertions that are in conflict with what we all believe:

'Material things are not real'
'Space is not real'
'Time is not real'
'The Self is not real'.

He admits that these expressions are ambiguous and that some philosophers who have used them did not put forward views which contradicted what we all believe – beliefs which he attributes to 'common sense'. However he is sure that *some* did and that they *meant* to do so.

His paper 'Proof of an External World' begins with a long discussion of what it is exactly that he intends to prove, a long discussion of what it *means* to speak of an 'external world', of 'things external to our minds and to be met with in space'. This is important for his proof – as we shall see.

The proof itself is extremely simple:

Premise: He holds up his hands saying 'Here is one hand and here is another' and claims that it is *absurd* to suggest that I don't know this. In other words, it is certainly true that two human hands exist.

Conclusion: It follows that it is certainly true that at least two material objects exist. In other words, there are material things, things outside of us and to be met with in space – in the sense explained in the earlier part of the paper.

Moore argues that for a proof of this kind to be valid three conditions at least must be satisfied:

(1) The Premise and the Conclusion *must be different*.
(2) I *must know* the premise to be true.
(3) The Premise *must entail* the Conclusion.

He argues that all these three conditions are in fact satisfied in the case of his proof and that, therefore, he has given a valid proof of what philosophers like McTaggart have denied.

Are these three conditions satisfied?

(1) Moore says that the premise and the conclusion are different since the premise could have been false while the conclusion could have still been true. There may not have been two human hands here, or any human hands at all, but there may still have been material things – tables, chairs, sticks and stones. I shall not query this now, though I think there is something wrong about putting it this way. This will become clear when I consider condition (3).

(2) Does Moore know the premise to be true? He says: 'How absurd it would be to suggest that I did not know that here is one hand and here is another, but only believed it, and that perhaps it was not the case! You might as well suggest that I do not know that I am now standing up and talking – that perhaps after all I'm not, and that it's not quite certain that I am!' (pp. 146–7).

I shall consider this later in connection with scepticism.

(3) Does the premise entail the conclusion? (This is related to the question whether they are different. For the claim that they

are different is that if C is true it does not follow that P is true, while the claim that P entails C is that if P is true then C must be true.)

Moore thinks that the answer to the question whether his premise entails his conclusion is an obvious Yes. His claim is that his conclusion follows from his premise in the same way in which 'There are three misprints on this page' follows from 'Here's one' (pointing to a misprint on the page in question) and 'Here's one' and 'Here's another':

> Are there any other conditions necessary for a rigorous proof, such that perhaps it did not satisfy one of them? Perhaps there may be; I do not know; but I do want to emphasise that, so far as I can see, we all of us do constantly take proofs of this sort as absolutely conclusive proofs of certain conclusions – as finally settling certain questions, as to which we were previously in doubt. Suppose, for instance, it were a question whether there were as many as three misprints on a certain page in a certain book. A says there are, B is inclined to doubt it. How could A prove that he is right? Surely he *could* prove it by taking the book, turning to the page, and pointing to the three separate places on it, saying 'There's one misprint here, another here, and another here': surely that is a method by which it *might* be proved! (p. 147)

We see that Moore thinks that the philosopher's doubt about the existence of material things is *like* B's doubt as to whether there are any misprints on a certain page. He thinks that the assertion that there are material things is *like* A's assertion that there are three misprints on that page. So his view is that the existence of material things follows from the assertion that here are two hands *in the same way as* that 'there are three misprints on this page' follows from 'here's one, here's another, and here's yet another' uttered while pointing to the page.

These are not three different comparisons or alleged analogies, but three different aspects of the same comparison. I shall begin by considering the third aspect of this comparison. We shall see that Moore's claim that his premise does entail his conclusion turns on its adequacy.

2 Is a Material Thing a Kind of Thing?

Let us begin with Moore's example. A says that there are three misprints on p. 240 of this book. B says: 'I have just read that page carefully and I can say confidently that there are no misprints there.' Obviously both A and B are literate people and know what a misprint is. Both know how to spell and they agree on the spelling of words. For instance, it is not the case that one is English and one American so that when they see a word spelt 'color' one thinks it is a misprint and the other thinks it is not. Still it is possible for B to have read the page in question and to have overlooked some misprints. Now that A points them out to him B sees them and has to admit that there are three misprints on that page.

Here B is shown something and he recognises it as an instance of a misprint. So he admits that he was wrong in saying that there are no misprints on that page. Why had he said this? Because he had read the page and, being a proof-reader, had looked for misprints there, but he had seen none. Obviously he could neither miss misprints, nor come to recognise them later, unless he knew how to read and write, how to spell words, and therefore what it means to misspell them. So it is presupposed that he knows what a misprint is – and this means that he *can* recognise misprints when he sees them, or more pedantically that he can recognise instances of misprints. But what is it to be able to do so? To be able to tell when a word is spelt or printed incorrectly and when it is spelt or printed correctly.

Take another example. If there is a car, a lorry, and a bus in the car park then there are three motor vehicles there. Why? Because each is an instance of a motor vehicle.

Now is a hand an instance of a material thing? If we have read any philosophy we may want to say that it is. For it is usually in philosophy books that we meet the expression 'material thing', and there the meaning of this expression is explained in the first place by means of such examples as tables and chairs, sticks and stones, bodies and their parts. So if we are asked whether a hand is an instance of a material thing, it will be natural for us to answer Yes.

But is there anything wrong in saying that a hand is an instance of a material thing? If it is wrong, how is it wrong? Is it wrong in the way that if we said that a whale is an instance of a fish we would be saying something wrong? Surely not. Is it a mistake in logic – one which a logic book would help us to detect and correct? Surely not.

Someone who admits that a hand is a material thing may nevertheless refuse to speak of it as an instance of a material thing. He may say that one would be wrong to take the copula here to indicate class-membership. This is at best a warning and as such, I think, sound. But the man who speaks like this cannot enlist the support of any logic book for what he says. His claim, if it is to remain abstract, will be doctrinaire. For whether someone who says that a hand is an instance of a material thing is saying something objectionable or not depends entirely on what he goes on to do with his words. The remark is perfectly innocent and carries no commitments beyond those which the speaker wishes to embrace. If I criticise Moore on this point, it will be for the construction he put on this idea, for what he went on to do with it, and for what this way of speaking, natural and understandable in itself, blinded him to.

What does saying that a hand is an instance of a material thing amount to and how does it differ from saying that a car is an instance of a motor vehicle, or that this (in Moore's example) is an instance of a misprint? I think that there is an important difference which Moore did not recognise. He knew that there are differences and admitted this in his reply to Miss Ambrose-Lazerowitz, but he did not recognise that they have far-reaching implications for his proof. In his reply to Miss Ambrose this is what he says:

She insists that the conception of 'external object' is a very different sort of conception, in important respects, from such conceptions as 'human hand' or 'coin'; and seems to suggest that though you can *prove* that at least one coin exists by producing a dime, you cannot prove that at least one external object exists in the same way. Now I have no doubt that she is right that there *are* extremely important differences between 'external object' and 'coin'; but as regards at least one respect in which she alleges that there is a difference between them, she is, I think, suggesting, if not saying, something false. She says (p. 406) 'Consider now teaching someone the phrase 'external object'. The difficulty would be that one could not *point out* anything to him which was not an external object.' Now if 'point out' is taken literally to mean 'point with the finger at', this may be true. But in a sense, which is, it seems to me, very relevant to our problem, it is not true. One *can* point to a person an object which is *not* an external object by the method which I suggested just now for finding an object of the sort which I should call a 'sense datum'. You can say to him: 'Look at a bright light for a little while; then close your eyes; the round blue patch you will then see is not an external object.' After-images, seen with closed eyes, are *not* external objects; and you *can* arrange that a person should see an after-image. And it seems to me that the contrast with objects of this sort enters into the meaning of 'external object'. But, whatever be the important differences between the conception 'external object' and such a conception as 'coin', I cannot understand what argument can be given to show that, *owing* to these differences, whereas producing a dime *can* prove that at least one coin exists, it *cannot* prove that at least one external object exists. ('A Reply to My Critics', *Philosophy of G. E. Moore*, p. 671)

Miss Ambrose had asked if 'external object' (or for that matter 'material thing') is a *general name*, and whether one can *point to* an external object as one can point to any kind of thing – e.g. a coin. If you can point to something, for instance a penny, and say that it is a coin, or an instance of the kind of thing we mean by 'coin', then you must be able to point to things that are not of that kind, but which perhaps one might confuse with it, such as a counter, a jetton, or even a button. A person who knows what a coin is can distinguish one from such other things, though he sometimes makes mistakes and takes for a coin what is not one. When you teach someone, say a child, what a coin is you generally point to coins and also to other things and indicate differences. Miss Ambrose asks how all this applies to 'external object' or 'material thing'. She says: 'The difficulty would be that one could not *point out* anything to him which was not an external object.' A bit further down she continues:

> The order 'Bring me an external object' has the peculiarity that anyone who brought one anything at all could not fail to carry it out. Carrying out the order would provide no means of testing whether the person had learned the use of 'external object'. We have not provided for the possibility of making a mistake, and hence there is no way of testing whether we have taught him. In fact there is no way of teaching him if there is no possibility of testing whether he has learned what we have taught. These considerations show, it seems to me, that 'external object' is not a general name for some kind of thing, designating features distinguishing that kind of thing from some other kind. One can only bring something which this names if one can fail to bring it. If this is the case then one cannot *point out* an external object, so that no argument about the existence of external objects could be settled by 'pointing out an external object'. (*Essays in Analysis*, pp. 222–3)

Can one point to or point out a material thing? One is at first inclined to say 'Of course' – pointing to e.g. the ashtray in front of one. But this is not a pedestrian question and the answer to it is by no means obvious. In fact I don't think that there is a short answer Yes or No to it – just as the earlier question 'Is a hand an instance of a material thing?' has no short answer Yes or No. When does one ever point to a material object – under that description? When is one ever asked to point to a material thing? For whose benefit?

Compare with whether one can point to the colour of a thing? Certainly one can point to a red thing and then to a blue thing. Then while one's finger is still pointing someone entering the room may ask: 'What are you pointing at?' One may answer: 'I am pointing to the colour of this vase. I was saying: Look how blue it is.' But here there is the possibility of being misunderstood. He might have thought I was pointing to its shape. I might have said (while pointing): 'Look at its curves – how pleasing its shape!' Notice that here I have provided a context to give sense to the words 'pointing to the colour of a thing'.

I can point to a blue thing because I can point to a thing that is not blue – e.g. a red thing. Similarly, I can point to the colour of a thing because I can point to another quality of that thing – e.g. its shape, its size, etc. But in contrast with what would I be pointing to a material thing? Its shadow? In that case what would I say? I am not pointing to the shadow, I am pointing to the ashtray. *Not* to the material thing.

What about an after-image, or a sense-datum? 'I don't want you to describe your sense-data; I want you to describe the material thing!' Moore thinks that this is a genuine contrast and that it makes it possible for the words 'pointing to (or pointing out) a material thing' to have sense. I would agree with Moore this far. It is a genuine contrast and *where it is applicable* one can genuinely point out a material thing to someone. But is it applicable in the context in which Moore sets out to prove that there are at least two material things? I do not think so. Let me explain.

Perhaps during a psychological experiment on perception the experimenter may direct the subject's attention to his visual field and its contents. Say the subject is looking at a penny from an angle. He is asked whether what he sees is round or not. He replies that it is round. The experimenter then asks him whether it *looks* round. Again, and quite correctly, he answers that it looks round. The experimenter now says: 'Yes, that is because you know that what you are looking at is a penny. But try to forget that. Concentrate on how it appears to you – that is all we are interested in.' The subject may end up by saying that what he sees is elliptical – or in technical jargon: 'The shape in my visual field is elliptical.' Here when he describes what he sees what the subject refers to is *not* a material thing. In these *special circumstances* perhaps one can say 'Tell me what you see – I mean in your visual field', and then 'Now tell me what you see – I mean on the table'. Here, perhaps, one may be said to point from a material object, or its shape, to the contents of the subject's visual field, and then back to the shape of the object before his eyes. In *these* circumstances if I say, 'Now describe this', pointing to the penny, I may be said to be pointing to a material thing. For they provide a special context in which it makes sense to talk of 'pointing to a material thing' *in contrast with* a sense-datum.

The circumstances I have imagined, however, are very different from those in which Moore lifts up his hands to prove the existence of material things. The subject of the experiment understands the contrast between what he is supposed to describe in the two cases – the contrast between what he sees and how what he sees appears to him if he can forget what it is that he is looking at. This latter notion, in any case, involves the notion of 'what it is he is looking at' – something which the subject is asked deliberately to forget. One can only grasp that latter notion if one already understands what it means to describe or refer to what one sees when one looks at such things as ashtrays and shadows. There would be absolutely no sense in pointing to an ashtray for such a person, as Moore does, and saying 'Look, here is an ashtray. Therefore at least one material thing exists.' For if we can genuinely direct his attention from his visual field to the thing in front of his eyes in the special circumstances I have imagined, then he already knows there is an ashtray when he sees one. If he didn't, then no amount of pointing to ashtrays could bring him to see anything.

The point I am trying to make is this: If anyone is to understand that Moore is pointing to an ashtray or a cloud, when he does so, then he must already know that there are such things as ashtrays and clouds. Understanding how Moore's pointing is to be taken is at least part of what we would be thinking of if we said of anyone that he 'possesses the concept of a material thing'. Possessing this concept *is* knowing that there are such objects as ashtrays, clouds and soap bubbles – unlike possessing the concept of unicorn, dinosaur or cow. For a person who possesses the concept of unicorn, or knows what a unicorn is, or knows the meaning of the word 'unicorn', is one who would recognise a unicorn if he saw one, one who can tell the difference between a unicorn and other beasts, who could sort out unicorns in a field, if there were any, from other beasts, one who can do so in pictures, one who can describe and perhaps draw unicorns, etc.

Whereas a person's possession of the concept of a material thing does not show itself in this way.

It shows itself in almost everything he says and does – in the way, for instance, he follows with his eyes a ship in the distance and takes it for granted that his friend beside him can see it; in the way he reaches for what is before him; in the way he looks for the keys he put in his drawer the previous evening; in the various expectations he has, the judgements he makes, investigations he carries out, hypotheses he puts forward, explanations he gives. That is why it is queer to talk of 'possessing the concept of a material thing'. Certainly there must be numerous occasions where he says something true, and himself believes to be saying something true, with such words as 'ashtray', 'pencil', 'chair', 'table' – e.g. 'I have a pencil in my pocket', 'That chair is rickety', 'Pass me an ashtray'. Here there is no distinction between 'possessing the concept of a material thing' and 'knowing that there are such things as ashtrays, chairs and tables'.

You cannot test whether a person possesses the concept of a material thing apart from testing whether he is a complete cretin or not, knows or understands anything. If he can take any test whatsoever then he 'possesses the concept of a material thing'. Certainly you would not ask him to point to anything, bring you anything, sort out one kind of thing from another, draw or describe anything. I certainly cannot think of any circumstances in which someone may say 'Bring me a material thing', 'Show me a material thing', 'Point to a material thing', or 'This is a material thing'.

The meaning of such words as 'material thing' (and also 'colour', 'number') is not and cannot be taught *directly*, by pointing to anything, or by definition or description – by learning what characteristics material things possess which other things do not. You can point to an ashtray or to something blue. But if you are to be understood, the person to whom you are talking must already understand what it means to refer to such objects as ashtrays, vases, pencils, or what it means to talk about the colours of these things. As Wittgenstein puts it: 'An ostensive definition can be variously interpreted in *every* case' (*Inv.* sec. 28). He points out that how such a definition or pointing is to be taken 'depends on the circumstances' (sec. 29). But

there must already be a custom, an established use, a way of
taking it, and this is what the person to whom it is given must be
familiar with if he is to learn the meaning of a new word such as
'ashtray' or 'blue'. Being familiar with this *is* what I called 'possessing the concept of a material thing' – or at least it is an important part of it. As Wittgenstein puts it: 'The ostensive
definition explains the use – the meaning – of the word when the
overall role of the word in language is clear. Thus if I know that
someone means to explain a colour-word to me, the ostensive
definition "This is called 'sepia'"' will help me to understand
the word' (sec. 30). Wittgenstein talks of this overall role of the
word in language as the *grammar* of colour words. Possessing the
concept of colour is thus knowing or being familiar with this
overall role of words such as 'blue' and 'yellow' in language,
being able to use such words correctly – and that means use
them to say *true* things with them on numerous occasions – also
being able to respond appropriately to other people's utterances. This goes as much for possessing the concept of a material thing – whether or not one has a word for it. (In English I
suspect that this word is by and large philosophical in origin – it
bears the imprint of the philosopher's seal. Unlike Austin, however, I do not think that this means that there is something
wrong with it.)

   You point to a stone and say 'This – I mean this stone – is
called "granite"'. Imagine that I didn't know that. You then
tell me its most characteristic properties, so that if I find any
stone which has them I shall be able to identify it as granite. But
if I am to understand what you mean by 'this' or 'this stone' I
must already be familiar with a practice – a familiarity which
will show in the many things I say and do, in the way I respond
to other people's utterances on many occasions. This will include saying many true things and also judging the truth of
what other people say on a great many occasions with such
words as 'ashtray', 'cloud', 'soap bubble' etc. That is what I
meant earlier by 'knowing that there are such objects as ashtrays, clouds and soap bubbles', when I said that possessing the
concept of a material thing is knowing that there are such
things as ashtrays, clouds and soap bubbles. It is not a matter of
being able to distinguish one kind of thing from another – as
with the concepts dog, cat, unicorn, red, blue and sepia –

though being able to make such distinctions is part of possessing the concept of a material thing. This is what I take Miss Ambrose to mean when she says that 'material thing' or 'external object' is *not a general name*.[1] This is very important and has far-reaching implications for Moore's proof. One could say that words like 'material thing', 'external object' do not designate a kind of thing but mark a grammatical category – the place in grammar where a whole host of words are stationed.

Moore's claim that his premise 'Here is a hand and here is another' *entails* 'There are at least two material things' rests on his idea that the relation between these two propositions is like that between the propositions 'There is a poodle in the garden' and 'There is a dog in the garden' – where 'dog' is the name of a kind of thing or, more precisely, animal, i.e. a general name, and 'poodle' is the name of a thing or animal which is an instance of that kind. I have supported Miss Ambrose in arguing that 'material thing' is not a general name but a category word. This does not mean that Moore's premise doesn't entail his conclusion – at least I have not shown this in what I have said so far – but that Moore's reason, or chief reason, for thinking this is a bad one. The question, therefore, whether Moore's premise does or does not entail his conclusion needs to be further investigated. I shall do so in Chapter Four below. Before that, however, I want to consider what kind of claim philosophers make when they say that material things are 'external to our minds', that they have 'continued and independent existence'. This will be the subject of Chapter Three.

There is one point that has emerged from our discussion in this chapter which is worth emphasising. It is this: Moore lifts a hand for his audience to see, or he points to an ashtray. His audience is supposed to understand (as indeed they do) how this pointing is meant. On the other hand they are supposed to need convincing that material things exist. It is this distinction or separation for which there is no logical room in the case of formal or logical concepts – just as with logical propositions there is no distinction between sense and truth, so that grasping the sense of such a proposition guarantees that one recognises

---

[1] Not an ordinary genus word, as Prof. Wisdom puts it, but a category word – 'Moore's Technique', *P.P.A.*, p. 136. Not a concept proper but a 'formal concept' as Wittgenstein would put it in the *Tractatus*.

its truth.[2] Thus, for instance, where you may be said to point to a thing's colour, as opposed to its size or shape, there is no distinction between how the pointing is to be understood or taken and what it points to. Whereas, in contrast, you may know that I am pointing to something on the table, but you may not know *what* I am pointing to. That is you may understand how my pointing is meant but not know what I am pointing to in particular. Here, in this latter case, understanding how my pointing is meant is one thing and knowing what it points to is another. It is *this* distinction that is not possible where you say that I am pointing to the object's colour, not its shape or size; or that I am directing your attention to an object in space, not to a figure in your visual field. So if Moore's audience is to understand and follow his proof they must know how his pointing is meant. But they cannot know this and need convincing that material objects exist.

[2] In Wittgenstein's words, 'one can recognise that it is true from the symbol alone' (*Tractatus* 6.113). See Dilman, *Induction and Deduction, A Study in Wittgenstein*, Chapter Eleven, sec. IV, pp. 184–190.

3 The Concept of Externality

I argued that 'material thing' or 'external object' is not a general name. Moore treated it as such and on that basis thought that the conclusion he wanted to prove logically follows from his premise – or any other premise of the kind. Accordingly he started by trying to state as clearly as he could the defining properties or distinguishing criteria of ,the kind of thing he wanted to prove exists:

> Material things are things of such-and-such a kind – i.e. are
> external to the mind.
> Here is a hand and, therefore, a thing of the kind in question.
> Hence there is at least one material thing.

The first step or definition is crucial to Moore's proof. That is why he devotes more than one third of his paper to stating as clearly as possible what kind of thing a material thing or external object is.

The model that guides Moore is something like the following: Take a chemical substance like sulphur. One can certainly explain what sulphur is to someone who has never seen or heard of it. One would do so by telling him what it is like, by describing some of its most distinctive properties. For all this man knows we may be deceiving him; there may be no chemical substance which has the properties we have described. We could, however, *prove* to him that there is. What we do is to isolate a substance which has the properties described. The crucial point here is that the properties in question can be identified or specified independently of whether or not one knows that the substance in question exists. One can understand the descriptions in question, know what it would be like for the defining criteria to be satisfied, without knowing whether or not they are satisfied, without knowing whether or not all the descriptions in question fit any existing substance or object.

Now is this true in the case of what Moore wishes to prove? He tries to describe meticulously the distinguishing features of material things. Not surprisingly he finds this a singularly difficult thing to do. The words and expressions in which he tries to characterise the features of material things have no clear, unambiguous meaning. Hence other words have to be used in trying to clarify their meaning. Most of the words Moore begins with are common enough – 'external', 'space', 'experience', 'consciousness', etc. But, as he himself appreciates, he is not using them in the kind of connection in which we normally use these words, and hence what he means by them is not at once apparent. When he tries to clarify their meaning he finds himself in the same situation all over again. He substitutes one word for another, and he contrasts the sense of one expression (e.g. 'external to the mind') with that of another (e.g. 'in the mind'). But these new words and their senses call for clarification – and for similar reasons. Each time a word, distinction or contrast is clarified only when Moore produces *familiar examples which speak for themselves*. So when having given such examples Moore asks: 'What is the resemblance between these various things we are thinking of when we use the expression in question – for instance, "having an experience"?' he can only say: 'This is left to be gathered from the instances given'. (p. 142)

This clearly shows that he begins in the wrong place,[1] that he cannot begin where he must begin *if* he is to give a 'proof of the existence of external objects'. An understanding of what he is trying to describe presupposes a familiarity with the examples he comes down to in the end which, in turn, involves the ability to make and test various judgements and distinctions – e.g. between seeing a star in the sky and 'seeing stars', judging that what one sees is a perceptual illusion and making corrections. To have this ability *is* knowing that there are such objects as stars, hands and soap bubbles (see Chapter Two above). Here,

[1] 'It is so difficult to find the *beginning*. Or, better: it is difficult to begin at the beginning' – Wittgenstein, *On Certainty*, sec. 471.

unlike the previous case, we cannot understand what 'properties' we are meant to look for without knowing that there are a great many objects which possess them. So when Moore says, 'There is at least one star (pointing to one); therefore there is at least one external object' (p. 144), this means no more than 'There is at least one star; therefore there is at least one object which is the kind of object of which a star is an instance'. But this is hardly a step forward.

'There are objects of the kind of which a star is an instance.' Surely this is not what is in question. What Moore wants to establish is the existence of 'objects of a certain kind'. If, therefore, a star is mentioned in his premise, he has to be able to explain that it satisfies certain criteria – i.e. of externality. Obviously, it is no good his saying that the criteria in question are just those that objects like stars satisfy. That is it is crucial that he should be able to specify the criteria without referring to stars, etc., in order to give them content – i.e. without presupposing an understanding of what it means to talk about stars and other such objects. He has to be able to show that a star satisfies certain criteria which can be understood independently of the instances that Moore uses to illustrate their meaning. And this cannot be done – as Moore's attempts illustrate. But if not, then Moore's proof is bound to be circular. For if he begins by elucidating what is meant by 'externality' by referring his audience to stars, hands and the like, then he is presupposing what he is trying to prove. If his premise requires a grasp of what 'and the like' means, if it presupposes an understanding of what it means to talk of a star as opposed to an after-image, then it requires from the audience the kind of 'conviction' which would be exhibited in their accepting Moore's conclusion.[2]

This is the same as the point I made in the last chapter. For, obviously, if 'material thing' is not a general name, then one

---

[2] Let me put this point more crudely: Moore's aim is to prove that there are objects of a certain kind – 'external objects'. He hopes to convince his audience by showing them instances of objects that satisfy the criteria of externality. Surely if there is any step forward in this proof it consists in its claim that objects (e.g. stars and hands) whose existence in certain circumstances we cannot doubt without absurdity do satisfy the required criteria. But if the criteria in question are ultimately defined as 'the kind of criteria which stars, hands and like objects satisfy' then the step has been guaranteed only by collapsing its destination into its point of departure.

would hardly expect 'externality' to be an ordinary predicate, the name of a property which the kind of thing named possesses. Certainly what is in question has nothing to do with spacial relations or anything analogous to it, but rather – as we shall see – with relations between different parts of speech or grammars. This is what I now wish to bring out.

II

'Chairs and tables, and also shadows, rainbows and mirror images, are external to our minds. They continue to exist when they are not perceived; they have an uninterrupted existence. They can be perceived more than once and by more than one person. Most of these things can be perceived by more than one sense.' (Certain qualifications have to be made here which do not affect the main point at issue. For instance, a shadow cannot be touched, smelt or heard, and it disappears when it is dark. A rainbow too cannot be touched and one can fly through it in an aeroplane. A mirror image is different in other ways as well.)

What kind of thing are we saying here? Are we ascribing properties to these things – as if we were saying 'These chairs are made of wood' or 'They are solidly made' or 'There is a phosphorescent paint on them and you can see them in the dark'? Are we saying something about what they are like? Are we stating those common features which define and differentiate a large class of things – namely material things?

If you think so, as Moore did, you will be in trouble. For how can one know that anything has these properties? You may find out that you cannot touch what you see, as you expected, and also that no one else sees it. You may suddenly stop seeing it. In that case you will conclude that it was an hallucination, or perhaps an illusion. But that is not what I mean. My question is: How can you know that the chair or table continues to exist when no one is looking at it? If a man wants to know what goes on behind his back, when he has left his home or place of work, he can hire a 'private eye' to find out. If he wants to find out what goes on in a locked room when he is not there to see he can set up a cine-camera. But how can anyone know that the table continues to exist when there is no one there to see it? Nothing that we find subsequently upon re-entering the room would be reason or evidence for the 'continued existence' of the table if we were not willing to accept the 'continued existence' of something without proof or reason. This is not a question of having to take something on trust under unfavourable circumstances. The point concerns what is involved in any intelligible reference to what goes on behind one's back, what it means to have reason for a belief about something for which one does not have the evidence of one's eyes or of other witnesses – what underlies the possibility of even thinking about what goes on behind one's back, of having any conception of it.

We do say such things as 'My car has not been out of the garage, where I left it, while I was away' and base such claims on reason or evidence, because there is a great deal in what we find on our return that we are unwilling to question. Imagine the police investigating whether the car has been on the road while I was away:[3] Has the milometer reading changed? If not, could anyone have tampered with it? How old is the dried-up mud on the tyres? Exactly how much petrol was there in the tank when I left it in the garage? If these and a thousand other such questions make sense and can be investigated, then it makes no sense to question the 'continued existence' of physical things.

We do not treat the 'continued and independent existence of material things' as an hypothesis, as something that is open to doubt, something for which we need reason or justification. We could not regard it as such coherently – given the kinds of question we ask, the ways in which we investigate them, our ways of speaking about almost everything. The possibility of asking most of these questions that interest us, investigating them, and generally of the ways of going on in the ways we do, demands that we treat the uninterrupted existence of material things as beyond question. What we have here is not an hypothesis about a kind of thing we meet instances of in our life, but – as we shall see – part of the conception we take of what confronts us in our life on innumerable occasions, as well as of what 'being confronted' means in these connections.

Russell thought otherwise; he thought that what we have here is some sort of very general explanatory hypothesis – some-

---

[3] Perhaps someone alleges to have seen it on the road, though he is not sure of it, and the question is: Could it be that the car he saw was my car?

thing we assume to be true in order to make sense of a host of familiar phenomena in a simple and economic way, though strictly we cannot prove it:

> If the cat appears at one moment in one part of the room, and at another in another part, it is natural to *suppose* that it has moved from one to the other, passing over a series of intermediate positions. But if it is merely a set of sense-data, it cannot have ever been in any place where I did not see it; thus we shall have to suppose that it did not exist at all while I was not looking, but suddenly sprung into being in a new place. If the cat exists whether I see it or not, we can understand from our own experience how it gets hungry between one meal and the next; but if it does not exist when I am not seeing it, it seems odd that appetite should grow during non-existence as fast as during existence. (*The Problems of Philosophy*, p. 23 – italics mine)

Contrast Russell's 'I cannot say where the cat was when I was out at work, but it was surely somewhere – in existence. It did not just pop into being on my return home' with the following genuine suppositions:

(a) 'The cat must have been in the house when I was away, though there was no one in the house to see it. It must have got in through the open window. How else can you explain the fish bowl being tipped over and the missing fish!'

(b) This is an imaginary example from a ghost story in which the dead uncle 'materialises' at midnight some evenings and on one such occasion knocks down books from a shelf. On finding the books on the floor the following morning one of the characters asks: Was it the wind that knocked them down during the storm last night or was it the ghost?

In the second example whether or not it is the case that the dead uncle 'sprung into being' in the library is a genuine question. That he existed 'in material form' when others could have seen him but, in fact, did not, is a genuine hypothesis because it can be false. But what is in question is very different from what Russell thinks we all suppose to be false, though strictly we cannot prove it. What we have here is a transformation – the uncle takes on a different form, where previously he was invisible he 'materialises', in other words becomes visible and tangible. This is based on the analogy of water vapour in the air, invisible to the eye, condensing into water and freezing into ice. But even if it were not, we could still make sense of the idea of something or someone springing into being at certain times and ceasing to exist altogether in the intervals. But if we can understand such a suggestion in particular cases, this still requires our not regarding as possible that material things may not have a continued and uninterrupted existence.

To return to our wicked old uncle. We could easily suppose that he never 'materialises' when someone could see him. Wicked he may be, we could imagine, but he is shy of the gaze of the living. He becomes invisible if he thinks there is any danger that he might be seen. Still it would make sense to suppose that someone could see him.

Why could we not suppose the reverse of this in connection with material objects – that they 'spring into being' or 'materialise' only when some human being can see or touch them? Otherwise they become invisible? That is, why can we not imagine that Russell's 'supposition' is false? We should be able to do this if it is really a supposition or very general hypothesis.

There are a great many difficulties here. First of all, we could of course imagine a particular object disappearing when our back is turned to it. But then we could imagine it disappearing and reappearing when we are actually looking at it – that is before our very eyes. In this latter case what would we say? If we are alone we would not believe our eyes. Or we might think that we were having a negative hallucination – some sort of selective hysterical blindness. If there are other people in the room and what they say they see agrees with what I see, then we would seek some explanation. If the object reappeared again, we might wonder about the possibility of a collective negative hallucination. If it does not reappear, we might wonder whether it might have suddenly disintegrated – whether, as it were, it might not have burnt up so quickly that we did not actually see it burning. Given ideas that we have come to accept in physics, this hypothesis would raise questions about the energy during the process – questions which would need investigating and upon the answers to which the acceptability of our hypothesis would depend. I am, of course, imagining way out hypotheses which we would not now take seriously. If, on the other hand, what I am imagining were a common occurrence we would want an explanation, preferably consonant with ideas accepted in physics. If we could find no such satisfactory explanation, however, we may find ourselves forced to revise some of those ideas. (Notice that the possibilities I have suggested have been put within the framework of the 'postulate' of the conservation of matter – where matter is imagined as being transformed, but its destruction is ruled out. At the very most these possibilities may be considered within the framework of the 'postulate' of the conservation of energy. I use the term 'postulate' advisedly; they belong to the framework of physical investigation. But their *intelligibility* in turn presupposes the ideas which we take for granted outside physics, in our daily lives – those ideas the status of which is the subject of the present chapter.)

What I have imagined are *strange* phenomena and, as I said, if we were to meet them commonly, this might force us to revise our ways of thinking in physics. But what would it be for *everything* to disappear while I am asleep? The idea of something disappearing, as in the former case, makes sense only against a background of things which we trust do not disappear. (If a physicist were to suggest that perhaps one day *all* matter would be transformed into energy in accordance with Einstein's law E = mc² I would not understand him. How is this energy to be manifested and how is it to be measured?)

So what about supposing that everything save our visible surroundings may have disappeared? To be clear about what supposing this involves and whether we can think it through, we have to consider how taking such a supposition seriously would affect the numerous activities we may carry out from our little corner – for instance, speaking on the phone with a friend in a distant town, listening to the radio or watching a television programme, or detonating a bomb outside our field of vision. If the rest of the world has gone up in smoke I certainly cannot do most of these things; and if I can still do them regardless, and no special explanation is needed in each case, for instance of the voice from my radio set announcing 'this is radio Luxembourg', then what is it that I am supposed to be imagining? In the latter case, do we not have an idle hypothesis, a wheel in the mechanism that is not connected to the rest?

I do not now wish to consider this 'supposition' in detail. I have suggested that however we take it we cannot think it through or fill it with content. Everything in our life that we need to rely on in order to make sense of it blocks our attempts to give it some content. If it has no connection with the rest of the mechanism, if it does not move with it and help other parts to move, then it is devoid of content. If, on the other hand, it is connected then the whole mechanism jams. It is in some ways like Russell's 'hypothesis' that the world came into existence five minutes ago complete with records and memories of an unreal past.

The supposition I have briefly considered was meant to be the contradictory of Russell's 'supposition' that material things have a continued existence. If it is not a coherent supposition, if it cannot be given content without upsetting us in all sorts of ways, then Russell is wrong in thinking that what it stands opposed to is a supposition or hypothesis.

To see this more clearly let us return to the first of our two examples of genuine hypotheses: 'The cat must have been in the house when I was out, though no one saw it there.' You could say that the remains or pieces of the fish bowl, in the absence of any other plausible account, points to the cat as the most likely culprit, as responsible for the state of affairs we discover when we return home. We notice the open window, we know that the cat sometimes comes in through it and we know that it likes fish. This enables us to make sense of the disaster: How else would the fish bowl have been knocked down? And fish don't walk away out of open windows!

Now take Russell's example. We feed the cat before we go out to work. We come home late to find it ravenous. Do we need an explanation for this? If we found it ravenous half an hour after we fed it, that would be different. Perhaps we haven't given it enough to eat. Or perhaps it has worms. We take it as *normal* that animals and human beings get hungry when they have not eaten for a long time. It is true that we can tell a physiological story of what happens to the food after it has been swallowed and how the body needs food at regular intervals to replenish its energy. But we learn about hunger in men and animals long before we have any conception of physiology, and what the physiological story does is to link what we already know with these new and interesting facts about the body. It does not give what we have learned to expect and trust any extra support. On the' contrary, the possibility of developing any physiological account presupposes that such regularities are themselves trusted or taken for granted.

But does our trusting such regularities presuppose a belief in the continued existence of material things? Does the latter 'belief' support, give foundation to, or in any way make intelligible the content of my belief that a cat that hasn't had anything to eat for a long time will be hungry? The situation is very different in the case of our belief that the cat was in the house while I was out at work. For even if in this case no one actually saw it in the house and our only reason for thinking this is the missing fish, still someone could have seen it. That is (1) we can have independent evidence for what we suppose. (2) Even where we don't have such evidence, we can have evidence, apart from the facts explained, which makes our supposition plausible or reasonable – e.g. the open window. (3) The supposition in question can be false, and even where we don't know it to be false, it may not be plausible. (4) What is tentatively advanced as an explanatory hypothesis here represents the actualisation of a number of different possibilities any of which, if realised, would explain the facts which we seek to explain. The surrounding facts may make it unplausible to suppose that a thief broke into the house, knocked down the fish bowl, and took the fish with him when he left. E.g. What else did he steal? Why should he want to steal the fish? But this alternative hypothesis could have been true and if so would explain the facts in question.

None of this is true in the case of our 'belief' in the continued existence of material things. What we have here is not anything over and above our trust in the kind of regularities which, according to Russell, it explains. We do not trust those regularities 'because' we believe in the continued existence of material things; nor does the general belief justify our trust in particular instances. Rather our trust in the case of those numerous instances, as this is exhibited in our reactions and behaviour, is what gives content to the general belief. To trust in those regularities *is* to believe in the continued existence of material things. We acquire the 'general belief' *indirectly*, by acquiring many specific expectations – e.g. that the cat will get hungry in time whether we see it or not. As I said, the general belief is not something *additional* to the specific expectations. It can have no independent support other than what it derives from the particular expectations – which is not 'support' but 'content' – and so it can give no support or justification to those expectations. In any case they need no support. The behaviour and reactions in which these expectations find expression in our life form part of the framework on which the working of our language is based. It is in this sense that those expectations and the 'general belief' to which they give content are *fundamental*, or belong to the foundations of thought and language. Not as hypotheses that we are forced to take on trust.[4]

III

Take another example. You live in the vicinity of Whipsnade. You wake up one morning, look out of your window, and lo and behold – a lion in your garden. For a moment you cannot believe your eyes but you hear it roar and are soon convinced. You *assume* that it must have escaped from the zoo. Under the circumstances this is a reasonable assumption. But there is logical room for such an assumption only because you are convinced that what you see is a real, physical lion and not an hallucination. If you thought it was an hallucination there would be no question about where it was before you saw it. You would not need to account for how it came to be where you now see it. That this question does arise is part of what it *means* to talk about a real lion as opposed to an hallucination. What you *assume* is that the lion you now see must have escaped from the neighbouring zoo and so, presumably, will be recognised by the keeper there as one of the animals kept in the zoo. The assumption may prove to be mistaken. But you do *not* assume that the lion was somewhere, in existence, before it appeared in your garden. 'Somewhere' – this says nothing. All you are trying to

---

[4] I have developed this same point further in connection with our 'belief' in the uniformity of nature in *Induction and Deduction, A Study in Wittgenstein*, Part One, Chapter Three, 'Unreasoned Beliefs'. The substance of these discussions comes entirely from Wittgenstein – see especially *On Certainty*.

say is that it is not an hallucination.

Is what I see a real lion or an hallucination? This is a genuine question. If you are not sure you may try to find out. 'But one thing is sure, if it is a real lion it must have been somewhere. Surely, you are not going to believe that it suddenly popped into being in the garden.' What you are trying to say is that if it is a real lion, it *makes sense* to ask: where did it come from? where was it before you saw it in the garden? It makes sense to ask such a question in connection with a real lion, but not an hallucination. This is one difference between what talking about a real lion amounts to and what it means to talk about an hallucination. It is not a difference between one kind of thing and another, but a difference between grammars, a difference in grammar.

(a) 'It must have been somewhere – in existence.'
(b) 'It must have been in the zoo – from where it must have escaped.'

It looks as if the relation between (a) and (b) is like the relation between 'It must have been in Whipsnade' and 'It must have been in the zoo'. If (a) were the most general form of (b), if as Russell might say it had 'absolute generality', then it would mean nothing. But, in fact, what one who speaks like this is trying to say is that it makes sense to ask questions about its previous whereabouts, that it makes sense to relate what one sees on different occasions if it satisfies certain criteria and speak of seeing the same thing on those occasions. If so, then clearly what is in question is what is involved in speaking about a material thing, the possible ways of going on starting from an utterance like 'a lion!' which make it into an utterance about a material thing.

Consider the response of the person in the above example when he looks out of his window and exclaims 'a lion!'. For instance, he thinks that it must have escaped from the zoo, rings up the zoo and asks to speak to one of the keepers. Surely this shows that he doesn't doubt his eyes, that he doesn't think he may be having an hallucination. Imagine you are writing a story which begins with the hero's exclamation in the circumstances in question. Now ask yourself *how he would have to go on* in order to have meant a real lion. How he goes on, how he acts, what else he says, what he regards as the proper conclusion to draw at this point or that – all this is what we anticipate when we take it that he meant or was speaking of a real, physical lion. It is an important part of what constitutes speaking about, meaning or referring to a real, physical lion. If starting at this point you were to continue: 'He exclaimed "a lion!"'. A look of worry clouded his face. He remembered the previous evening, and the evenings before. He hesitated, picked up the receiver and dialled Alcoholics Anonymous.' You are clearly talking about a man who realises he is seeing an hallucination. If you now make him say on the phone '. . . and I saw a lion in the garden' there would be no doubt that he is talking about his hallucination. The point is that whether he means a real lion or an hallucination depends partly on his subsequent behaviour – including what he thinks and what he is prepared to say. This is what he commits himself to for the future when he speaks about a lion. The commitments in question are part of the logic of the kind of statement he makes.

This kind of subsequent behaviour and words as opposed to that – this is part of what we mean when we say, 'He meant a real lion', 'He thought – rightly or wrongly – that he was seeing a real, physical lion'. Here we are speaking about what makes a reference a reference to a material thing, about some of the conditions that must be satisfied for words to describe a physical reality. This is what the words 'the continued and independent existence of material things' bring to our attention; they do not indicate any assumption we all make.

IV

'If it is a body then it hasn't sprung into being. It will disintegrate after we bury it, but it will not just disappear. If you look at it you too will see it.' Contrast: 'It will disintegrate after it is buried' and 'It will not simply disappear'. The former proposition, that flesh rots when covered with earth, is based on experience. But is the latter proposition also based on experience? Could it be? Could cameras prove or disprove it? We have seen that the desire to see it proved, the disappointment in our failure to justify the confidence we have in it, the idea that therefore it must lie beyond any reason or evidence we have, lead us to misconstrue it as an assumption or hypothesis.

When you hide a child's toy he looks for it. Does he have any reason for thinking that it must be somewhere, that it has not simply disappeared? He may have reason for thinking that it is still in the room – just as the police may have reason for thinking that the bullion that was stolen the previous evening is still in the country, or that the robbers could not have had time to melt it down. But that is different. This is the kind of thing you can infer, have reasons for or against, assume and be right or wrong about. However 'if it is bullion, then it must be somewhere, even if in the form of liquid gold' – this is not a step or link in any chain of reasons.

The child looks for his toy when you hide it; and he is pleased when he finds it. The infant does not at first do so when you take away his rattle and hide it behind his pram. The dog goes back to the spot where he buried his bone the previous day. If we did not come to behave in these ways *as a matter of course* then could we carry out any investigation, make any inference, put forward any hypothesis, give any explanations? This is what is in question when a philosopher talks of the continued and uninterrupted existence of material things. As Wittgenstein puts it:

> Every language-game is based on words 'and objects' being recognized again . . . If, therefore, I am uncertain about this being my hand (in whatever sense), why not in that case about the meaning of these words as well? (*Cert.* secs. 455–6)

Or take: 'If he looks at it, he will see it too.' What reason do I have for thinking this? I might say: 'I don't believe he is blind' – meaning that in the absence of special circumstances I don't need any reason for this. 'I believe he will see it': – this is something I might say of someone who is just coming out of an eye operation, or when his bandages are being removed. My reason for thinking this is as follows: he couldn't see before because he had cataracts in both eyes. They have now been removed. The doctor tells me the operation was a success and that he found nothing else wrong with his eyes. Here, in these special circumstances, I have good reason for believing that he will see the flowers by his bedside which I am looking at now. But that doesn't mean to say that in the normal case I have reason to believe that he will see what I see.

'If there is nothing wrong with his eyes he will see it too.' We all learn to expect this very early in life. If we did not, pointing could have no sense for us and we could hardly come to speak. Such matter-of-course expectations lie at the foundations of all speech and thought, and they are what give content to the philosopher's claim that material things exist independently of being perceived, or that they are external to the mind.

(1) 'What I see now is the same thing that was before me yesterday.'
(2) 'It will not disappear when I turn away from it and stop seeing it.'
(3) 'When he comes in he will see it too.'

What these three propositions point to are intertwined. Unless I can take all three for granted in a particular case I am not speaking about a material thing. In this sense what is in question belongs to our conception of a material thing; it underlies the possibility of referring to 'external objects'. But unless we can point to, recognise, refer to, speak about material things, we could not speak at all – about anything. Therefore the possibility of being brought to take for granted, in particular cases, what is in question above is fundamental to all speech and thought.

v

In the last chapter I argued that when philosophers speak about material things they are not speaking about a kind of thing, that whether they speak of 'material things' or 'external objects' the expression in question is not used as a general name. I said that this has serious consequences for Moore's claim that his premise entails his conclusion. In this chapter I have argued that the independent and uninterrupted existence of material things is part of the *grammar* of 'material thing' and that, therefore, Moore's elucidations at the outset of his paper are *grammatical* elucidations. As such they are not, of course, a waste of time. On the contrary, unless we are clear about the grammatical points Moore begins to elucidate here we shall not find it easy to put our finger on what is objectionable in what Berkeley and McTaggart asserted.

On the other hand, unless we are clear that in the long

discussion that precedes his proof Moore gives *grammatical* elucidations we shall not recognise that they cannot form a basis to Moore's proof in the way he imagined. For what is in question are not criteria or defining properties of a class which may or may not be null. If that were the case, as Moore thinks, then on finding objects which as a matter of fact satisfy these criteria or exhibit these properties we would have proved that the class in question is not empty. However, as I have argued, what Moore elucidates are features of a way of talking central to our language, features that are exhibited whenever we refer to a table, stone or cloud, attribute properties to it, or seek an explanation for its present condition. They are realised in our ways of talking and are grasped or recognised only by someone who can make sense with the kinds of expression in question and understand what is said by means of them – and this involves a recognition of the possibility of using the expressions to say what is true. Hence if there is anything to be elucidated here, then what Moore seeks to prove needs no proof.

4 The Relation between Moore's Premise and His Conclusion

I stated earlier one of the conclusions I argued for as follows: The expression 'material thing' or 'external object' is not a general name but a category word.[1] It does not signify a kind of thing but is used by philosophers to focus on a grammatical category. This doesn't mean that Moore's premise doesn't entail his conclusion, but that his main reason (and I think his only one) for thinking that it does is a bad reason.

In other words, I have not argued that Moore's premise does not entail his conclusion. But now is the time to ask whether or not it does. Once more, however, there is no short answer to this question, no answer of the form Yes or No – as there is in the case of the logician's 'Does p entail q?', 'Is the inference from p to q valid?'.

I have tried to show that the relation between Moore's premise and his conclusion is not like the relation between 'Here is a whale' and 'Here is a mammal'. If it is True that there is a whale in this marine-land pool then it is *necessarily* True that there is a mammal in that pool; and if it is False that there is a mammal there then it is *necessarily* False that there is a whale. On the other hand from the Falsehood of the antecedent clause nothing follows as to the Truth or Falsehood of the consequent: Even if there is no whale there, there may be dolphins which are also mammals. Equally from the Truth of the consequent nothing follows as to the Truth or Falsehood of the antecedent

[1] '. . . "physical object" is a logical concept. (Like colour, quantity, . . .) And that is why no such proposition as: "There are physical objects" can be formulated. Yet we encounter such unsuccessful shots at every turn'. (*Cert.* sec. 36). '"There are physical objects" is nonsense. Is it supposed to be an empirical proposition?' (sec. 35). Also see secs. 476–7.

clause: the mammals in the pool may include whales, on the other hand they may not; there may only be dolphins in the pool. What is in question here is a *truth of logic* or a *logical principle* and where it is applicable the question 'Does p entail q?' has a definite answer Yes or No – even if that answer may not be at once apparent and may take some logical manipulation to become apparent. This question 'Does p entail q?' is a logical question, not a philosophical one.

Now when we ask whether Moore's premise entails his conclusion our question is not like this, and no amount of logical manipulation will help us to answer it. We have already seen that if anyone accepts Moore's premise he may be said to have thereby accepted his conclusion. I say 'may be said' since Moore's conclusion is not the sort of thing we normally either accept or reject. It is true that philosophers have sometimes rejected it; but we have yet to examine what 'rejecting' means in this connection. So let me initially put this point by saying that if anyone accepts Moore's premise *we* have at least *some* reason for saying that he has accepted Moore's conclusion – though, as we shall see, if he is a philosopher and denies that he has thereby accepted Moore's conclusion, we cannot say *definitely* that he has contradicted himself, nor yet that he has not. We have already seen what makes me say that if anyone accepts Moore's premise we have at least some reason for saying that he has accepted Moore's conclusion. For, as I argued, if anyone is to understand what Moore is pointing to or showing when he points to an ash tray or lifts a hand (and he would have to understand this if he is to accept Moore's premise) he must already know that there are such things as hands, tables and ashtrays. However, if this makes me say that if he has accepted Moore's premise then we have some reason for saying that he has accepted Moore's conclusion, it does not make me say that accepting Moore's premise has *convinced* him of Moore's conclusion, or has given him reason, which he did not have before (until then), for accepting Moore's conclusion. For again, as I have argued, if he had not *already* accepted Moore's conclusion (whatever this may mean), if he did not already possess the concept of material thing or physical reality, he could not understand Moore's premise and so could neither accept nor reject it.

Let us, before going further, remind ourselves of what we are doing. I stated the logical relation between 'There is a whale in this pool' (let us call it p) and 'There is a mammal in this pool' (let us call it q) as follows:

(1) If p is T then q is T
(2) If q is F then p is F
(3) If p is F then q is T or F
(4) If q is T then p is T or F

Then I tried to compare the relation between Moore's premise (capital P) and his conclusion (capital C) to it. This is a dangerously formalistic procedure; but I shall not stick to it for long. Any dangers it involves will, I hope, be averted by what further I shall have to say.

Now with regard to the relation between P and C so far we have seen that:

(1) If anyone accepts P we have some reason to say that he accepts C.

(2) But if he accepts P and denies that he accepts C we cannot definitely say that he is contradicting himself. (I shall return to this.)

(3) We cannot say that accepting P has convinced him of C, or that it has given him reason for accepting C – for rejecting McTaggart's ∼ C. (I shall return to this too.)

But now to proceed,

(4) If someone could intelligibly say that P (Moore's premise asserted in the kind of circumstances Moore asserted it) is False, then in this case too *we* would have *some* reason (perhaps not as good as in the case where he agrees that P is True) for saying that he accepts C.

This last point would be clearer in the following case: Suppose Moore points before him and says 'Here is a horse' when there is no horse before him. Now if someone in the audience says 'Surely that is false, Moore is mistaken. Perhaps he is having an hallucination' this would be enough to show that this person accepts Moore's conclusion. My point is that the *possibility* of either agreeing or disagreeing with a claim like 'There is a horse in the field' *presupposes* one's acceptance of Moore's conclusion, if 'accepting C' means 'possessing the concept of material thing'. (This is a restatement of points (1) and (4) above together.)

Professor Malcolm, in his Lecture on Moore, expresses what I have tried to point out under 4 as follows:

> When he [Moore] said, against the sceptics, such a thing as 'I now see that door', it did not matter whether he was actually looking at a *door*. He did not have to produce an example of a *true* perceptual statement. In order to refute the claim that there is an absurdity in the concept of seeing a body, Moore did not have to present a *paradigm* of seeing a body, as I once thought [in 'Moore and Ordinary Language' in the Schilpp volume *The Philosophy of G. E. Moore*, p. 354]. He only had to remind his listeners and readers that the sentence 'I see a door over there' has a correct use and, therefore, *can* express a true statement'. (*Knowledge and Certainty*, p. 179)

What is in question is not a connection between the Truth and Falsity of two propositions P and C – as in the case of p and q of our earlier example – but a connection between the possibility of the truth and falsehood of a large number of things we say everyday of our lives and what Moore wishes to affirm, namely C. If so, we are, I think, well out of the realm of deductive connections, since deductive connections hold between the truth-values of propositions of the same kind.[2]

Agreed, then, that the relation between P and C is not one of entailment, is it not one of presupposition? This fits better what I described by saying that if anyone accepts P then we have some reason for saying that he accepts C, though this does not mean that accepting P gives him a reason for accepting C which he did not have before. But there are serious difficulties to taking this view and it too must be rejected. To begin with, it is not clear what it means for anyone to accept C. Secondly, as we have seen, if anyone rejected P (and it is difficult to see how he could – see Chapter Ten below) we could still have some reason for saying that he accepts C (point 4 above). So we see that if C is presupposed at all, it is not presupposed by the truth of P, but by both its truth and its falsity. In other words, if P makes sense

---

[2] This last is what Wisdom calls the realm of the 'domestic logic' of these propositions – in contrast with what he calls their 'ultimate logic', or what Wittgenstein calls their 'grammar'.

at all there must be material things – i.e. C must be true. But this is a rather grand and over-formal way of saying that if P makes sense there must be a language in which it is intelligible, and if anyone can accept or reject it he must understand that language.[3] This fits in with what I said earlier when I argued that 'material thing' is not a general name but the expression of a formal concept or category.

However if you put it like this it becomes difficult to understand what philosophers like McTaggart, whom Moore combated, were denying, and so what it is that Moore thought he proved. Were they denying that there is a language in which propositions like P make sense? I do not think so.[4] Moore would have certainly said that to think that this is what they were denying is to distort their words and to twist their sense – and, I think, with justification.

I should now like to add this to what I have said so far about the relation between P and C: '~C', or the form of words 'Material things don't exist', does not have a stable, established meaning. I don't mean simply, as Moore himself admitted, that different philosophers have meant different things by these words, but that what any one philosopher meant by them is subject to change under pressure. Hence you cannot say, without qualification, that they were used by this or that philosopher (Berkeley or McTaggart) to mean this or that. Philosophers who have said such things as 'Matter doesn't exist' were trying to say something, some of them were trying to say something important. But they were not clear about what they wanted to say. Hence the meaning of '~C' and, therefore, the reaction to 'C' and to Moore's proof of a philosopher who wishes to assert it, is bound to shift in discussion. That is what I mean by saying that the form of words '~C' doesn't have a

[3] '"There are physical objects" – this assertion, or its opposite, is a misfiring attempt to express what can't be expressed like that'. – *Cert* sec. 37

[4] We shall see what they were denying further down – see Chapters Six and Eight below. Malcolm thought that they were denying that a whole host of expressions and sentences that we use everyday are self-contradictory ('White on Moore', *Mind*, Jan. 1960). He says: 'It is surprising that anyone should think that, for instance, the sentence "I see the moon" has not a correct use: but philosophical reasoning has a peculiar power to blind one to the obvious'. (*K. C.*, p. 180) I think that this view is crude – see my 'Paradoxes and Discoveries', *Wisdom: Twelve Essays*, ed. Renford Bambrough.

stable meaning. Since Moore's conclusion 'C' is meant to be the contradictory of '~C' it will not have a stable meaning either (see Chapter Six below).

One could say that insofar as Moore took the philosophical assertion he opposed as an empirical claim in which the existence of a large class of things is denied (like 'Unicorns do not exist', 'Dinosaurs no longer exist'), insofar, therefore, as Moore's conclusion C *approaches* an existential assertion about a large class of things, then the relation between P and C *approaches* a deductive relation. In arguing that 'material thing' is not a general name, a class name, I have argued that this is an unattainable limit, that the words 'Material things exist' cannot be used to make an empirical claim. On the other hand, Moore *took* the assertion he was opposing as a negative existential claim like 'Unicorns do not exist', and not without some justification, and meant his own conclusion C to be a denial of this. We cannot say, without qualification, that Moore's words mean something different from what he himself intended them to mean. That is why I say that the meaning of his words 'approaches' the meaning he intended them to have as a limit without, however, reaching it. Since that limit is logically unattainable, we could say that Moore was confused insofar as he intended his words to express an empirical existential affirmation.

Summary   I have compared the relation between P and C with the relation between p and q – where p entails q. The comparison may be schematically represented as follows:

A.	p *entails* q	B. P C
(1)	$T \rightarrow T$	(1) If x accepts P we have some reason for saying that he has accepted C.
(2)	$F \leftarrow F$	(2) If x is a philosopher and denies that he accepts C, we cannot definitely say that he has contradicted himself. e.g. Berkeley.
(3)	$F \rightarrow TvF$	(3) But we cannot say that accepting P has convinced x of C, or has given him reason for accepting C.
(4)	$TvF \leftarrow T$	(4) If someone says that P is false, then

again we would have some reason for
saying that he accepts C.

Combining (1) and (4): The *possibility* of either agreeing that
P is True or denying it *presupposes* that one accepts what Moore
wishes to prove, namely C – if we recognise (as I argued in
Chapter Two) that 'accepting C' means 'possessing the concept of a material thing'.

So if there is a connection between P and C, it is a connection
between the possibility of the Truth or Falsity of a large number
of propositions like P and what Moore wishes to affirm, i.e.
what some philosophers have denied, namely C.

Hence we are well out of the realm of deductive relations.
The relation between P and C (i) is not one of entailment, nor
(ii) one of presupposition.

(iii) If C is presupposed at all, it is not presupposed by the
truth of P, but by its intelligibility.

(iv) Does this mean that what is presupposed, namely what
'C' means, is that there is a language in which P makes sense? It
cannot be said that this is what is denied by those philosophers
who assert ∼ C.

(v) The difficulty in saying what '∼ C' and, therefore, also
its denial 'C' mean is that those philosophers who affirmed one
or the other (e.g. McTaggart and Moore) were themselves not
clear about what they wanted to say. We can, therefore, represent the relation between P and C as follows:

deductive relation: *unattainable limit*: existential assertion about
. . . . a large class of things
↑   ↑
P. C
                                               ↓
                              . . . . assertion that there is
                                      a language in which
                                      P-like propositions
                                      make sense

The two arrows pointing away from C represent the range of
oscillation, with Moore's idea of what he was proving at the
upper limit and Malcolm's interpretation of it at the lower
limit.

The question remains about what those philosophers whom

Moore opposed were troubled by and meant to comment on –
even if this involves conceptual confusion – when they asserted
that ∼ C. The question about the sense of 'C', as Moore
affirmed it and believed to have proved, cannot be divorced
from this question, since Moore meant it as the denial of ∼ C.
These two questions will occupy us in the following three chapters.

5 Can Moore's Opponent be Proved Wrong?

In 'A Defence of Common Sense' Moore writes:

> The strange thing is that philosophers should have been able to hold sincerely, as part of their philosophical creed, propositions inconsistent with what they themselves *knew* to be true; and yet, so far as I can make out, this has really frequently happened. (*Philosophical Papers*, p. 41)

Moore would not have found this strange at all if the connection between what these philosophers held 'as part of their philosophical creed' and the things they knew to be true consisted of a complex chain of a great many links so that it was easy to fail to detect the inconsistency. In such a case a deductive proof would have been just what is needed and, if valid, would have forced the philosophers in question to give up what they held. This would then be the end of the matter.

What makes it strange is that if there is any inconsistency between the kind of philosophical claim Moore had in mind (e.g. that Time is unreal, that material things don't exist) and the kinds of thing Moore rightly claimed these philosophers must know, then it is an inconsistency which is too obvious for anyone to fail to see. In that case there would be hardly any need to bring it to their attention. For it is hardly credible that they should have failed to see it. As Wisdom puts it:

> It is quite incredible that the reason why philosophers have found 'Matter exists' questionable whereas they have found 'I have just raised my hands' unquestionable is that they have failed to see a connection between the two. ('Moore's

Technique', *P.P.A.*, p. 130)

Wisdom goes on to explain that with a good deductive proof in which one argues from p to q one has very good reason for thinking that p is true, and by connecting p with q one shows that this is equally good reason for thinking that q is true. If one had no reason for thinking that p is true but good reason for thinking that q is false, then by connecting p with q as above one would show that one had equally good reason for thinking that p is false.

Where the connection between p and q is complex and so easy to miss, a proof that brings out this connection serves a useful purpose. For one who is certain of the truth of p but doubtful about the truth of q sees, thanks to the proof, that he ought to be certain of the truth of q. In other words, the proof serves to convince him of something about which he was doubtful before the proof.

But the shorter or simpler the proof is, the more difficult the connection is to miss, the more likely it is that if a man is doubtful about the truth of q then he has independent reasons for doubting it. In that case, he will have equally good or bad reasons for doubting the truth of p. Here the reasons he has for thinking that p is true will raise the level of certainty of q. But equally those independent reasons he has for doubting the truth of q will lower the level of certainty of p. 'Proof [says Wisdom] is like putting a pipe between two tubs of water.' Here the proof shows that the two sets of reasons (the reasons for believing that p is true and the independent reasons for doubting the truth of q) are inconsistent; it forces this to our attention. But it cannot resolve the conflict of reasons.

Moore believes that his premise is incontrovertible and, therefore, that any reason which a philosopher may have for denying his conclusion *must* be a bad reason. So he does not feel the need to consider these reasons.

But a philosopher who denies Moore's conclusion and believes that he has good reasons for doing so may thereby deny that Moore's premise is incontrovertible. This is, perhaps, McTaggart's position. At any rate this is one possibility. Moore says that he cannot prove his premise but that this does not show that it is not incontrovertible. I think that Moore is right here – as we shall see – but this does not mean that there is nothing further that can be said. As long as Moore does not say anything further on this point, the philosopher he is opposing may remain unmoved. He may reply as Wisdom imagines he would:

> Of course *some* things are known without proof. One knows without proof that 1+1 makes 2, and one knows immediately that one feels sick or that one sees the appearance of a dagger. But it's different with 'There's a real dagger there'. That is not known immediately. If it is known, it is known on the basis of other knowledge which collected together establishes it. But is there anything we know from which we can really establish for certain that there is a real dagger there? If so what is it? This is what we are concerned with. We know well enough what we mean when we say 'There's a dagger in the air – a real dagger'. The question which interests us is 'How do we know that what we mean is so?' (*P.P.A.*, pp. 121–2)

Now I think that Moore invites these questions and he does not meet them, though I believe that it is possible to do so. I shall return to this question when I consider the sceptic and Moore's arguments against him (see especially Chapters Ten and Eleven below).

I said that where we have a proof of the form P ∴ C, like the one Moore gives us, there are three possibilities.

(i) One who, for good or bad reasons, wishes to deny C, may accept the connection, and for the same reason deny P, deny that Moore is right in thinking that P is incontrovertible. This is, perhaps, McTaggart's position.

(ii) The proof may brow-beat one into thinking that one's initial reasons for denying C must be bad reasons. I say 'brow-beat' advisedly, since this needs showing and the proof does not do so, nor anything else that Moore says. Let me restate my reason for saying this.

If one had denied C, not recognising the connection between P, which let us imagine one does not dream of denying, and C, then a proof which brought out this connection would understandably make one think that one's reasons for denying C must be bad reasons since they ignore the connection which the proof brings out. But if one had denied C, in the full knowledge of the connection between P and C, then if one's reasons for denying C are bad reasons this could not be because one had failed to recognise the connection between P and C. Hence something more than Moore's proof is needed if one is to be convinced that one's reasons are bad reasons. So if, in such a case, one is led by the proof *alone* to think that one's reasons for denying C must be bad reasons one will have been brow-beaten by the proof to think this. This is why, I think, Wisdom says that Moore's proof is 'suspect'.

(iii) One may not question Moore's premise, but the connection between the premise P and the conclusion C; or – and this comes to the same thing – not question P, nor question the connection between P and C, but deny that what one has asserted is the contradictory of C. This was Berkeley's position:

> I do not argue against the existence of any one thing that we can apprehend, either by sense or reflection. That the things I see with mine eyes and touch with my hands do exist, really exist, I make not the least question. (*Principles of Human Knowledge*, sec. 35)

In other words, Berkeley is saying that when he denies the existence of Matter he is not denying Moore's premise or anything that follows from it. One could put it like this:

> Either (a) C follows from P, but Berkeley's claim is not the contradictory of C, although it seems to be so,
>   or (b) Berkeley's claim is the contradictory of C, in which case C does not follow from P.

So Moore cannot say of Berkeley that he held 'as part of his philosophical creed' a proposition inconsistent with what he himself *knew* to be true. Berkeley said:

> If any man thinks this [i.e. the denial of the existence of matter] detracts from the existence or reality of things, he is very far from understanding what hath been premised in the plainest terms I could think of. (*Principles*, sec. 36)

Equally, Wisdom reports Wittgenstein, on hearing Moore's proof, to have said:

Those philosophers who have denied the existence of matter

have not wished to deny that under my trousers I wear pants. (*P.P.A.*p. 129)

This needs qualifying. Moore's view of what philosophers like McTaggart, and even Berkeley, wanted to deny has excuses and even justification. For at least some philosophers who denied the existence of matter *thought* they were denying a very general hypothesis and saying something similar to 'Unicorns don't exist'. As Moore pointed out to Wisdom, McTaggart said: 'So matter is in the same position as the gorgons and the harpies' (*P.P.A.*, p. 137). Many more philosophers who have denied the existence of matter have been undecided or divided in their reactions to the implications of their words.

If we want to get clear about what their denial ('∼C') amounts to, what kind of assertion they were making when they said that material things don't exist, it is not enough to consider what they themselves thought. We have to consider the context of the discussion, the kind of difficulties they were trying to meet, and the kind of considerations which led them to say what they said. Certainly in the case of Berkeley what led to his assertion was the kind of difficulty that Locke and Descartes raise.

One may be led, as Locke was, to think of matter as the support of all its qualities. We find this idea also in Descartes – remember his example of the piece of wax which he brings close to the fire:

> What remains of the taste evaporates; the odour vanishes; its colour changes; its shape is lost; its size increases; it becomes liquid; it grows hot; one can hardly touch it; and although it is knocked upon it will give no sound. Does the same wax remain after this change? We must admit that it does . . . What is it then in this bit of wax that we can recognise with so much distinctness? Certainly it cannot be anything that I observed by means of the senses, since everything in the field of taste, smell, sight, and hearing has changed, and since the same wax nevertheless remains.

This then leads Descartes to say:

> This wax was neither that sweetness of honey, nor that pleasant odour of flowers, nor that whiteness, nor that shape, nor

that sound, but only a body which a little while ago appeared to my senses under these forms and which now makes itself felt under others.

In this way a wedge is driven between a thing and its qualities. But then (one will want to ask) what is a thing apart from its qualities? One may then be inclined to answer 'Nothing' and to say that the thing apart from all its qualities is a fiction and does not exist. This is not what Descartes said.

One can reach such a conclusion through a somewhat different route – through difficulties about the nature of perception. This was the route that led Berkeley to it. When I look in front of me and see, for instance, a table, there is some inclination to say that it is not the table itself that I see but a visual impression. This inclination has many sources, and if it is to be resisted, as I think it must, these sources need to be examined. For the moment I shall simply indicate two such sources and later examine the second.

The inclination to say that it is not the table itself that I see comes partly from the scientific account of what happens when we see anything. When I see something in front of me I do so only because the light reflected from it strikes the retina of my eyes, start electrical impulses along the optical nerve which reach my brain, and this in turn brings about some further changes in my brain. So far so good. But this gives one the inclination to think that in seeing what is before me I am like a man at the end of a telephone line listening to his friend. We say that he hears his friend's voice. But is that true? He only hears the vibrations in his telephone receiver which copy or resemble his friend's voice. In the same way, when I look at the table before me what I see is not the table itself but the end product of the perceptual process described, namely my visual impression or sense-datum.

Thus a wedge is driven between material objects and our so-called sensations. But then what reason have we for thinking that material objects are as we experience them in perception? And, in any case, if what we see is not the same as what makes us see, if the sensation we have when we see is not the same as what causes that sensation in the first place, what reason have we for thinking that it is caused by anything outside us?

In *Some Dogmas of Religion*, following this line of thought, McTaggart writes: 'What reason can be given for a belief in the existence of matter? I conceive that such a belief can only be defended on the ground that it is a legitimate inference from our sensations.' (sec. 66) 'It is evident that sensations are not themselves the matter in question.' (sec. 68) As to their cause there is no reason to suppose that they resemble the sensations in the way that we think when we think of any material thing:

> A man who boils a lobster red may have a red face – there is nothing to prevent it. But his action in causing the redness of the lobster gives us no reason to suppose that his face is red.
>
> The result is that matter is in the same position as the gorgons and the harpies. (sec. 73)

The conclusion is that we have no more reason for thinking that there exists material things *as we normally conceive these things* than we have for believing in the existence of the gorgons and the harpies.

This conclusion is different from Berkeley's, since it seems to say that we have absolutely no reason for thinking that there exist the kind of things we constantly think exist. But presumably we could have had such a reason. Whereas Berkeley's claim is that we *could not*.[1] Berkeley's reason for thinking so brings us to the second source of the inclination to think that we can never perceive material things themselves.[2]

Here we have the famous 'argument from illusion'. Very briefly it goes something like this: Stage 1 – Sometimes it seems to me that I see a dagger before me. I subsequently find out that there was no dagger there at the time for me to see. Yet I must have seen something at the time. What I saw was an hallucination, a sense-datum. Stage 2 – But there is no intrinsic difference between what I see when I see a hallucinatory dagger and what I see when I see a real dagger. Since what I see in the first case is a sense-datum, it must equally be a sense-datum in the second case. Hence what I see when I say I see a dagger or a

---

[1] McTaggart too is pulled this way – See p. 54 below.

[2] Berkeley had thought that we cannot perceive material things in any pure sense of perception, divested of any judgment and inference (*New Theory of Vision*). Later he came to the conclusion that none of the judgements and influences that enter into perception, in the impure sense of that term, can be justified (*Principles of Human Knowledge*).

table and there is a dagger or table before me is never the dagger or table itself but a sense-datum.

Here we have been made to swallow a great deal that we need to examine, and in *Sense and Sensibilia* Austin pulls this argument to pieces.[3] I shall return to the question of the existence of sense-data further down – see Chapter Ten.

Berkeley was very much influenced by this idea that what we see are sense-data, sense impressions, or 'ideas' as he called them. If you start from this point,[4] you will naturally ask what reason your sense-data or visual impressions could possibly give you ever, on any occasion when you seem to see a dagger or a table, for thinking that there *is* a dagger or a table there, over and above your impressions, present and future, and those of other people. If you reflect on this question and you follow through the line of thought that led you to ask it, you will be forced to conclude that if your sense impressions give you any reason at all for thinking that there is a dagger or a table there, they can *at best* do so in the way that the images you see in your driving mirror give you reason for thinking that there is a car behind you getting ready to pull out.

Berkeley saw clearly that this conclusion inevitably points in the direction of scepticism, and for good reasons he wanted to reject it. We can know from the images in our mirror something about the car behind us only because we can look away from the mirror to the car itself, and because others on other occasions have done so and have seen besides the reflection the thing itself. 'Besides the mirror images we can see the car itself whose images we saw in our mirror; but we can never see besides our visual impressions those material things themselves whose visual impressions we see.' I think that Berkeley recognised the fatal implications of this lack of parallel, and he blamed our conception of matter for them, whereas, I think, he should have blamed his notion of an idea or sense-datum – in particular his notion that what we see is always and necessarily a sense-datum or sense impression: his notion of *esse* as *percipi*.

If material things exist independently of our sense im-

[3] See especially Chapters Three and Five of *Sense and Sensibilia*.

[4] You shouldn't start here. But you can only avoid doing so by examining critically the ideas and assumptions which you take for granted in your philosophical arguments.

pressions, and surely this is of the very essence of what we mean by a material thing, he thought, then we can at best have only inductive reasons for what we claim about chairs, tables and the like on particular occasions. At best only inductive reasons? This destroys the intelligibility of the whole class of claims in question. I think that Berkeley recognised this and in order to avoid this consequence he denied that material things are anything over and above our sense impressions – i.e. he claimed that Matter is ideas. But if material things exist independently of our sense impressions, does it follow that we can at best have inductive reasons for what we say about chairs and tables? Berkeley thought so and *this* is what led him to deny that material things exist independently of our sense impressions. But the answer which forced him to this conclusion is questionable. (I shall question and reject it in Chapter Ten below.)

Now we see two things: (i) That when Berkeley denied the existence of matter he was denying that matter is something over and above what he called ideas, that the existence of material things is something over and above the existence of a manifold of sense impressions. (ii) That whether this is so or not, whether Berkeley is right or wrong, has nothing to do with whether or not he would have accepted Moore's premise. Let me first consider the second point.

A philosopher who says that material things don't exist may be saying that a thing apart from all its qualities is a fiction. Or he may be saying that the existence of a material thing is not anything over and above our sense impressions – the sense impressions we would have under certain conditions. Whatever there is to be said for or against this, does accepting Moore's premise commit one to rejecting this claim? This is the question we asked earlier: If '∼C' means what I suggested it means, is ∼C incompatible with P? Berkeley may have answered this question as follows: 'If the word "hand" is meant to refer to something over and above and independent of the sense impressions anyone in such-and-such a position may have then someone who accepts Moore's premise has committed himself to something that is inconsistent with what I, Berkeley, maintain. But if the word "hand" is not to be understood in this way, then from Moore's premise the contradictory of what I claim does not follow, and I would be quite happy to accept his premise.'

That is whether C follows from P, if C is taken to be the denial of what Berkeley claimed, depends on what the correct *analysis* of words like 'hand', 'tree', 'soap bubble' etc., is. On this question Moore never subscribed to a recipe and always spoke with a great deal of caution and hesitation. Does C follow from P? I answered, provisionally, if such words as 'hand' and 'tree' are used to mean something over and above our sense impressions then it does follow, and if not then it does not follow.[5]

But are these words used to mean something over and above our sense impressions? This is a queer question and cannot be met head on. If one tries to do so, as Berkeley did, one will be pulled in two opposite directions. Hence Professor Wisdom would say that our question here is a 'conflict question' – like the question 'Is a tomato a fruit or a vegetable?'[6]

So Wisdom compares the issue of whether or not Moore's proof is valid to the following case:

[5] Even if one were to come out and say that when one speaks of a hand one is not talking about sense impressions, but about something that exists over and above them, and even if C is taken to be the contradictory of the analytical assertion that Matter is not anything over and above sense impressions, there would still be an objection to saying that P entails C. For can we say that the correct analysis of a class of propositions follows from the assertion of any one such proposition? I doubt it. That is why I qualify the above answer as 'provisional'. But putting this objection aside let me indicate schematically how this provisional answer to the question 'Does C follow from P?' compare with the answer I suggested to this question in the previous chapter:

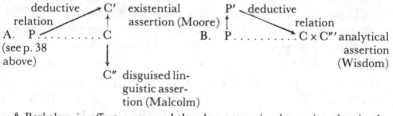

[6] Berkeley, in effect, answered the above question by saying that in the vulgar sense by 'hand' we do not mean anything over and above ideas/sensible properties, but in the philosophical sense, *vide* Locke, we do. But he also spoke of the philosopher's prejudice as deeply riveted in *our* thoughts. Similarly, one may say that according to botanical criteria a tomato is a fruit, but in common parlance it is spoken of as a vegetable – e.g. greengrocers sell it as a vegetable.

Consider the case of Smith who raises Jones' salary on the day he said he would but *only* because he fears Jones' leaving for another job. One philosopher may insist that this is not the keeping of a promise. Another philosopher may *prove* it is a case of promise-keeping. He proceeds somewhat as follows: 'Smith unquestionably has done that which he said he would do. A man who does what he has said he would do keeps his promise. Therefore Smith has kept his promise.' All this proof really does for us is to bring out where and how we are undecided even when fully informed about a case whether to describe it as a promise-keeping or not. But although this is all the proof does, it is to be noticed that it cannot fairly and plainly be called invalid. It neither involves a slip . . . nor is it a case of ambiguity. This is why even this sample dispute may puzzle us. (*P.P.A.*, p. 131).

Elsewhere Wisdom has given other examples – one of them William James' example of a squirrel or dog circling the place where a cow stands while the cow turns round itself always pointing its horns to the squirrel or dog: Has the squirrel or dog gone round the cow or not? ('Metaphysics and Verification')

The point is this: If the question 'Are there material things or not?' is really a question about whether the existence of material things is anything over and above the existence of sense impressions, then it cannot be settled by a proof in the way that Moore tried to do. As Wisdom puts it:

> In these cases the difficulty is not removed by doing any of the only three things to be done, namely (1) deny the premise, (2) protest at a step, (3) accept the conclusion. For, whichever one does, the repressed objectionableness of it leaves a haunting anxiety which in the end leads to rebellion in oneself or others. (*P.P.A.*, p. 132)

We cannot say that Moore's premise entails his conclusion and finish with the matter, as Moore thought he could do. But neither can we say that it does not entail his conclusion and dismiss Moore's proof, as Berkeley might have wished to do. There is another kind of work that needs to be done.

If we cannot dismiss Moore's proof, we need to consider what it is that it achieves. This will be the topic of the next chapter. Before turning to it, however, I should like to distinguish the

last point I made about whether one can prove that Moore's op-
ponent is wrong from the earlier one I made when I argued that
'material thing' is not a general name but a formal concept: (i)
The existence of material things is not anything that can be
directly stated. What is in question shows itself in our use of
language. It is not anything that can be said to be known, that
can be proved, justified or doubted. (ii) If a philosopher like
Moore finds the assertion that material things don't exist objectionable and wants to combat it, this cannot be done by offering
a proof of its contradictory.

Summary   (I) A proof of the kind Moore purports to offer is
useful, i.e. it can bring conviction to a person who lacks it, only
where the connection between P and C is complex and, therefore, easy to miss.

Where this is otherwise, the reason why a man doubts C is
more likely to be that he has independent reasons for wanting to
deny C. A proof which connects P with C will give him some
reason for wanting to accept C, but equally some reason for
doubting the truth of P. The proof, here, can at best force this
conflict to his attention. It cannot resolve it.

(II) Confronted with Moore's proof a philosopher who
asserts that $\sim$ C can do one of three things which may be represented schematically as follows:

    (i)   P deny that P is incontrovertible
                ↓ accept the connection
        ∴ C wish to deny C

    (ii)   P One may be brow-beaten by the proof
                ↓ and retract what one wanted to say,
        ∴ C i.e. retract $\sim$ C.

(iii) (a) P not question this   or (b) P not question this
          ↓ question the connection   ↓ not question
                                        the connection
        ∴ C insist on retaining $\sim$ C ∴ C deny that what one
                                                wishes to assert
                                              is the contra-
                                                dictory of C

      Or more briefly:

(a) P   (b) P
     ↓ question the connection   ↓
     ∴ C"   ∴ C' × ∼ C"
                                          question the incompatibility

(a) C' is the limit at which C destroys itself.
(b) C" is not entailed by P; it is presupposed by the
     intelligibility of P.

(III) But what were philosophers who asserted that ∼ C
denying? Were they asserting the contradictory of C' as Moore
thought, or of C" as Malcolm thought? Neither – though both
Moore and Malcolm had excuses for what they thought. I
suggested that if we want to get clear about what they were
denying, it is not enough to consider the form of words they
used, nor what they themselves thought they were saying –
though we cannot completely ignore either. We have to consider the context of the discussion, the kind of difficulties they
were trying to meet, and the kind of considerations that led
them to say what they said. I considered three cases: ∼ C"' (1),
(2), (3).

(1) 'A material thing apart from all its qualities is a fiction.'
(2) 'A material thing, as we experience it in perception, is a
fiction of the mind. We have no more reason for thinking that
there are material things, as we normally conceive them, than
we have for believing in the existence of the gorgons and the
harpies' (McTaggart).
(3) 'Material things as having a reality over and above our
sense impressions don't exist. The idea of such an existence
involves a contradiction' (Berkeley).

What is being rejected in (1) is a model for the logic of matter or
of the relation between a substance and its qualities. Locke and
Descartes were captives of it. This was *part* of what Berkeley
wanted to reject (see *Principles* sec. 37). In (2) a model is foisted
on us for what we mean by perception – the so-called causal
theory of perception is carried to an extreme where it destroys
itself. In (3) what is rejected is a model of the logic of the reality
of matter and of its relation to our sense impressions (see *Principles* sec. 36). (These are oversimplifications and at the core of
each denial is a conflict between the attraction to the model and

the reasons for wanting to reject it. On both sides of the conflict may be intermingled conceptual confusion as well as penetration.)

(IV) Does accepting Moore's premise P commit a philosopher to rejecting what he asserted, namely $\sim C'''$ $_{(1)}$ or $_{(2)}$ or $_{(3)}$? Is $\sim C'''$ incompatible with P? No. But I suggested earlier that a philosopher who asserts $\sim C$ is often not clear about what he wants to say and that he may oscillate in what he means — thus:

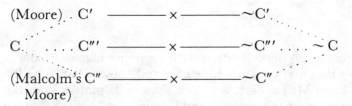

If the question 'Do material things exist?' is a question about whether $\sim C'''$ is to be accepted or rejected, then (1) it cannot be settled by any proof like the one Moore gives. (2) If one wishes to reject it, then (a) one needs to appreciate what makes any one put it forward and (b) that it often is, in part, an attempt to say something correct and, therefore, something one must be careful not to deny when rejecting it. (This is what Wisdom has in mind when he characterises questions like 'Are there material things?' as conflict questions.)

6 What Moore's Proof Achieves

I said that when Berkeley denied the existence of matter he was denying that matter is anything over and above what he called ideas. Even McTaggart, when he says that 'matter is in the same position as the gorgons and harpies', and means that we have absolutely no reason for thinking that there are chairs and tables in the ordinary sense of these terms, isn't really saying that we are all under the kind of misapprehension that a man is who is seeing an hallucination of a dagger and thinks wrongly that there is a dagger there. For his arguments boil down to this: If by matter we understand something other than and over and above our 'sensations', and our knowledge of material things, if we had such knowledge, is based on our sensations, as it must be, then what kind of reason could our sensations provide us with? Not inductive reasons; nor yet deductive ones. It follows that they can provide us with no reason at all. The argument is purely *a priori* and so is, therefore, its conclusion. In fact, it is very reminiscent of Hume:

> That our senses offer not their impressions as the images of something *distinct*, or *independent*, and *external*, is evident; because they convey to us nothing but a single perception, and never give us the least intimation of anything beyond. A single perception can never produce the idea of a double existence, but by some inference either of the reason or imagination. When the mind looks farther than what immediately appears to it, its conclusions can never be put to the account of the senses; and it certainly looks farther, when from a single perception it infers a double existence, and

supposes the relations of resemblance and causation betwixt them. (*Treatise*, Bk. I, Pt. IV, sec. 2)

What is in question is surely not a contingent matter – of whatever generality. If I say 'There are no unicorns' then I am speaking about a class of animals and deny that such animals exist – that they are to be found anywhere on earth. We have seen that one could not, in the same way, intelligibly deny the existence of material things. What is in question is not a class of things at all. Yet Moore fails to appreciate this. In 'A Defence of Common Sense' he says:

> It seems to me quite clear that it *might* have been the case that Time was not real, material things not real, Space not real, selves not real. (*Phil. Papers*, p. 42)

In 'Four Forms of Scepticism' he says: 'Descartes' malicious demon is a logical possibility.' (*ibid.* p. 222) In other words, we may all be deceived all the time. This is what Moore takes a philosopher like McTaggart to have claimed – i.e. that whenever we say anything like 'Here is a hand' we are saying something false. In 'A Reply to My Critics' he mentions Wittgenstein's remark, 'Those philosophers who have denied the existence of matter have not wished to deny that under my trousers I wear pants' and he insists that *some* have:

> If by this Wittgenstein meant that *no* philosophers who have ever denied the existence of matter have ever wished to deny that pants exist, I think the statement is simply false . . . That *some* have *sometimes* meant this, is, I think, certain (*The Philosophy of G. E. Moore*, p. 670).

He is right only this far: That some philosophers have sometimes *wanted* to say that whenever anyone ever says something like 'I have got some pants on' they are saying something false – in the same way that if Macbeth had said 'This is a dagger that I see before me' he would have been saying something false. They *wanted* to say this, they *tried* to say it, and they *thought* that it could be said. But – and this is where Moore is wrong – they couldn't have succeeded. Moore's interpretation of what they sometimes meant and, therefore, succeeded in saying is ruled out by logic. One cannot intelligibly claim that all assertions

like 'I wear pants' are or may be false. The reason for this, very
briefly, is this:

(A) If one could *never* utter such words as 'I am wearing
pants' or 'I am sitting on a chair' and say something true, then
what would be the point of uttering them? What would be the
difference between uttering the words 'I am sitting on a chair'
and 'I am not sitting on a chair'? If it made no difference which
of these two sentences I uttered, would I be saying anything in
uttering them – true or false? If the answer is No, then this
plainly contradicts the claim that I would be saying something
false whenever I uttered such words. Moore's claim, therefore,
that it is conceivable that a malicious demon is deceiving us all
the time in the way that Macbeth was deceived when he
thought there was a dagger before him, may be said to hide a
contradiction. If one can never use sentences of the kind in
question to say something true, then one cannot use them to say
something false either.

(B) I must *understand* a form of words before I know whether
it says something true or false. But what is it for me to understand these words? How do you know whether I understand
them? Surely, I understand them only if I can make true statements with them. If this is ruled out of court, then how would
my understanding of what they mean find expression? If, for
instance, I know what the word 'chair' means then you expect
me to bring you a chair when you ask for one – and not bring
you something else, or just look at you vacantly. But if all statements like 'Here is a chair' were false, then there would be no
way in which I, or anyone else, could show an understanding of
these statements, or of the words in which they are made.

(C) It follows that the words 'Matter doesn't exist' could not
intelligibly be taken to mean that all assertions like 'Here is a
hand' are false – i.e. '$\sim C'$' doesn't make sense. They can *at best*
mean that all such assertions are meaningless – '$\sim C''$'. But we
have only to look at the difference these utterances make to our
actions, the role they play in our life, to see that this is a ridiculous claim.

I do not think that this – i.e. $\sim C''$ – is what philosophers who
claimed that matter doesn't exist wanted to say. Why should
they have wanted to say anything like this? It is more understandable that some of them were confused and wanted to say

what Moore took them to be saying – i.e. $\sim$ C'. We have seen, however, that there is more to their words than this and that at least part of what they wanted to say was that material things are not anything over and above our sense impressions – i.e. $\sim$ C'''. We have seen something of why they should have wanted to say this. And whether we agree with it or not, surely we can agree that *if* this is what they were saying then they were concerned with the *concept* of matter or physical reality, and not the truth or falsity of anything we believe or say. This is very different from what Moore took them to be concerned with and thought they had said. (Although, as we have seen, in his long *preparation* to the proof he gave, Moore himself was concerned with these conceptual issues – with elucidating the concept of externality, the difference between the kind of reality that a shadow has and the kind of reality that belongs to an after-image. See Chapter Three.)

Still we cannot say without qualification that they were making a conceptual statement, that they were concerned with the analysis of our concept of material existence or physical reality. For, as is often the case in philosophy, a philosopher may not be clear about what he wants to say, he may be divided in his reactions to the many familiar things he says everyday of his life.

The virtue of Moore's proof is that it forces such a philosopher to a corner and obliges him to reflect on what it is he wants to say, and so to become clear about the issues he is trying to come to terms with. For if, as Moore thought, he wants his words 'Matter doesn't exist' to be related to 'Here is a hand' in the way that 'There are no vehicles in the park' is related to 'Here is a motor cycle', uttered by someone walking in the park, then he is in trouble – though Moore himself was not clear about the kind of trouble in which he finds himself. If, on the other hand, on reflection he says, 'What I want to say is that Matter is not anything over and above our sense impressions', then he steers clear of this particular trouble – which is not to say that the path ahead is a rosy one. For what he now says, his transformed assertion, may still be open to objection, though of a different kind.

As Wisdom points out in 'Moore's Technique', the philosophical statements 'Matter doesn't exist', 'Matter doesn't really exist', 'Matter isn't anything over and above our sensations', 'Matter is a logical fiction', 'Statements about material things can be analysed into statements about sensations' form a series (*P.P.A.*, p. 145). The question whether or not they mean the same is a conflict question. There are good reasons for saying that they mean the same thing, but also equally good reasons for saying that they don't. As such these conflicting reasons cannot be reconciled – that is *qua* reasons for and against speaking of *equivalence of meaning* in this connection. But the facts themselves which give us these conflicting inclinations are not incompatible. So instead of forcing an answer Yes or No on ourselves, we should try to get an undistorted view of them. If we can do this,[1] we shall understand better the nature of the enterprise in which these extravagant assertions are made and then reformulated until much of the initial sting vanishes.

One difficulty at the heart of this question has to do with the use of the word 'meaning', and therefore 'equivalence of meaning', in connection with philosophical utterances. How far does the philosopher's intention form part of what he means by his words and how far is his meaning to be found in the considerations with which he backs up what he says? I mean, what weight must we attach in our considerations of what he means to what he says he means? If he is confused in his intentions, how far does this enter into his meaning, and in what form can it do so?

There are many occasions outside philosophy where we say to someone, 'You could not have meant what you say you mean' and get him to agree. We may describe this as *discovering* what he meant. But in philosophy this kind of questioning is part of the philosophical inquiry itself. When the philosopher, subjected to this kind of criticism, admits that he could not have meant what he thought he meant and proceeds to use different words, we have as much reason for saying that he now expresses

[1] Wisdom describes what is in question as giving an a-septic description of those facts, or letting the conflicting voices speak their fill. This is one respect in which he likens a way of dealing with philosophical problems to an aspect of psycho-analytic method that is central to it. Both bring the appropriate kind of insight and enable one to move forward, instead of oscillating back and forth repetitively.

what he originally meant to say in more appropriate and less
misleading words, i.e. says the same thing only better, as we
have for saying that he has modified his original assertion.
There is good reason for giving the latter description, since his
modified assertion may contain a perception into the issues that
trouble him which his original assertion lacked. The reverse
may be also true, and at the same time. But where one assertion
shows greater insight than the other you cannot say, without
qualification, that they mean the same – especially when the
insight in question is precisely what the inquiry in which these
assertions are made seeks to obtain.

Wisdom does not say that these different statements made by
the philosopher are equivalent, that they mean the same, nor
yet that they don't mean the same. He says that 'as the formulations become more and more logical and analytic . . . something is gained and something is lost' (*P.P.A.*, p. 145). What he
has in mind, briefly, is this: When the formulations are such as
to make it seem that the philosopher is a kind of master-
scientist, advancing extremely general hypotheses, they mislead us with regard to what is in question.[2] Hence Wittgenstein
often insisted that the questions he was writing about are conceptual questions and not empirical ones. When, on the other
hand, the formulations become more and more logical they
make it seem that the philosopher is concerned to map, as completely as he can, the logic of certain areas of discourse, that he
is a kind of informal logician – an idea of philosophy that has
had much influence in Oxford.[3] Wisdom thinks, as I agree, that
there is much to be said against such a conception of philosophy. When the formulations of a philosophical thesis become
progressively more logical, what is lost sight of is the extent to
which a philosopher is concerned to overcome certain sorts of
difficulties and to combat certain kinds of illusion and misapprehension. As he puts it: 'What he does [the philosopher who
says that matter doesn't exist] is in many ways like what one
who corrects a popular illusion does, and unlike the mere trans-

[2] See my criticism of Russell's view that the continued and independent
existence of material things is a very general assumption which, strictly
speaking, we cannot prove – Chapter Three above.

[3] See, for instance, Professor Ryle's lecture 'Formal and Informal Logic',
Dilemmas.

lation of one class of sentences into others which are not applicable in exactly the same cases' (*P.P.A.*, p. 141). Berkeley, certainly, gives us a strong sense of this – a sense of the fact that he is combating misapprehensions, what he calls 'prejudices', from which the 'vulgar' is not altogether immune. (In 'The Metamorphosis of Metaphysics' Wisdom questions the view to which Ayer subscribed that metaphysical issues as traditionally expressed are logical issues in disguise: 'Was this all a mistake?' – *Paradox and Discovery*, p. 71.)

Secondly, the view of philosophy as informal logic (Ryle), or as a logical enterprise (Ayer), threatens to obscure the difference between philosophy and logic, between the kind of misapprehension the philosopher attempts to redress and the kind of misapprehension from which the logician is concerned to free us. It was partly to bring this difference into relief that Wisdom distinguished between the 'domestic logic' of expressions and their 'ultimate logic'. Thirdly, the view of philosophy as informal logic makes philosophy systematic[4] in a way that makes it flat and loses sight of its big questions. Obviously this is a topic that needs separate treatment.

To recapitulate. In giving his proof Moore assumed that the proposition 'Here is a hand and here is another' *entails* the proposition that 'Matter exists'. The proof is supposed to show that one cannot *consistently* accept a proposition like Moore's premise and assert that there are no material things. We have seen that if one who asserts that there are no material things means no more by this than 'Material things are not anything over and above sense impressions' then he can with perfect consistency accept Moore's premise and still deny his conclusion. This is precisely what Berkeley did. Often, though, the reactions of one who says 'I don't believe Matter exists' are very much like those of someone who says 'I don't believe there is anyone aboard that ship' (*P.P.A.*, p. 140). It is not until we trace the concrete consequences of 'Matter doesn't exist' (as Berkeley does quite explicitly) right down to what the man expects to see and what he doesn't expect that we begin to feel the inclination to say that

---

[4] See, for instance, Russell's idea of a 'scientific' philosophy in 'Logic as the Essence of Philosophy', *Our Knowledge of the External World*, and in 'The Philosophy of Logical Atomism', *Logic and Knowledge*, ed. Robert C. Marsh.

though he appears to advance a negative hypothesis, he is doing no such thing. But until then his reactions are often undecided – e.g. over 'Are there no cherries on the tree, and no tree in the garden?' 'Moore's proof [writes Wisdom] forces him to decide, forces him to become unmuddled, to gain a grasp of what he wishes to do with his words "Matter doesn't exist", what he wishes us to understand by them.' (p. 140)

This is what Moore's proof achieves. It does not settle the question about the existence of material things as it purports to do; but it helps to transform it in such a way that its conceptual character becomes plain and the conceptual preoccupations that lie beneath the surface are allowed to emerge so that they can be given direct attention.

7 What Moore's Opponent Denies

We have seen that we cannot deny the existence of all material things *in the way* that someone may deny that there are pink rats before him when, under the influence of alcohol, it seems to him that there are. For we find out that a perception is deceptive by reference to other perceptions – our own and other people's. To deny, for instance, that there is water in the distance, when travelling in the desert it seems as if there is, is to say that when we get to the right spot we shall see no water, feel no wetness, etc. If we claimed those perceptions to be equally deceptive, what sense could we attach to our first claim? It doesn't make sense, then, to claim that all our perceptions may be deceptive. Similarly, neither can we claim that all physical object propositions are false without denying that it makes sense to talk about chairs and tables, sticks and stones.

Hence insofar as a philosopher who denies the existence of material things *thinks* that he is denying the truth of all propositions like 'Here is a chair' he must be confused. What needs to be done here is not to prove him wrong, but to expose his confusion. This, however, would rarely be the end of the matter. In most cases it would serve the purpose of getting him to reformulate his claim: 'I see that I couldn't intelligibly have meant what I thought I meant. But that doesn't mean that I meant nothing. I was really trying to say that material things are nothing over and above our sense impressions.' Here we would have to raise *new* objections.

Professor Wisdom reminds us that words like 'The average man doesn't exist' are quite commonly used to mean 'The average man is not anything or anyone over and above individual men'. Here the existential denial forcibly combats the idea that the relation between the average man and individual men is like the relation between a member of Parliament and the men in his constituency whom he represents. He says that it is muddling to express oneself like this since it may mislead us to suspect the everyday remarks we make with the help of such expressions as 'the average man', 'the average tax payer', 'the average plumber'. Nevertheless it is natural to talk like this, to say that the average man doesn't exist, and it does not constitute a misuse of language (*P.P.A.*, p. 133). But how far are the philosopher's words 'Matter doesn't exist' like the words 'The average man doesn't exist'? The question is a comparative one.

You may say that the point made by someone who says 'The average man doesn't exist' is obvious and indisputable, so that what he says is a platitude. This is true. You may say that no one needs to be reminded of what these words are used to say. But still there are occasions when they are informative and useful – e.g. in conversation with a child. Here telling the child that the average man doesn't exist will be part of an attempt to teach him how to understand such words as 'the average man prefers a bitter to a gin and lime', part of an attempt to correct or prevent misunderstanding – one that may show itself in such questions of the child as 'Where does he live?', 'What does he look like?', 'How can I meet him?'. It helps the child to learn to make sense of such remarks as 'The wages of the average man are low'.

If the child asks where the average man lives, that is because he has not yet firmly grasped how statements like 'The wages of the average man are low' differ from and how they are related to such statements as 'Tom's wage is low'. And this is a matter of logic. Yet the child is not concerned with logic, or asking a question of logic: How are these two kinds of statement related? How does the former differ from the latter? If he asks, 'Can I meet the average man?' and you answer 'You cannot', you will have to explain why – explain, for instance, that this is not because the average man is invisible. Explaining why one cannot meet the average man is explaining to the child a bit of logic. When the child grasps the logical points we explain to him his questions will have been met – although he was not asking any question of logic. His questions will have been met because they come from a misunderstanding of the logic of the expression 'the average man'. So an explanation which clears the misunderstanding will meet his questions. It will make him see not only that he cannot meet the average man but also why he cannot meet him – that it doesn't make sense to speak of meeting the average man.[1]

But now to what extent are the philosopher's questions 'Are there material things?', 'Can we know them?' like the child's questions 'Can I meet the average man?', 'What does he look like?'. We have seen how the child's questions come from his mistaken idea that the average man is related to individual men whose tastes, habits and wages he represents, in the way that a member of Parliament is related to his constituency. Can we say, in the same way, that the philosopher's questions come from logical misapprehensions, from mistaken ideas about the logic of statements about chairs and tables?

Unlike the child, in the case of the philosopher we cannot say that he doesn't know or hasn't grasped the logic of statements about chairs and tables. It would be ridiculous to suppose that like the child his grasp of the logic of the expressions in question is weak or inadequate. But if so, in what sense can he be said to be under a logical misapprehension, to misunderstand the logic of these expressions? He does not misuse them, nor does he reason badly. But, to use a metaphor, one could say that the shadow which the logic of these expressions casts on his mind makes him uneasy; it leads him a metaphysical dance. So, on the one hand, we have his proper grasp of the logic of these expressions as it is exhibited in his use of them. On the other hand, we have the shadows which their logic casts on his mind when they begin to idle, when, in Berkeley's words, we begin 'to meditate on the nature of things'[2] – in this case on the nature of material existence and our knowledge of it. What I called 'shadow' Wittgenstein calls 'picture'[3] ('A picture held us captive' – *Inv.* sec. 115) and Berkeley calls a 'prejudice' ('a prejudice deeply riveted in our thoughts'). The 'prejudice' in question is the idea that material things have an existence dis-

---

[1] Unless one uses this expression in connection with its instances, as with 'the typical English gentleman', 'l'homme moyen sensuel'.

[2] *Principles of Human Knowledge*, Introduction, sec. 1

[3] See Part Two, Chapter Three, sec. 1 below.

tinct from and independent of our sense impressions; and we have already seen that, adequate or not, this is a *grammatical* or *logical* characterisation. Berkeley is saying: This cannot be a correct characterisation, for it makes unintelligible much that we are familiar with – for instance, that when we open our eyes in the morning we know that the sun is shining.

We have noted a similarity and a difference between the child who asks whether the average man exists and, if so, where he is to be met, and the philosopher who asks whether matter exists and, if so, how we know the various things we claim to know about sticks and stones, tables and chairs, on particular occasions. I want to note another difference. The logical questions about which the child is not clear, though he does not ask them, namely 'Is the average man someone over and above individual men?', 'Is he related to individual men as a member of Parliament is related to his constituency?' have a definite answer, namely No. The corresponding 'logical' questions about Matter do not have a definite answer, and in fact part of our difficulty with these questions come from their very formulations. Given the particular formulation, which itself needs questioning, the question 'Are material things anything over and above our sense impressions?' is one to which both the answer Yes and the answer No meet with insuperable objections. Very briefly, on the one side, if material things are not anything over and above our sense impressions, how do we manage to communicate with each other? Isn't the notion of a sense impression parasitic on the notion of a material thing? On the other side (and this was Berkeley's difficulty), if matter is something over and above our sense impressions, how can we ever form a conception of matter? Berkeley couldn't see how and so he took the heroic course of denying that matter is anything over and above our sense impressions. His words that Matter doesn't exist, as we have seen, express just this denial.

To put it differently. The correct answer to 'Is the average man anything over and above individual men?' is No. In *this* sense, there is no correct answer to 'Is a material thing anything over and above sense impressions?'. We wish to say, quite rightly, that unlike mental images, sensations and after-images, physical objects do not depend for their existence on being perceived (see Chapter Three above). This favours an affirmative answer to our question. But the affirmative answer suggests that our knowledge of physical objects is like our knowledge of what is hidden from us, in other words inferential and indirect. It suggests that I know that the sun is shining when I open my eyes in the morning in the way that I know from the images on my driving mirror that there is a car behind me. And this makes the affirmative answer objectionable.

I said that unlike the child the philosopher is familiar with the logic of the expressions in question and does not draw invalid inferences. In that sense he neither fails to understand their logic, nor misunderstands it. But I added that the shadow which this logic casts on his mind leads him a metaphysical dance. There are two shadows here which alternate, two models or pictures of the logic of matter: (i) A material thing is to the appearances or sense impressions from which we know it *like a substance is to its shadows*. This, by and large, dominated Locke's thinking, and Berkeley *rightly* wanted to oppose it. (ii) A material thing is to the appearances or sense impressions from which we know it *like an abstraction is to the individuals from which it is abstracted* – e.g. like the average man is to individual men. The trouble is that *both* these models are unsatisfactory, and yet they are diametrically opposed. Therefore any attempt to turn our back on one of them faces us with the other, and *vice versa*. The unsuccessful attempt to come out into the open is the metaphysical dance which Wittgenstein compared to the antics of the fly in the fly bottle.

Let me summarise. Having seen that the philosopher's assertion 'Matter doesn't exist' (which Moore wanted to reject by trying to prove its opposite) is not and cannot be like the assertion 'Unicorns don't exist', I asked whether it is like the assertion 'The average man doesn't exist'. We have seen that the latter, though somewhat misleading, nevertheless makes a logical point which is perfectly acceptable. The philosopher, without recognising this clearly, is trying to make a similar point about the notion of matter. But the point he is making is not acceptable, nor yet is its contradictory. So arguing for or against the answers possible to the questions which Berkeley or McTaggart were answering when they said 'Matter doesn't exist', will not take us any further. It is the questions themselves we need to scrutinise and the concepts in terms of which these questions are asked. One of these concepts is the concept of sense-datum or sense impression or idea (in Berkeley's sense).

One important question here: There is certainly a difference in grammar between the notion of e.g. a spot on the wall and the notion of an after-image seen against the background of the wall. Part of this difference may be indicated by saying that the spot exists whether I see it or not, whereas the after-image cannot exist unseen – in Berkeley's words its *esse* is *percipi*. If this is a correct characterisation of the grammar in which we speak of a spot or stain on the wall, does it follow (as Berkeley thought) that we can at best have inductive reasons for the claim that there is a spot on the wall? I don't think so – see Chapter Ten below. Wrongly thinking that this is an inevitable conclusion, Berkeley concluded (and this was a perfectly valid step to take) that the notion of matter as something over and above our sense impressions involves a contradiction. In other words, his reasons for denying the existence of matter, conceived as something over and above our sense impressions, were purely logical, and a good part of his reasoning was both impeccable and penetrating.

8 Scepticism and Moore's Premise

Moore says that a proof of the kind he has given must satisfy three conditions if it is to be any good:

(i) The premise and the conclusion must be different.
(ii) I must *know* the premise to be true.
(iii) The premise must *entail* the conclusion.

In connection with (ii) he insists that he knows the premise:

> How absurd it would be to suggest that I did not know it, but only believed it, and that perhaps it was not the case! You might as well suggest that I do not know that I am now standing up and talking – that perhaps after all I'm not, and that it's not quite certain that I am! (pp. 146–7)

He doesn't go far beyond insisting that he *knows* what the premise says and that it would be *absurd* to deny it. He says that he cannot offer a proof of the premise that would satisfy the sceptic. But his tone of voice is hesitant; he half-thinks that he ought to be able to do so.

(A) On the one hand he says 'I can know things which I cannot prove' (p. 150) and this suggests that he thinks that to ask for a proof of these things is to labour under a confusion. If so, he *ought* to have explained why. But this he does not do anywhere.

(B) On the other hand he says that in order to satisfy the sceptic he has to be able to prove, among other things, that he is awake and not dreaming. He goes on:

But how can I prove that I am not? I have, no doubt, conclusive reasons for asserting that I am not now dreaming; I
have conclusive evidence that I am awake: but that is a very
different thing from being able to prove it. I could not tell you
what all my evidence is; and I should require to do this at
least, in order to give you a proof. (p. 149)

This gives the impression that he thinks there is something he
could have done which he has failed to do, namely list all the
evidence that he has in order to see how conclusive it is.

He returns to this question at the end of his paper 'Certainty'
and there too it is clear that he does not think he has been able
to counter the sceptic's 'I cannot be sure that I am not now
dreaming'. But there his reason for thinking that he has failed is
different and less relevant to the point under discussion. It is
this, namely that he cannot prove or show that what the sceptic
says is logically possible is not so:

The conjunction of my memories of the immediate past with
these [present] sensory experiences *may* be sufficient to
enable me to know that I am not dreaming. I say *may* be. But
what if our sceptical philosopher says: It is *not* sufficient; and
offers as an argument to prove that it is not, this: It is logically
possible *both* that you should be having all the sensory experiences you are having, and also that you should be remembering what you do remember [having the memories that you
have], and *yet* should be dreaming If this *is* logically possible,
then I don't see how to deny that I cannot possibly know for
certain that I am not dreaming: I do not see that I possibly
could. But can any reason be given for saying that it *is* logically possible? So far as I know nobody ever has, and I don't
know how anybody could. (Phil. Papers, p. 250)

Here what Moore seeks to show is that what the sceptic
claims is incoherent, or that what leads him to think that he
may now be dreaming does not justify this conclusion.[1] This is

[1] This is what Professor Malcolm provides in his book *Dreaming* – though
with an important difference: (i) He states the so-called argument from
dreams which aims to establish that no one can ever be sure whether the experiences he is having are those of a dream or those of waking life. (ii) He
examines, finds unsatisfactory, and dismisses one common answer to the
sceptic who puts forward this argument, i.e. the counter-argument from cohe-

what he thinks he has failed to demonstrate; *not* the truth of his premise and our knowledge of it. Ought he to be able to prove the latter? No. But he should have been able to do something else, namely to show that in the given circumstances it makes no sense to doubt his premise.

Moore missed this by a very narrow margin. He said that he *knows* his premise to be true and that it would be *absurd* to deny this. He also said 'I can know things which I cannot prove'. But he was troubled by his inability to state the *evidence* on which his premise is based. This prevented him from concentrating on the absurdity involved in denying that we know the kind of thing he insisted we know.

In 'A Defence of Common Sense' he says:

> We are all, I think, in this strange position that we do *know* many things, with regard to which we *know* further that we must have had evidence for them, and yet we do not know *how* we know them, *i.e.* we do not know what the evidence was. (*Phil. Papers*, p. 44).

Here we have a perfectly valid and, I think, important distinction in philosophy. To *know* something is one thing, to be able to characterise the kind of knowledge one has is another. Epistemology is largely concerned with providing an account of the kinds of knowledge we have. There is, then, (1) the question 'Can anyone ever know that he is sitting on a chair? or that his friend is angry?' which the sceptic raises. If the sceptic's doubts can be shown to be unfounded and to come from conceptual confusion, there is (2) the further question 'Given that we can know these things, *how* do we know them?'

Moore was confident that we all know the kinds of thing which the sceptic says we can't know. But he was hesitant with regard to the second question. He was right to be critical here. However, he tended to think of his inability to give a satis-

rence. (iii) Malcolm does not answer the sceptic on the sceptic's own grounds. What he argues is *not* that I can know what the sceptic doubts (p. 118), but that the question 'Can I know whether I am awake or sleeping and dreaming?' involves logical incoherences and comes from confusion.

The sceptic asks, 'Can I know . . .?' and answers 'I cannot'. Moore wants to be able to argue 'I can and do know'. Malcolm, on the other hand, rejects the question itself. The first fifteen chapters of the book, leading to the last three, contain a detailed discussion which enables him to reject this question.

factory answer to it as a form of ignorance.[2] This shows, I think, that Moore was not clear about the character of his second question.

He tended to take it as simply a more general form of the question, 'You tell me that the enemy is preparing for an attack; how do you know this? what makes you think so? what is the basis of your claim?' This is not a philosophical question at all. It is a request for the scout's evidence so that it can be evaluated. Once this is done, one would know how much weight to attach to what he says. One is trying to decide whether one can rely on it. There are also cases where one finds one cannot answer such a question. For instance, I hazard an opinion about a friend which I feel confident about. You ask me for its basis: 'What makes you think so?' I reflect and decide that I do not know the basis of my conviction on this matter – from which it does not follow that it has no basis.

The difficulty Moore feels in answering his second question is very different. What that question calls for is not some piece of knowledge which Moore lacks, nor even simply the reflective articulation of something he knows obscurely but has so far failed to articulate. It calls for philosophical work that is at the same time creative and critical – of the kind we find examples in Moore's writings. But if one has further to go in this work, if one is dissatisfied with some of the conclusions one has reached, this does not mean that one is in a state of partial ignorance, that one lacks some knowledge.

The question which calls for this kind of work is very different from the question we put to the scout or the man who ventured an opinion about a friend. That question asked for the man's evidence. Moore's question is a request for 'analysis' and aims to get clear about the *logic* of the claims to knowledge in question: 'How do we know these things *in the end*?', 'What is our *ultimate* evidence for claiming these things with confidence?' In *some* cases answering these questions will take the form of bringing out the 'groundlessness' of our claims and their connections with other things we take for granted. In *other* cases it will take the form of elucidating the sense in which the kind of basis we have for our claims justifies them. In either case we shall be

---

[2] Wisdom discusses this question in 'Mace, Moore and Wittgenstein', *Paradox and Discovery*.

bringing out what belongs to the grammar of the forms of knowledge under scrutiny. This is obviously very different from stating our evidence and, in this sense, supporting our claims in the face of doubt and criticism.

Moore's lack of clarity about the question 'How do we know what the sceptic says we can't know?' is reflected in the way he was divided in his reactions when he said 'I can know things which I cannot prove'. For insofar as he takes the above question as a common-or-garden request for evidence, his dissatisfaction with the account he provides makes him think that he has failed to give a proof that would show the sceptic to be wrong. He is thus inclined to think that while our inability to state (all) our evidence does not show that we don't know what we claim we know ('I can know things I cannot prove'), nevertheless if the sceptic is to be silenced *the philosopher* ought to articulate what most of us are unable to articulate. He is further inclined to think this because of an idea he shares with the sceptic, namely that if we know the things which the sceptic doubts we know them *indirectly*. (I shall return to this point in the following section of this chapter.)

Insofar as Moore is pulled in this direction when he says 'I can know things I cannot prove' he is prevented from recognising the full force of what he is saying. He does not recognise fully that what is in question is not an inability that is harmless outside philosophy though a short-coming in a philosopher, but an *impossibility* which has implications for the kind of scepticism he is opposing. One could sum them up by saying that where there is no room for a proof, a doubt doesn't make sense either, and that the sceptic's 'We cannot prove', 'We cannot justify' does not imply 'We cannot know'. As I said, Moore went a good way towards bringing this out, but he was pulled back by confusions in his own thinking, some of which he shared with the sceptic.

In short, Moore is divided between saying (a) that it makes no sense to doubt certain things, e.g. the truth of his premise, in the circumstances sketched out in his paper, and that where this makes no sense there is no room for a proof,[3] and (b) that if

[3] Compare Moore's 'You might as well suggest that I do not know that I am now standing up and talking' with Wittgenstein's 'What would stand upright if that were to fall!', 'it would be a piece of unreason to doubt it' (*Cert.*

the sceptic is to be silenced he has to be offered a proof. He wavers between (a) the idea that there is no logical room for a proof where the sceptic asks for one and that the demand for it comes from confusion, and (b) the idea that not being able to offer a proof is a philosophical defect, though it is not needed outside philosophy since we can know things which we cannot prove. Insofar as Moore was drawn towards the latter idea he tended to disparage his own achievement and he was prevented from recognising that to meet the sceptic's doubts what is needed is not a proof of what he doubts, but argument to show that the sceptic's demand for a proof comes from confusion. In many places in his writings Moore did develop such arguments – for instance, in a long paper entitled 'Four Forms of Scepticism'.

II

Where exactly does the philosophical sceptic demand a proof in connection with Moore's premise? What does he want proved before he concedes that we can and do know it? He would say to Moore:

> Of course *some* things are known without proof. One knows without proof that 1 + 1 makes 2, and one knows immediately and without proof that one feels sick or that one sees the appearance of a dagger. But it's different with 'There's a real dagger there'. That is not known immediately. If it is known, it is known on the basis of other knowledge which collected together establishes it. But is there anything we know from which we can really establish for certain that there is a real dagger there? If so, what is it? (Wisdom, 'Moore's Technique', *P.P.A.*, pp. 121–2).

In other words, the sceptic is contrasting Moore's premise with '1 + 1 = 2' and 'I feel sick', 'I see an after-image', i.e. sense-datum statements in the first person. Moore would agree with there being a contrast here and, I think, *rightly*.[4] But the sceptic

---

sec. 325), 'If I doubt that this is my hand, why should I not doubt the meaning of these words as well?' (sec. 456), 'I cannot doubt this proposition without giving up all judgment' (sec. 493), and 'If that's false, then I'm crazy'.

[4] On this point Malcolm is right as opposed to Austin. See p. 86, n. 1 below.

is saying *more* than this and Moore goes along with him further than he should have. For he is saying (a) that if we know P at all we must do so on the basis of evidence and (b) that our knowledge is indirect. Thus after having said emphatically that both he and others *know* the propositions or 'truisms' he has listed at the beginning of 'A Defence of Common Sense', Moore goes on:

> It is, indeed, obvious that, in the case of most of them, I do not know them *directly*: that is to say, I only know them because, in the past, I have known to be true *other* propositions which were evidence for them. If, for instance, I do know that the earth had existed for many years before I was born, I certainly only know this because I have known other things in the past which were evidence for it. And I certainly do not know exactly what the evidence was. Yet all this seems to me to be no good reason for doubting that I know it . . .(*Phil. Papers*, p. 44)

And Moore continues with the famous words I have quoted on p. 70 above. Further down, in the same paper, he makes the same point in connection with our perception of material things:

> I hold it to be quite certain that I do not *directly* perceive *my hand*. (p. 55)

I think that both Moore and the sceptic are right in wanting to contrast 'Here is a hand' or 'I see a hand' with 'I see an after-image' and '1 + 1 = 2'. It is particularly the contrast between 'I see a hand' and 'I see an after-image' that Moore wishes to emphasise when he says that we do not perceive a hand directly. Part of what he wishes to say is that we cannot see a hand in the sense in which we see hallucinations and after-images. But he also says that 'we do constantly *see directly* parts of the surfaces of physical objects', and *prima facie* this conflicts with his former claim. Moore was himself troubled by this:

> I am strongly inclined to take both of these incompatible views [i.e. that we do see the surfaces of physical objects directly, and that we cannot see them directly]. I am completely puzzled about the matter, and only wish I could see any way of settling it. ('A Reply to my Critics', *The Phil. of G. E. Moore*, p. 659).

In a penetrating paper entitled 'Direct Perception' Malcolm argues that in one sense of 'direct perception' (a technical sense we find in philosophy) it is true that we cannot see physical objects directly. What this comes to is that we cannot see e.g. a spot on the wall in the same sense in which we see an after-image against the background of the wall. Malcolm discusses how the sense in which we see the former differs from the sense in which we see the latter. His point is that it is these differences that exercised Moore when he said that we cannot see any physical object directly. Malcolm goes on to point out that there is another sense of 'direct perception' in which it would be false or misleading to say that we cannot or do not see physical objects directly. (I shall return to this last point in Chapter Ten below.)

Now although I like Malcolm's paper very much, I think that on this point he attributes to Moore more insight than he had. Certainly here Moore was pulled in two opposite directions, and behind each pull was something that ought to be retained and not rejected – these not being incompatible. Malcolm brings this out with lucidity. But behind the inclination to say that we cannot perceive a hand directly there is a commitment to a 'theory of sense-data' which needs to be rejected – I mean particularly the view that whenever we see a hand or an ash tray we are immediately aware of sense-data:

> Whenever I know, or judge, such a proposition [e.g. 'This is a hand'] to be true there is always some *sense-datum* about which the proposition in question is a proposition – some sense-datum which is *a* subject (and, in a certain sense, the principal or ultimate subject) of the proposition. ('Defence', *Phil. Papers*, p. 54).

And again:

> When I am said to 'perceive' it [i.e. my hand], that I 'perceive' it means that I perceive (in a different and more fundamental sense) something which is *representative* of it [this something being a sense-datum]. (p. 55)

Insofar as Moore's claim that we cannot see and know physical objects directly comes *partly* from his commitment to this view, which I shall later criticise, it involves serious confusions. In

'Direct Perception' Malcolm makes light of them. In other words, while I agree with Malcolm that it was for good reasons that Moore said that we cannot perceive a hand directly, I want to emphasise that he said it *also* for bad reasons. This point holds equally of Moore's idea that our knowledge of material things is indirect and that our claims about them are always based on evidence.

It is true that we can *know* things indirectly and from evidence and, in such cases, we are justified in saying 'It is certain that so-and-so'. For instance, I could say now 'I know that my car is in the Meadow car park'. You may ask me 'How do you know?', to which I answer 'I parked it there only five minutes ago'. This is a sufficiently good reason for thinking what I just claimed. It is true that my car may no longer be there; it may have been stolen or towed away. If that is the case then, of course, I did not know what I said I knew. I only thought I knew it. But this possibility does not make it impossible for me to know what I claimed I knew. Philosophers have not always appreciated this point. They have been inclined to think – and this is an inclination we all share to some extent – that where the possibility of error exists, knowledge is impossible. (Hence the search for the indubitable from Descartes to Russell, and the idea that it can only be found by a person (i) in his own so-called immediate experiences, and (ii) in logic and mathematics. The idea, in a nut shell is this. (i) If I say 'I feel pain' then nothing can prove me wrong. (ii) If I say that 2 and 3 together make 5 then I am saying something that cannot conceivably be otherwise. In both cases doubt seems to be excluded.)

Now although I am *justified* in asserting confidently that my car is in the car park, in saying that I know this, it would *not* be absurd for me to lack this confidence, to express myself with some caution: 'I believe it is there', 'It is there very probably'. Still I would be *wrong* to deny that anyone can ever know such a thing, wrong to think that where there is the possibility of error, where a doubt is intelligible, there can be no knowledge. I shall not argue this last point here, but will just say this: Of course if I have *grounds* for doubt, if I have *grounds* for thinking that I *may* be mistaken, then that far I cannot claim that what is in question is certain or that I know it. But the mere logical possibility of error, the intelligibility of doubt, does not give me such grounds. Moore explains this point very lucidly in 'Certainty' (see *Philosophical Papers*, pp. 230–5).

The situation with Moore's premise, however, is different – as Moore well appreciates. For here, as he points out, caution, hesitation, lack of confidence would not merely be groundless or unjustified, but logically out of place, 'absurd'. If I really did lack confidence here, this would show not that I was extra cautious, but that I did not understand or appreciate what was being said:

> How absurd it would be to suggest that I did not know it, but only believed it, and that perhaps it was not the case! You might as well suggest that I do not know that I am now standing up and talking. (*Phil. Papers*, p. 146)

Moore makes the same point – and it is an important one – in his lecture 'Certainty' (see pp. 227–8).

There is an important difference, then, a difference in logic, though not one that you will find in a book on logic, between (a) 'Here is a hand and here is another' said as I lift my hands one by one, and (b) 'My car is in the car park', said during a lecture, where this is based on 'I have parked it there only five minutes ago', plus the surrounding circumstances, namely my knowledge that normally cars are not towed away from the car park in question, that theft of cars is an extremely rare thing, and so on. In the latter case, I have *reasons* for thinking that my car is where I say it is. But I could be mistaken. At any rate, a doubt is intelligible here. Even though I made the assertion that my car is in the Meadow car park with confidence, and my confidence was justified, nevertheless if I had not been confident, if I had spoken with some hesitation, this would not have been absurd. Besides, I could now make sure that my car is where I say it is, and if you don't believe me I could prove it to you – by taking you there and showing you the car.

In contrast, where I lift my hand and you are close by, where the light is good, your eyes in order, and there is no question of my being a conjurer, what more can I do to convince you? I could do something in the case of the car, namely take you there and show you. And here if the light was not good, I could switch the light on or change the bulb. But this not being the case, on what grounds could you possibly distrust your eyes? There are three reasons why a philosophical sceptic wants a proof even in this case:

1. He thinks that Moore's premise must be based on evidence – the evidence of the senses, the eyes particularly. What does that evidence amount to? No more, he thinks, than the presence or existence of certain sense impressions, or sense-data as Moore called them. But if so, does that evidence justify Moore's premise? When I accept Moore's premise on the basis of my sense-data, the sceptic thinks, I take a step or make an inference from the sense-data to 'Here is a hand'. If so, what justifies that step? The sceptic wants a proof that the inference from the existence of the sense-data to the existence of the hand is warranted.

Here what needs to be done, if the sceptic's doubt is to be met, is to show that there is no inference, that Moore's premise is not based on evidence, that our knowledge of it is not indirect. This is a very different procedure from giving a proof.

2. The sceptic recognises and is troubled by the *predictive* character of empirical propositions, including Moore's 'Here is a hand and here is another'. Supposing that I raise my two hands and say 'One is a real hand and the other is an artificial hand'. Let us imagine that the two hands look exactly alike to you. My words have altered your expectations. Now that you have heard me you expect, as you did not expect before I spoke, that one of my hands will feel hard and leathery, that if you knock on it with a hammer it will make a sound such as you would hear if you knocked the back of a leather chair with a hammer, and also that it can be twisted all the way round and be pulled out. My point is that when Moore says 'Here is a hand' he raises expectations in you and that it is these expectations that he would alter if he were to add 'but it is only an artificial hand'. Further more, if you don't have the right expectations when you believe him, then you don't understand Moore's words.

The sceptic recognises this and it troubles him because he thinks that any such proposition can turn out to be false, that it is always on the cards that I may have to correct myself tomorrow or the next minute, and that therefore its truth is for ever on probation. This is another reason why he thinks that strictly speaking we cannot be said to know even as well assured a proposition as Moore's premise – although we can know that we are in pain, since 'I am in pain' makes no claims about the future, and also '2 + 3 = 5' which is timelessly true.

We have to meet the sceptic's first difficulty *without denying the independent existence of material things*. Similarly we have to meet his second difficulty *without denying the predictive character of propositions about material things*. In other words, we have to show (i) that we can deny that our knowledge of material things must be indirect without denying their independent existence. This is what Berkeley failed to see. But to bring it out one needs to do considerable spade-work. (ii) We have to show that there are circumstances in which the truth of propositions about material things is not vulnerable to the challenge·of the future, that one can admit this without denying their predictive character – in other words, that while '2 + 3 = 5' is *true come what may*, 'Here is a hand' can be *true come what further may*.

3. The sceptic's third reason for wanting a proof of even Moore's premise is this. He thinks that when I say (or think) that there is a chair before me (a) I may be dreaming, or (b) I may be having an hallucination. 'If I am only dreaming that there is a chair before me, then there is really no chair before me.' 'If Macbeth's dagger was only a dagger of the mind, then he did not see a real, physical dagger, and there was no such dagger before his eyes.' So he wants a proof that when he sees a hand this is not just a dream, or simply an hallucination. If he has been satisfied on the former two points then he has been satisfied that what he sees is not an hallucination. But the possibility that he may be dreaming raises *additional* difficulties. Hence if one is to come to terms with scepticism here one has to recognise (or show) that the sceptic's question 'Can I know that I am awake now and not dreaming?' comes from confusion and is not a question that one can ask intelligibly. I shall omit a discussion of this question. (Malcolm discusses it well in his book *Dreaming*.)

Summary   Moore insists that he and his audience know his premise to be true, though neither he nor they can prove it. Moore says that the fact that he cannot prove his premise in no way shows that he doesn't know it to be true: 'I can know things which I cannot prove.' Still, rightly, Moore thinks that this will not satisfy the sceptic and he feels he ought to be able to do something to meet his doubts. But he is divided in his views about what ought to be done; he half-thinks that he ought to be able to give the proof which the sceptic demands. Such a proof, he thinks, is not something that we need; but it is needed to dispel the sceptic's doubts.

I argued that insofar as Moore is inclined to think this he is confused and I indicated the source of this confusion: (i) Moore's idea that he surely has evidence for his premise and that if only he could articulate it this would constitute a proof: 'We do *know* many things, with regard to which we *know* further that we must have had evidence for them, and yet we do not know what the evidence was.' (See Part One of the present chapter.) (ii) His idea, shared by the sceptic, that in contrast with 'I am in pain', his knowledge of 'Here is a hand' is indirect and, therefore, that it must be possible to justify the inference from the sense-data propositions to his premise.

These ideas, and what is at the root of them, constitute a pull on his thoughts which prevent him from moving ahead on the road he was opening. Both Wittgenstein and Malcolm, who saw through these confusions, were able to take Moore's thought forward in the direction which he faced. Although it is an over-simplification, it could be said that Moore's contribution here consists in his having turned in the right direction, though he was not able to free himself from philosophical commitments which held him back and hampered his progress. In *On Certainty* Wittgenstein takes his start from Moore and is able to follow his lead far beyond where Moore could have travelled. He also makes his own very distinctive contribution – *one* of these being the way he brings out how Moore's 'truisms' form a network in which they give each other support and how Moore subscribes to a 'world-picture'[5] when he says of any one of them that he *knows* it to be true: 'What I hold fast to is not *one* proposition but a nest of propositions' (sec. 225). 'We shall stick to this opinion [e.g. that the earth is round], unless our whole way of seeing nature changes' (sec. 291). 'If I wanted to doubt the existence of the earth long before my birth, I should have to doubt all sorts of things that stand

[5] What Moore called 'common sense', though he did not recognise the logical peculiarities of what he was referring to.

fast for me' (sec. 234 – see what he says about Moore and the king in sec. 92). (See my Critical Review of *On Certainty* in *Philosophy* April 1971.)

How then is the sceptic's doubt to be met, if not by a proof of Moore's premise? To see how it is to be met, one has to ask: Why does the sceptic doubt that anyone can know, even in the best possible circumstances, a proposition like Moore's premise? What is it that troubles him when he asks for a proof of it? I indicated three difficulties which he finds insurmountable:

(1) How can the proposition 'Here is a hand' be based on what we see without our knowledge of it being indirect and inductive?

(2) How can one know that Moore has lifted a hand in the strict sense that one will not have to correct oneself later when Moore's assertion of this is predictive in character?

(3) How can I know that I am not dreaming when I say 'Here is a hand'?

Notice that in each case the sceptic's considerations start from a formal feature of the concept of matter, a feature of the grammar in which we talk about chairs and tables. It is these that seem to make it impossible that we should know the kinds of thing we all normally claim to know.

9 'Doubting has an End' (Wittgenstein)

We saw that the philosophical sceptic thinks wrongly that where doubt is not impossible, i.e. where it is intelligible, there knowledge is impossible. It is true that where there are *grounds* for doubt there is, indeed, no knowledge. For instance, if I have reason for suspecting that my car may have been towed away, even when I parked it there only five minutes ago, then that far I cannot be certain that it is to be found where I parked it. But I am thinking of positive grounds or reasons and not merely of a logical possibility. Only the former excludes knowledge; not the mere possibility of doubt. As Wittgenstein puts it: 'That is not to say that we are in doubt because it is possible to *imagine* a doubt' (*Inv.* sec. 84).

Still the philosophical search for the indubitable points to something important. For, as we shall see, unless there are things that we find indubitable, situations where we do not take a doubt seriously and find it absurd, we can neither doubt nor know anything elsewhere. The sceptic does not recognise this. Moore, on the other hand, came very close to drawing the sceptic's attention to it. For he had the good sense (perhaps the common sense) to appreciate that there are certain things which we cannot doubt in certain circumstances without absurdity. So he insisted that it would be ridiculous to suggest that we do not or cannot know these things. His premise, given the circumstances in which he asserted it, is a good example:

> 'How absurd it would be to suggest that I did not know it, but only believed it, and that perhaps it was not the case!' (p. 146)

In different circumstances, however, the same proposition can be doubted and then the doubt can be dispelled by a proof:

> If one of you suspected that one of my hands was artificial he might be said to get a proof of my proposition 'Here's one hand, and here's another', by coming up and examining the suspected hand close up, perhaps touching and pressing it, and so establishing that it really was a human hand. (p. 149)

In *those* circumstances we can make sure or establish that what we see is really a human hand. How? Namely, by coming closer, touching and pressing it.

If, on the other hand, there *is* still something you haven't thought gives content to that doubt? It may be that I think: 'Perhaps it is an artificial hand.' What does that mean? Roughly something like this: 'If you look at it from close quarters you will find it leathery, if you press it it will not feel like flesh, etc.' But if when you look at it from close quarters and touch it you still express doubt, what does *that* doubt come to, what gives it content? Perhaps there is something else you haven't made sure! If there isn't, then your doubt is empty, it has no content, it is no doubt at all – the words 'I doubt' are now without meaning.

If, on the other hand, there *is* still something you have'nt made sure, then there is something you are content to rest with, something that removes your doubt, brings it to an end.

In his *Memoir* Professor Malcolm reports Wittgenstein to have said that physical-object statements like 'This is a tree' *in some circumstances* play a role similar to that of mathematical propositions (see pp. 87–92). This is further developed by Wittgenstein in his last notes *On Certainty*. If I put 5 beads in a box and then another 5 and then on counting the beads I find 9 I would say that one of the beads must have disappeared. Have I seen one disappear? No. I say this because I treat '5 + 5 = 10' as invulnerable; I use it as I use a measure for describing what happens. For instance, my jeans no longer fit me. Have they shrunk or have I put on weight? I measure them or I measure my waist. The length of an inch on the tape is what I treat as constant, and it is that which enables me to make the kind of comparison in question.

Similarly, if I am sitting under a tree in the garden, a tree that

I can see clearly and recognise well, then normally nothing would convince me that there is not a tree there. I could walk up to it in dense fog, try to touch it, in order to make sure. But on a clear day, in broad daylight, when I am standing only three yards away from it, and it is clearly visible to my friends, I would not need to go up to it and touch it. Touching it, under those circumstances, cannot make it more certain that there is a tree before me. It would be an idle ceremony.

Moore says 'Here is a hand and here is another', 'I am standing up, and not either sitting or lying down; I have clothes on, and am not absolutely naked', 'I know that that is a tree and this a finger' in circumstances where it does not have any sense to make sure, where there is nothing further that we would call 'making sure'. That is why he says: 'I should have been guilty of absurdity if, under the circumstances, I had *not* spoken positively about these things, if I spoke of them at all'. ('Certainty', *Phil. Papers*, p. 225).

In these circumstances we are not prepared to allow anything as counting against the truth of the proposition that this is a tree. We do not take seriously the possibility of being mistaken. We do not admit such a possibility here. To the sceptic this is yet further evidence of our being creatures of instinct and habit. Wittgenstein anticipates this reaction: 'But if you are *certain*, isn't it that you are shutting your eyes in the face of doubt?' His answer is: 'They are shut' (*Inv.*, p. 224). And what we need to appreciate here is that we do not have reasons for shutting our eyes in the face of doubt in those situations where we do so, agreeing with each other in where we do so, and that there is nothing irrational in our doing so. On the contrary, it is the sceptic who is confused in finding these reactions irrational unless they can be justified.

That we react in this way in the kind of situation on which Moore focused, that we take this sort of attitude to a great many propositions about trees and stones, or to what these propositions say, whether or not they are asserted, is an *important fact* about us. It underlies the possibility of our talking and reasoning in the way we do. Wittgenstein said that 'a language-game [he meant a way of speaking and of reasoning] is only possible if one trusts something' (*Cert.* sec. 509). He added: 'I did not say "can trust something".' 'You can trust this material; it won't shrink.' 'Why can I trust it?', 'Why should I? Give me a reason why I should.' The answer may be: 'It has been tested.' Here our trust is based on reasons. Whereas Wittgenstein meant: if one trusts something without reason – naturally, instinctively, as a matter of course. 'Language [he said] did not emerge from some kind of ratiocination' (sec. 475). The trust he was thinking of is pre-logical. To try to base it on reason (as the sceptic would like to do) is like trying to lift yourself by your boot-straps. Wittgenstein writes:

> One cannot make experiments if there are not some things that one does not doubt . . . The *questions* that we raise and our *doubts* depend on the fact that some propositions are exempt from doubt, are as it were like hinges on which those turn. That is to say, it belongs to the logic of our scientific in-vestigations that certain things are *in deed* not doubted. But it isn't that the situation is like this: We just *can't* investigate everything, and for that reason are forced to rest content with assumption. If we want the door to turn, the hinges must stay put. (*Cert*. secs. 337, 341–343)

Thus if it is to be possible for us to doubt or wonder whether what seems like palms and water in the distance is an oasis or a mirage, if there is to be a finding out that it is the one or the other, then when we are drinking the water and bathing our hands in it we must regard it as senseless to continue to doubt. At that point nothing that could be countenanced must be counted by us as evidence that we are having an hallucination. In other words, unless we take this attitude on such occasions as when we are drinking the water, we cannot doubt, wonder, or even assume or tentatively believe and try to make sure about anything on other occasions. As Wittgenstein put it: 'If there is a making sure *here* [e.g. when we are actually drinking the water, where Moore insists that I know that here is a hand and here is another] then there is no making sure at all' (Malcolm's *Memoir*).

When the sceptic says 'I don't know' or 'I can't know' he implies that we are debarred from making sure. In other words, the very intelligibility of what he is saying depends on and, in that sense, presupposes that there is a making sure. But if there is a making sure *here* then there is no making sure at all. That is he presupposes the very thing which he rejects. His position is, therefore, incoherent.

Malcolm writes: 'One statement about physical objects *turned out to be false* only because you *made sure* of another statement about physical objects. The two concepts cannot exist apart. Therefore it is impossible that *every* statement about physical objects *could* turn out to be false' (*K.C.*, p. 69). Yet this is precisely what the sceptic claims: For all we know there may be no physical objects; all the trees and stones that we see and touch may be hallucinations.

We have already seen this to involve one kind of incoherence. Now we see that it involves another:

(i) Perhaps we are all mistaken all the time. Perhaps all physical object propositions are false.

(ii) There are no physical object propositions that cannot turn out to be false, none that are beyond the reach of doubt, none that are indubitable.

We have seen that Moore did not find anything incoherent in (i). He said: 'It *might* have been the case that material things [were] not real' (*Phil. Papers*, p. 42). And again: 'Descartes' malicious demon is a logical possibility' (p. 222). Although he did not recognise fully the kind of incoherence we have in (ii), he did recognise that there are physical object propositions which in some circumstances are beyond the reach of doubt.[1]

---

[1] One question here which I shall not discuss now is this: Are they beyond the reach of doubt *in the same way* in which 'I am in pain' or 'I see a blue after-image' is beyond the reach of doubt? Professor Austin thinks so in *Sense and Sensibilia*, Chapter Ten, and Malcolm, I think rightly, criticises him in his paper 'Direct Perception' and brings out the difference in the way each is beyond the reach of doubt. In other words, Austin swings too far to the opposite extreme from the sceptic and loses sight of something important which the sceptic keeps in focus by responding to it – even if his response shows that he has a distorted apprehension of it. See *Knowledge and Certainty*, pp. 91–92, n. 22.

10 Moore's Premise: Known Directly

I

I think that we are in a position now to return to the two questions Moore evaded when he rightly said that he cannot prove his premise however much the sceptic may challenge him to do so.[1]

We have seen that the sceptic is wrong in wanting a proof of Moore's premise. Nevertheless we owe him an explanation on two points. These explanations are part of what constitutes 'showing the fly out of the fly-bottle'. It is no good simply telling the sceptic that what he wants proved cannot be proved. After all this is the conclusion the sceptic himself has been forced to embrace. We must also remove the urge in him to seek a proof here. We must show him that we can know things that we cannot prove, or rather that where we cannot prove p it doesn't always follow that p is doubtful.

Why then does the sceptic want a proof? (i) Because he thinks that if Moore's premise is based on the evidence of our eyes and ears then our knowledge of its truth, if we can have such knowledge, must be indirect. (ii) Because he thinks that if Moore's premise, like any other physical object proposition, is predictive in character, it must be for ever open to the challenge of the future. So we have to show him (i) that although Berkeley was wrong to think that *esse est percipi*, nevertheless our knowledge of Moore's premise is not indirect, and (ii) that although Moore's premise is predictive, nevertheless we can know it 'in the strict sense that we shall not have to correct ourselves tomorrow' (Wisdom).

[1] See p. 81 above – questions (1) and (2).

The answer to the first question 'Can we know the truth of any physical object proposition directly and without inference?', 'Can we perceive physical objects directly?' leads to the question, 'Whenever we perceive a physical object, do we always and necessarily perceive sense-data?'. It is because we implicitly take the answer to the second question to be Yes that we find it difficult to answer the first question in the affirmative.

In *Philosophical Investigations* and also in the *Blue and Brown Books* Wittgenstein distinguishes between what he calls 'symptoms' and 'criteria'. If, for instance, you have an inflamed appendix your temperature goes up, you feel sick, and perhaps also you have dizzy spells. These are *signs* or *symptoms* of an inflamed appendix in the sense that because they are generally produced by an inflamed appendix they can be taken to indicate inflammation of the appendix – that is to indicate something that we cannot actually see at the time. Notice (1) that the appendix or its inflammation is one thing while the high temperature or the nausea is something else. The inflammation can exist apart from and without these symptoms, and what constitutes the symptoms, say the high temperature, can exist without the inflamed appendix – i.e. a person can have the one without the other. (2) The high temperature, together with the pain in a particular part of the body and the feeling of nausea, becomes a reliable sign of an inflamed appendix because it has been found to be generally associated with an inflamed appendix. How has it been found to be so associated? Presumably by operations which have revealed an inflamed appendix in people exhibiting these symptoms. In other words, when the doctor knows from the symptoms that the patient has an inflamed appendix, he doesn't actually see the inflammation, he only infers it; and there is a more direct way of knowing whether or not the patient has an inflamed appendix, namely by operating on him and examining his appendix. So when we know the state of a man's appendix from certain symptoms, we may be said to know it *indirectly*.

When the doctor actually operates on the patient and examines his appendix, he may find it looking red and perhaps also swollen. It looks characteristically different from the way a person's appendix looks normally, when there is nothing wrong with it. Here, on the basis of the way it looks, the doctor may say that the patient has an inflamed appendix. But this is *not* an inference. The inflammation of the appendix is not something over and above what the doctor sees here. He may show it to his pupils and, perhaps, describe how in this case the appendix looks different from a healthy appendix. He may add: 'You have all read it in your books, this is what we *call* an inflamed appendix.' You may, certainly, say that here he knows the appendix is in a state of inflammation *from the way it looks*, and it is true that when he says 'it is in a state of inflammation, as you can see' he is making claims about the future. But the way it looks is at least part of what is *meant* by its being in a state of inflammation. It is not something that is associated with inflammation, a symptom of inflammation. When on the basis of the way it looks we call it an inflamed appendix, or classify it as an inflamed appendix, this enables us to make useful predictions. We may predict, for instance, that a microscopic examination will reveal the presence of certain germs which would be killed if treated by such-and-such a medicine. Here you may say that the inflammation is itself a symptom of the appendix being attacked by germs.[2] But the look from which you know that it is inflamed and infer the presence of the germs is not a symptom of inflammation, it is a *criterion*. Where from the look of the appendix the doctor knows that it is inflamed his knowledge is not indirect. As Malcolm puts it:

> What makes something into a symptom of y is that experience teaches that it is always or usually associated with y; that so-and-so is the criterion of y is a matter not of experience, but of 'definition'. The satisfaction of the criterion of y establishes the existence of y beyond question. The occurrence of a symptom of y may also establish the existence of y 'beyond question' – but in a different sense. (*K.C.*, p. 113)

Now Moore is in a lecture room and I am sitting in the front row. He lifts up his hands one by one and says 'Here is a hand and here is another'. How do I know that what he says is true? Certainly if I were blind I would not know it, or at least not know it in the same way as I now do. If I were blind I would

---

[2] Although I imagine that the presence of the germs has by now become absorbed into what is meant by 'a state of inflammation' – an example of what Wittgenstein means by 'the fluctuation between criteria and symptoms'.

know that Moore had lifted his hands from hearing him say so. If I knew Moore well and knew that he wouldn't lie, I could say to you 'I know beyond the shadow of a doubt that Moore has lifted his hands'. But though I am justified in saying this, if I were not so certain, if I said 'Probably Moore has lifted his hands' this would not be absurd. Here Moore's saying 'I have lifted my hands' is one thing and his lifting his hands is another. Since, being blind, I cannot see his hands, when I say 'Moore has lifted his hands' I base this on what I hear him say. Trusting him as I do, from what he says I *infer* that he has lifted his hands. I may, of course, be mistaken, and if I am not mistaken then my knowledge may be described as *indirect*.

Being blind I based my claim that Moore lifted his hands on what I heard him say. If I were not blind I would base it on what I see. But, in contrast with the previous case, it cannot be said that what I see is one thing and Moore's lifting his hands is another, since Moore's lifting his hands *is* what I see.

The philosophical sceptic denies this and his reasoning (the argument from illusion) is very briefly this: I may see exactly what I see when I see Moore lifting his hands when he is not lifting his hands. This may be an illusion or even an hallucination. Therefore my seeing what I see when I see Moore lift his hands is one thing and his lifting his hands is another.

Wittgenstein states what has gone wrong here as follows:

> The fluctuation in grammar between criteria and symptoms makes it look as if there were nothing at all but symptoms. We say, for example: 'Experience teaches that there is rain when the barometer falls, but it also teaches that there is rain when we have certain sensations of wet and cold, and such-and-such visual impressions.' In defence of this one says that these sense impressions can deceive us. But here one fails to reflect that the fact that the false appearance is precisely one of rain is founded on a definition. (*Inv.* sec. 354)

He goes on:

> The point here is not that our sense impressions can lie, but that we understand their language. (And this language like any other is founded on convention). (sec. 355)

In other words, when I am having an hallucination and it seems as if there is a dagger before me, I am deceived and think there really is a dagger before me, because I know what a dagger looks like, because I know what it is to see a dagger. I know this because on numerous other occasions I have really seen a dagger. I have learnt what it means for there to be a dagger and other such objects before one's eyes, and what it means to see a dagger and other such objects, in connection with situations in which I was looking at these things and saw them. These are situations in which I also touched them, heard other people near me describe what they see, and so on. If I had not been in thousands of such situations in which I learned to talk about and describe what I see and how things look, (i) could I have or see hallucinations?[3] and (ii) could I be deceived by them?

This is what Wittgenstein means when he says that we are sometimes deceived by our senses only because we understand what they tell us. Just as you are deceived by someone who tells you a lie only because the lie is in a language you understand; and you understand that language in the sense that you know what it is like for statements in it to be true. You know that because you have heard many, many true statements in that language and were made to appreciate that it is in these situations that we *call* such-and-such statements true.

The situations in which we learn to say this or that, the situations in which it is correct to say this or that, constitute the fulfilment of the *criteria* for this or that – e.g. the criteria for there being a dagger, or for an appendix being inflamed, or for seeing a table. It is what we *mean* by these things that is in question. If I see an hallucination and am deceived then at least I *must* know that the appearance which deceives me is an appearance of a dagger. That is I must know what a real dagger looks like. This is part of knowing what is *meant* by there being a dagger in front of one, before one's eyes. It is in this sense that the false or deceptive appearance being the appearance of a dagger 'is founded on a definition'.

That is, the idea that *whenever* we make a claim about such things as chairs and tables we are making an inference from our

[3] I am thinking of the sense in which my knowledge of how these things look enters into not only the mental images I form deliberately, but also those that come to me, including hallucinations. I discuss this question very briefly in 'Imagination', *Analysis*, January 1968, pp. 94–6.

sense impressions, as from symptoms, to the existence of the chairs and tables which produce these symptoms in us is a confused one. It is true, of course, that we are sometimes deceived by our senses. But this does not mean that we may always be deceived. It is true that sometimes we have sense impressions of a dagger when there is no real, physical dagger before our eyes. But this does not mean that when there is a real, physical dagger before our eyes and we are not blind what we see is a sense impression, the same as what we see when we see an hallucinatory dagger. It does not mean that the dagger in space, before our eyes, is one thing and what we see is another.

The case where we know Moore is lifting his hands because we can see him doing so quite clearly is different from the case where a blind man knows the same thing from hearing Moore say so. As I argued, given that certain conditions are fulfilled – e.g. that the light is good, our eyes in order, and Moore not a conjurer – it is not conceivable that we may be mistaken and there is nothing that we would call 'making sure' that what we see are Moore's hands (see Chapter Nine above). This surely means that in that case there is no inference from what I see to what I know. If what I know is that Moore has lifted his two hands then this is just what I see.

My knowledge is based on what I see, in the sense that if I were blind I wouldn't know what I know, unless someone I could trust told me so, or I were near enough Moore to touch his hands. But what I see is not my evidence for what I assert. Nor do I conclude that there are two hands from the sense impressions of two hands. My knowledge is based on what I see only in the sense that, since I speak English, I know that what I see, in the given circumstances, is correctly described by saying 'Here are two hands before me'. What I see, in the particular circumstances, satisfies the *criteria* of there being two hands before me.

II

I said that what I see are Moore's hands, physical things, and not sense impressions or sense-data. This is not to say that I could not talk of sense-data, describe the contents of my visual field, even here. Earlier I considered an example in which you are asked to describe how a coin looks to you from a certain angle. I said that you might quite correctly say that it looks round. Here it looks round because you know that it is a coin and that coins are round. Someone might say: Try to forget that it is a coin and tell me how it looks to you. This is a move in the direction of getting you to describe the contents of your visual field, your visual sense-data. The description of how things look to you when you can forget or disregard everything that you know about them, when you can detach yourself from the different expectations which your perceptions have come to embody: this is a description of your sense-data. It is not always easy to give such descriptions. It requires a certain practice and training, and most of us are not prepared for it. On the other hand, when we switch from considering and describing an object before our eyes to considering and describing the contents of our visual field at the time, we are switching from one language-game to another. As Wittgenstein puts it:

> Physical object – sense impressions. Here we have two different language-games and a complicated relation between them. (*Inv.* p. 180)

What is more, you must have learnt a great deal before you can speak of sense impressions or sense-data. Certainly if you could not speak of physical objects you could not speak about sense impressions or sense-data.

I am saying the very opposite of what Professor Ayer maintained in his paper 'The Terminology of Sense-data'. For he spoke of an asymmetry between the language of physical objects and the language of sense-data and claimed that the latter is logically prior to the former, or that it is logically more primitive. He said: 'While referring to sense-data is not necessarily referring to physical objects, referring to physical objects is necessarily a way of referring to sense-data.' We have seen that Moore agrees with this. I have, however, argued the opposite, namely that talk about physical objects is logically more primitive. I have also argued that referring to physical objects is not necessarily a way of referring to sense-data. If we want to refer to or talk about sense-data we have as it were to 'alter the adjustment of the microscope',[4] to shift from one language-

---

[4] Wittgenstein uses this simile in another, though similar connection – see *Inv.* sec. 645.

game or grammar to another. But until we do so, when under normal circumstances we describe what we see we are talking about and referring to physical objects and not sense-data. In those circumstances what we see are physical objects and not sense-data. It would be a confusion to say here that what we see directly are sense-data and that physical objects are what we see indirectly.

Berkeley had thought, rightly, that if our knowledge of physical objects is indirect, if it is never direct, then scepticism is inevitable. He rightly wanted to be able to avoid scepticism and saw that if it is to be avoided we must admit that we have direct knowledge of physical objects, knowledge that is not inferrential. But, he reasoned, we cannot have such knowledge if physical objects exist independently of our sense impressions – that is if it is possible for there to be no sense impressions while there are physical objects. So he identified physical objects with sense impressions and said that 'matter is ideas'. He denied that physical objects have an existence distinct from and independent of the percipient's mind – 'esse est percipi'. In this way he got rid of any need for inference in perceptual knowledge – an inference not to further sense impressions, but one that goes *beyond* all sense impressions. But he got rid of it at a cost. For the claim that the existence of a physical object is constituted by its being perceived is as unpalatable as the claim that we cannot know whether or not there are physical objects.

Unpalatable. For we want to say: Surely it is the existence of an after-image that is constituted by its being seen or perceived, *not* that of a physical object. Berkeley realised that it would be going too far to deny this and he tried to allow for it – but not very successfully.

I have argued that one can avoid scepticism, that one can admit and even insist that we can and do often know directly, non-inferentially that before us stands a tree, or that there is an ashtray before our eyes, without having to deny that these objects exist independently of being perceived, that if we cease to perceive them this does not mean that they have stopped existing, in the sense that this is true of our after-images and our aches and pains. How? By recognising that when we look at trees and ashtrays what we see are these objects themselves and not sense impressions; or rather by recognising the confusion in the idea that 'whenever we perceive there is an *intermediate* entity *always* present and *informing* us about something else'.[5]

---

[5] Austin, *Sense and Sensibilia*, p. 11. As I pointed out earlier this idea is closely related to 'the model of a substance acting through the media of our sense-organs and nerves to throw shadows upon a screen in our brains' – Wisdom, 'Moore's Technique', *P.P.A.*, p. 133. But this latter involves further confusions, centring around the notion of a 'perceptual process', which I have not discussed.

11 Moore's Premise: True Come What Further May

We have seen how the idea that every time we see a physical object what we really see is a sense impression whose *esse* is *percipi*, whereas this is not true of physical objects, leads us to think that if we know a physical object proposition we can at best know it only indirectly. I have tried to show how you can reject the idea that physical object propositions are at best known only indirectly without rejecting that physical objects have an existence distinct from and independent of their being perceived – as Berkeley did. Very briefly, what I argued is this: When we know Moore's premise because we can see him lifting his hands what we see *are* his hands. The idea that what we see here are sense-data comes from confusion. Hence our knowledge is not indirect and inferential. But, of course, the existence of Moore's hands does not in any way depend on my, or anybody else's, seeing them. Their existence is one thing and their being seen quite another thing – unlike the existence of an after-image I may be seeing now.

I turn to the second difficulty which leads the sceptic to think that while we can know that $1 + 1 = 2$ and each of us knows when he feels sick or in pain, we cannot know that before us is a table or chair no matter what our eyes and other senses tell us. The sceptic says that we cannot know a proposition which states this because its truth is open to the challenge of the future. The gist of his reasoning is this: Propositions about chairs and tables, in contrast with reports about the after-images I see or the sensations I feel, are predictive, they make claims about the future. Therefore, even in the best of circumstances, when Moore or I say, 'Here is a hand and here is another' it is always conceivable that what is said may turn out to be false. I cannot be sure that Moore's premise won't turn out to be false and, therefore, I cannot know it to be true.

Why does the sceptic think that we cannot be sure that Moore's premise won't turn out to be false? Because it makes claims about the future. Here there are two things that trouble him: (i) How can I be confident that any prediction will come true? (ii) If even a simple statement like 'Here is a hand' makes an *infinite* number of claims about the future, how can it ever be conclusively verified? How can its truth be established once and for all? It was largely the latter difficulty that made Ayer, at one time, talk of all empirical propositions as mere hypotheses, and C. I. Lewis claim that we are never justified in saying that such a proposition is true, that we can at best say that it is 'probably true' – what Moore thought was an absurd thing to say. In *Mind and the World Order* C. I. Lewis expresses this difficulty in the following words:

> Obviously in the statement 'This penny is round' I assert implicitly *everything the failure of which would falsify the statement.* The implicit prediction of *all* experience which is essential to its *truth* must be contained in the original judgment. . . . What totality of experience would verify it completely beyond the possibility of necessary reconsideration? . . . It seems to be the fact that *no* verification would be absolutely complete; that all verification is partial and a matter of degree. . . . Is it not the case that the simplest statement of objective particular fact implicitly asserts something about possible experience throughout all future time; that theoretically every objective fact is capable of some verification at any later date, and that no totality of such experience is absolutely and completely sufficient to put our knowledge of such particulars beyond all possibility of turning out to be in error? (pp. 279–281)

I want to confine my attention to the difficulty raised by C. I. Lewis – namely that no amount of experience, no amount of seeing and touching, is absolutely and completely sufficient to put our assent to the truth of Moore's premise beyond all possibility of turning out to be in error.[1] This is sometimes put by

[1] The question 'Can anyone have a right to be confident about any predic-

philosophers in words to the effect that no descriptions of what I say I see ever *entail* the existence of what I say I see. As we shall see, the former statement, as Lewis has it, is unacceptable though it points to a grammatical feature of such statements as 'This penny is round'. The latter statement, on the other hand, is unexceptionable though harmless. It is no ground for saying that we cannot ever know the truth of physical object propositions.

It is perfectly true that physical object propositions are predictive and so make claims about the future. But this does not mean that they are predictions. If I say 'He sees a dagger before him – a real, physical dagger' I am speaking about what is the case now; whereas if I say 'He will see a dagger when he opens his eyes' I am speaking about the future. Nevertheless if I say, 'He is sitting next door, clutching a dagger, ready to strike' I raise certain expectations in you. For instance, you expect to see a dagger if you peep through the key hole; you expect to find a dagger in the room five hours later if the door is locked, the windows bolted, and the guards outside make sure that no one and nothing leaves the room. If these expectations are not fulfilled then you will rightly say that I was mistaken when I said that there is a dagger in his hand. If, on the other hand, I say that I see a dagger and mean that I see an hallucinatory dagger then I don't expect to continue seeing it after a little while, I expect to stop seeing it even if I don't turn away or shut my eyes. The point is a grammatical one, namely that if it is a real, physical dagger then I shall go on seeing what I see now unless I close my eyes, turn my head away, or have it removed. These expectations are built into or are part of what we mean and understand when we talk about physical things such as daggers and trees.[2]

But if physical object propositions in the present tense make claims about the future and if when these claims are falsified by what the future brings we admit that a physical object proposition we asserted was false, that we were mistaken in assert-

---

tion?' is part of scepticism with regard to inductive reasons. I have discussed this elsewhere – see *Induction and Deduction, A Study in Wittgenstein*, Part One.

[2] See my discussion of 'the continued existence of material things' in Chapter Three above. There are qualifications to be made in the case of shadows and mirror images.

ing it, does it mean that a physical object proposition can *always* turn out to be false – no matter what we have done to ascertain its truth? Does it mean that we can never do enough to make sure that it is true, that we can never know it or be absolutely certain that it is true? Moore thinks that this doesn't follow at all, and neither does Wittgenstein or Malcolm.

Professor Wisdom who brought out the predictive character of physical object propositions so well also insisted that we can and do often know for certain that a thing pointed to us is cheese or that Moore has raised his hands 'in the strict sense that we won't have to correct ourselves tomorrow'. He discusses this question in *Other Minds* VIII. The discussion is in the form of a dialogue between several characters. Gray, whose words on pp. 172–3 I want to quote, is replying to White who wonders whether we can say of a man or a dog that he knows there is a rat before him when in every way it seems to him that there is. He admits that 'when he snuffles and wags his tail we say, "He knows there's one there, good old Trusty, he knows".'

> But [White goes on] his smelling the smell he does and his having had the experience he has had don't *constitute* his knowing that there's a rat there or that things will continue to seem just as they should if there were. For his past experience and present sensations are compatible with any future pattern and with there being no rat there while knowledge that a rat is there is not. Therefore all about him that counts is not enough and he no more knows that the rat is a rat than the bloodstock expert knows that the grey is a Tetrarch or the doctor that the patient has chronic anaemia.

> White's point is this: When good old Trusty snuffles and it smells to him as if there is a rat, and even when he opens his eyes it looks as if there is a rat before him, *it doesn't follow* that he will go on smelling the smells and seeing the appearances that he would have to smell and see if there really is a rat there. But if he *knows* that there is a rat there then this does follow. Therefore he can't be said to know.

> And yet [Gray replies] undoubtedly men and dogs often know that there is a rat in the room. And we should often say, 'I knew he was a Tetrarch the moment I set eyes on him', and we should say, 'The doctor knew at once that there was no

hope'.

Besides, these cases are different. If someone says of the bloodstock expert that he doesn't know that the colt is a Tetrarch I understand very well what is meant. What is meant is that he hasn't done all he might have done to make sure. He has looked at the colt but he hasn't written to Weatherbys, and so on. And when someone asks me, 'But does the doctor really know?' again I understand very well what is meant. It is not merely the academic point that always anything *may* happen, it is the point, 'Do the doctors know in such a case?', in other words, 'Is this doctor's prediction well supported, that is as well as or nearly as well as an astronomer's prediction?' But if someone asks, 'Do you know that glass is fragile, that fire burns, that cheese is soft?' i.e. 'Do you know when you see a glassy looking thing that it is fragile [i.e. that it will break easily] or, if you like, that it is glass? Do you know when you see as it were a fire that it will burn, i.e. that it is fire? Do you know when you see a *cheesy* looking thing that it is cheese?' then I don't know what he means unless he wishes to contrast my case when I merely see cheese, with my case when I see, touch and taste it all at once. But if that *is* what he is doing then, though it seems to me that he is being eccentrically strict, I can still understand him, I still know what he would call knowing.

But if he says that even when I am seeing, touching and tasting cheese still I don't know that there is cheese in my mouth, then I don't know what he means. Then I am no longer surprised that he says not merely that we don't know but that we never can know. For then we cannot conceive of what it would be to know. It now isn't merely that the use of 'know' has been eccentrically narrowed, it has been narrowed to nothing . . .

Gray's point is this: If someone says 'You can't ever be sure that what you see is cheese until you've tasted it, you can't be sure that what you see before you is glass until you have hit it with a hammer and seen it break' then though he is speaking eccentrically I understand him. But if someone says, 'You can't know, you can't be sure, even when you have tasted the cheese and broken the glass' then I don't understand him. For we say 'we don't know' or 'we are not absolutely certain' where there is something further we might have done to make sure which we haven't done. When we have done everything possible by way of making sure that this is cheese and that glass, then there is no room left for doubt or hesitation.

The sceptic's difficulty here, however, is that we can never do, never complete doing, everything possible by way of making sure that this is cheese and that glass. For the predictive claims made by the proposition 'This is cheese' cannot ever be completely and fully confirmed or verified, since their verification cannot be exhausted. For he thinks that if I am really to know that this thing I see before me is a piece of cheese, not only must I touch it, smell it and taste it, but I must go on doing so for all eternity. If after I have watched, sniffed and tasted it for a whole day I suddenly stop seeing it or begin to smell and taste soap, then whatever it is that I have been looking at all day it cannot have been cheese, and when I said 'I see a piece of cheese before me', 'I know it is cheese' I was wrong. Surely these things *can* happen. Therefore I cannot know that there is a piece of cheese before me. It cannot be said of anyone that he has done everything possible by way of making sure. He can always watch it for another five minutes, however long he has watched it for, and you never can tell it may suddenly explode – in which case it wasn't cheese but a cheese-tasting time-bomb.

Do not shrug your shoulders and say that this is an academic point. Something stronger needs to be said and can be said – as Wittgenstein did in the *Investigations* and in *On Certainty*. He did not deny that propositions like 'This is cheese', 'Here is a hand' are predictive, make claims about the future. He did not deny that after we have made sure, as best we can, that here is a piece of cheese, the future, may be the next moment, may bring forth such eventualities which *normally* would give us reason against saying 'Here is a piece of cheese'. But he said that the possibility of speaking about cheese at all, of using the word 'cheese' as we do, rests on certain very general facts of nature that we take for granted, certain regularities of experience that we trust as a matter of course. Without these regularities we would not speak as we do.

Wittgenstein imagines someone saying 'There is a chair'. I go up to it, meaning to fetch it, and it suddenly disappears from sight. 'So it wasn't a chair, but some kind of illusion.' But suppose that in a few moments we see it again and are able to touch it, and so on. 'So the chair was there after all and its disappearance was some kind of illusion.' But suppose that after a time it disappears again – or seems to disappear. What are we to say now? (*Inv*. sec. 80). The answer is that we do not know; we have no ready-made rules or recipes to help us cope with such eventualities. Why not? Because they rarely occur. But if they were common, then we would presumably know what to say. Given our language as it has developed, then certain regularities are taken for granted in the use of this language. In certain circumstances, when certain conditions are fulfilled, when we have made sure that this is a piece of cheese, in the agreed sense of 'making sure' for this kind of situation, we commit ourselves with regard to the future, we ignore or disregard certain possibilities. As Wittgenstein puts it in the *Investigations*: 'We shut our eyes.' This is part of speaking, part of judging.

Wittgenstein writes: 'I can easily imagine someone always doubting before he opened his front door whether an abyss did not yawn behind it, and making sure about it before he went through the door (and he might on some occasion prove to be right) – but that does not make me doubt in the same case' (*Inv*. sec. 84).

This man's reaction is an abnormal reaction, in the sense that most of us do not share it. But even *he* does not doubt that before him is a door, that he is standing up before it, that it is to be opened by turning the handle and pushing it. If his doubts are confirmed so that when he opens his front door he sees before him a precipice, he does not doubt that if he were to walk out he would fall through and break his neck. The possibility of his very eccentric doubt presupposes that there is much that even he does not doubt.

I said that our trusting certain things, ignoring certain possibilities, 'shutting our eyes', is part of speaking and judging. That, in particular, to which we take this attitude, determines the *form* of our judgements and reasonings. Notice the *we* – this is the agreement in attitude and reactions that underlies the possibility of our disagreeing with each other. And if we were to express in propositions the things with regard to which we take such an attitude, these would be *grammatical* propositions. They would indicate part of the framework within which we make judgements, test their validity, carry out our reasonings and investigations.

One example which I gave and discussed at some length was: 'There is a table there even when I turn round, and even when no one is there to see it' (see Chapter Three above). I said that in certain circumstances (when the light is good, I am near to it and actually feel its hard surface under my hand or elbow) we do not take certain doubts that may be put into words seriously. We regard them as 'academic'. These are the circumstances in which Moore would say 'I *know* that what I see is a table'. Although there is a great deal that could happen in the following minute or later which in *other* circumstances would give me reason for retracting or modifying my statement about what is before me, in the *present* circumstances none of these need be regarded by me as a reason for retracting or modifying the statement I made. So it is part of the *attitude* I take towards this statement in these circumstances that I regard it as *true come what further may*.

So on the one hand I trust in certain regularities of nature, on the other hand I do not regard the possibility of their failure in an individual case as a reason for retracting or modifying a judgement that I made, and neither do others who speak the language I speak.

Professor Wisdom might sum up our discussion as follows: Propositions like Moore's premise are, indeed, *predictive*. This is a feature of them without which they would not be the kind of proposition they are – i.e. propositions about chairs and tables, hands and feet. So in what the future brings I shall necessarily have reasons which bear on the truth of such a proposition I may have asserted now. It could, therefore, be said that at any given time I cannot have every possible reason for claiming that the proposition I have asserted is true.[3] 'I cannot have every possible reason' – this means that I can always imagine *other* equally good reasons for making that same assertion. But although I cannot, in this sense, have *every* reason for claiming it to be true, I can have sufficient and absolutely conclusive reason for asserting it with complete certainty, for claiming to

[3] This is the truth behind the words I quoted from C. I. Lewis' *Mind and the World Order*.

know it.

If Wisdom speaks of 'reasons' in this connection, if he says that what I see, in these circumstances, gives me reason for what I say, namely that there is a table before me, he does *not* imply that what I see is one thing and what I claim to be before me is another thing, so that what I claim to know is supported by an inference. As we have seen, Wittgenstein prefers not to speak of 'reasons' or 'justifications' here at all – sometimes speaking of 'right'. For the kind of *trust* we have in what we see and touch is pre-logical and underlies the possibility of 'having reasons' for what we claim. All the same there is no conflict here between Wisdom and Wittgenstein.[4]

Let me sum up the discussion of the last four chapters where I concentrated on Moore's premise and his insistence that he and his audience undoubtedly know it to be true. Moore claimed that though he could not prove his premise he still knew it to be true. He insisted that it would be absurd not to be fully confident about it (see Chapter Eight).

We tried to understand why it is that there is no logical room for doubt here and we saw that the impossibility of proving Moore's premise (about which Moore was divided in his reactions) goes hand in hand with the impossibility of doubting it in earnest (see Chapter Nine). Or rather to speak of 'impossibility' is misleading – for think of Wittgenstein's man who doubts that a precipice may not confront him when he next opens his front door. Indeed if there is to be any doubt, it is impossible for there not to be certain things that are beyond the reach of doubt. But what they are is not determined by logic. We *trust* certain things. As Wittgenstein puts it: A language-game is possible only if we trust some things. This trust is not justified or unjustified; it is pre-logical. However, there are a whole host of questions here about the concepts of *possibility, impossibility* and *necessity* in logic which I cannot go into now.[5]

Although Moore's premise, given the circumstances in

---

[4] I have commented on the relative positions of Wisdom and Wittgenstein on this fundamental question of philosophy elsewhere – see *Induction and Deduction, A Study in Wittgenstein*, Part One, Chapter Six 'Explanation and Justification by Experience has an End', especially pp. 85–6.

[5] For a consideration of *some* of these questions see Dilman, *Induction and Deduction, A Study in Wittgenstein*, Blackwell 1973.

which he asserted it, is beyond the reach of doubt and so equally beyond the reach of proof or justification, we must not take lightly the sceptic's demand for a proof. It arises from certain deep-going difficulties which have to be met if the sceptic is to be satisfied. I have concentrated on two of these: (i) If our knowledge of what Moore asserts in his premise is based on perception or sense experience and if the truth of what it claims is independent of our perception of it, then this knowledge can at best be indirect and inferential. (ii) If Moore's premise is predictive in character then it can always turn out to be false so that we cannot be said to know it for certain.

I have argued that if our knowledge here is based on perception or sense experience and the truth of Moore's premise is independent of our perception it does not follow that our knowledge of its truth is indirect of inferential (see Chapter Ten).

I also argued that if Moore's premise does make claims about the future it does not follow that it can always turn out to be false, that it cannot be regarded as true come what further may (see the present chapter). There are numerous circumstances in which we regard propositions like Moore's premise in this way. That we do so, that our reactions agree, is a fact that belongs to the foundations of our language.

12 Conclusion: Philosophical Scepticism

We have confined our attention to Moore's proof which was directed *not* against the philosophical sceptic who denies that we can have *knowledge* of material things, leaving open the question whether or not material things exist, but against philosophers who have denied the *existence* of material things. We have seen that Moore's proof, his ideas about the kind of position he was directing it against, and what he claimed for his proof, raise many important philosophical issues. We discussed *some* of these at length. The last set of questions we discussed revolved around Moore's premise and his claim that he knows it to be true though he cannot prove it. These are questions about philosophical scepticism concerning our knowledge of material things.

We have seen that this kind of scepticism is radically different from ordinary scepticism, although at first sight they look very much alike. For where the ordinary, non-philosophical sceptic finds fault with the grounds of a claim made or theory advanced and is more critical than other people, less easily satisfied, the philosophical sceptic finds fault not with these grounds but with the accepted criteria of their adequacy:

A. *The ordinary sceptic says*: Perhaps this is the accepted opinion in this field. But if you examine the grounds on which it is accepted, you will find them wanting, inadequate. Therefore, on those grounds alone, we ought to be less certain, we ought to be prepared to find that we may be wrong.

B. *The philosophical sceptic says*: Admittedly we have what we *call* 'good grounds' for these claims. But ought we to call them 'good grounds'? Our criteria for good grounds here are loose, not sufficiently strict. If we were to make them stricter, as we ought to do, then we could no longer say that we have adequate grounds for these claims.

The non-philosophical sceptic questions the grounds for the assertions we make, the predictions, hypotheses, generalisations and theories we advance within an accepted framework. The questions he raises rely for their intelligibility on this framework and his criticisms presuppose criteria that belong to it. The philosophical sceptic, on the other hand, questions what belongs to the framework itself, the framework which underlies the intelligibility of the very notions in terms of which he frames his questions and conducts his criticisms. It is no wonder that he has been likened to a man who is trying to cut the very branch on which he is sitting. Thus Hume spoke of the 'extravagant attempt to destroy reason by argument and ratiocination' and said that the sceptic gives reason 'a diffidence of herself and of the ground on which she treads'. Kant spoke of him as 'setting reason at variance with herself'. But, of course, you can cut the branch on which you are sitting and, therefore, a more apt simile for what the philosophical sceptic is trying to do is trying to lift himself up by his boot laces.

I have already mentioned the contrast between the man in the desert who doubts that there is water in the distance when it seems to him there is and the philosophical sceptic who doubts that there is water before him when he is actually drinking it. The former doubts his eyes in these *special* circumstances. These circumstances *as opposed to others* give him reason for not trusting what his eyes tell him. If he says 'I doubt that there is water there' he has *positive* reason for saying this, and his claim is *based on experience*. Other men in similar situations thought that at last they would be able to quench their thirst and were disappointed. The philosophical sceptic's doubt, on the other hand, is not grounded on any special circumstances and exercises no such discrimination – these circumstances as opposed to others. He has no positive reason. For instance he says:

'Life may be one long dream.'

'None of our expectations may be fulfilled as from now – the bread we eat may poison us though no trace of arsenic has been detected in it.'
'All our memories may be completely delusive – the world may have come into existence five minutes ago with a population complete with memories of an unreal past.'
'The walking, talking figures around me may be automata.'

But not because he has any positive reason for thinking that this may be the case. Contrast with the scientist who may say:

'Though that bread looks all right and has not proved contaminated, I should not eat it if I were you. It may well poison you.' (He knows or suspects something which we don't know and have no grounds for suspecting.)

Or again contrast the philosophical sceptic who says: 'One can never know what other people think and feel', with the jealous husband who says: 'With Mary you never know; you can never be sure what she thinks and feels'. Or the philosophical sceptic who says: 'I don't think there is or can be any good reason why I or anyone should be moral, why I should be honest and just if it pays to lie and cheat', with the Catholic housewife who says: 'I used to think that one should not practise birth-control. But I no longer think there is any good reason to think so'.[1]

The philosophical sceptic has no positive reasons; his claim is that 'there are no good reasons'. He says:

For all we (or I) know life may be a dream, material things may not be real, the past may be wholly unreal, the walking and talking figures around me may be automata.

He has no reason for thinking or suspecting that this may be so. His trouble is that he can think of no good reason for denying this. Moore thought he could show us that we have good reason for denying that material things are or may be unreal. But we have seen that the philosophical sceptic's difficulties cut deeper than Moore realised – the philosophical sceptic who questions Moore's premise.

On considering these difficulties we saw that they are differ-

[1] See Dilman & Phillips, *Sense and Delusion*, Chapter One, Postscript sec. 4 'Philosophy and Life', pp. 31–5.

ent in character from those of the ordinary sceptic who finds he cannot accept what others cheerfully accept. We saw that they are bound up with various features of the *grammar* in which the claims he is sceptical about are made, and that if these features are a source of difficulty to him this is because of certain unexamined assumptions he makes, without clearly recognising them, or even recognising them at all, assumptions which embody certain logical confusions. Hence you cannot answer the philosophical sceptic by trying to provide the proof or justification he seeks. To try to do so is to commit the very fallacies which beset the sceptic's thinking and to evade examining what lies at their source. In any case the sceptic is at least right when he says that there can be no proof or justification of the reality of physical objects, of the so-called uniformity of nature, or of the moral beliefs that are active in a person's life. What he does not appreciate is that this does not make us irrational, that it does not reflect on the rationality of the different activities in which we engage, and that it does not, therefore, justify the alarm which the philosophical sceptic raises.

Certainly coming to terms with or meeting scepticism is of fundamental importance in philosophy. If our discussion so far hasn't thrown some light on why I say this, perhaps the discussion in the second part of the book will do so. But if I say that meeting scepticism is important in philosophy, this does not mean that it is 'fundamental to anything else'. It isn't as if we have to rescue fundamental assumptions from the attack of the philosophical sceptic before we can get on with our other business. The idea that philosophy should refute scepticism so that, for instance, the scientist can build on more secure foundations is, as we have seen, a misconception. It misunderstands the character of the philosophical sceptic's doubts, and also the character of the so-called 'foundations' of our knowledge. The reason why it is so important for philosophy to meet scepticism can only be appreciated when we are clear about the object of the sceptic's concern.

The philosophical sceptic (as we have seen) is not himself clear about this. He thinks that he is concerned with very general *assumptions* for which we ought to be able to give reasons. We have seen that he is wrong about this. Think back, for instance, to what I said about the continued existence of physical objects and how the idea that this is a very general assumption is bound up with the idea that the expression 'physical object' or 'material thing' is a general name – ideas which we have seen to be operative in Moore's thinking when he offered a proof of the existence of material things and insisted that his proof is valid. We should appreciate now that what the philosophical sceptic is concerned with are features of the framework within which we make assumptions, embark on investigations, engage in various forms of reasoning, sort out what is true from what is false, distinguish appearance and illusion from reality. Wittgenstein talked of this as *grammar*.

What is at issue, then, is whether the grammars within which we talk and reason, raise and settle doubts, are themselves responsible to any reality, whether the grammatical frameworks within which we distinguish between what is real and what is not are *arbitrary*: Are our ways of thinking, reasoning, inferring, calculating in any way grounded in nature or are they bounded for us by arbitrary definitions? I may have touched on this question, but I did not discuss it. It is perhaps the most fundamental question behind those controversies in different areas of philosophy between realism, intuitionism and conventionalism – in the philosophy of mathematics, in ethics, and in discussions of the so-called problem of universals.

This question, whether what belongs to grammar and cannot be proved or justified is arbitrary, is I think the most fundamental question raised by philosophical scepticism.

Rhees once quoted Socrates' statement in the *Phaedo*: 'Let us beware of admitting into our souls the thought that probably no arguments are sound.' He said that what this statement emphasises especially 'is the rather extraordinary fact that people ever do have the idea that some arguments are sound. That they have so to speak got to be guided by arguments, or got to accept certain conclusions.' It is just *this* that the philosophical sceptic wonders at, just *this* that he wants to come to grips with. Behind his arguments and conclusions lies a concern to understand man's relation to reality and how his diverse activities are governed by this relation: How does an arrangement of signs which says something differ from, say, an arrangement of bricks? How does drawing a conclusion or calculating differ from the sequence of steps in a dance? How do the movements of a builder on a building site differ from those of an ape imitating him? In short: What is a proposition? What is an inference? What is a thought?

His desire to see clearly how we can know the many things we claim to know, how we can reason to and support or justify these claims, stems from this concern – a concern with the conditions of rationality and intelligibility, criteria of knowledge and understanding. It is not so much that he wishes to understand these things as that his questions are rooted in difficulties about them. These difficulties are at once the motive power that drives him on and also the stumbling block to his efforts – insofar as they are directed to a better understanding of man's relation to reality. Therefore, to meet or oppose scepticism means to resolve these difficulties, to remove the implicit contradictions to which they commit the sceptic, and so to move towards a better understanding. Insofar as the understanding in question is what the philosopher seeks, one could say, with Rhees, that 'the refutation of scepticism is the whole business of philosophy'.

The reason why meeting scepticism is of fundamental importance in philosophy is that meeting it *is* advancing or deepening one's understanding of the difference between and the relations to each other of different kinds of human knowledge and types of reasoning and argument and also of the kind of difference a man's understanding of his environment, his relation to reality makes to his life. If Wittgenstein spoke of 'solving puzzles' and 'resolving difficulties', if he used such similes as 'undoing the knots in our understanding' and 'showing the fly out of the fly-bottle' let this not obscure from us that in philosophy, as a result of reflection and discussion, we gain a better understanding of the things we are concerned with than we did before.[2] But the search for a better understanding in philosophy *is* a struggle with difficulties.[3] Our gain lies in what we come to understand *en route*. In St. Augustine's words, quoted by Wittgenstein: 'The search says more than the discovery' (*Z.* sec. 457). One could say that the discovery is in the search, in the struggle with difficulties. It has no independent life and cannot

[2] See Wisdom, 'Mace, Moore and Wittgenstein', *Paradox and Discovery*, especially pp. 165–6.

[3] See Rush Rhees, 'The Study of Philosophy', *Without Answers*.

be expressed directly – in the form of theses.

In the first seven chapters of this essay we have been concerned with what Moore thought he had proved, what he had set out to refute. We saw that the target of his attack here was *not* the sceptic's position, but a position arrived at in a philosophical attempt to counter scepticism:

> If a material thing is something over and above our sense impressions then we cannot know its existence at all and neither could we have formed any conception of it.
>
> But we do understand references to material things and know whether or not there is a chair or a hand before our eyes.
>
> Therefore it cannot be that a material thing is something over and above our sense impressions.
>
> I.e. The idea of a material thing as something over and above our sense impressions involves a contradiction – since we can have no conception of the very thing we are talking about.
>
> Material things, in this sense, don't exist.

This is a feasible way of countering scepticism only if one shares the sceptic's assumptions, namely the exhaustive dichotomy between material things and sense impressions and the idea that whenever we make any claim about a material thing this is based on our sense impressions. Hence an examination which will clear the confusions that make such assumptions irrestible will at one stroke free us from the temptation towards *both* scepticism *and* the kind of position Moore wanted to refute by means of his proof. Hence when a consideration of Moore's premise and his claim to know it for certain turned our attention to scepticism we did not turn away from the topic of our discussion up to this point, namely the assertion that material things don't exist, which Moore rightly wanted to oppose, and what it is that is wrong-headed about such an assertion.

We have seen (i) that what is wrong-headed about it is not what Moore took it to be and (ii) that it cannot be refuted in the way Moore tried to – and also why it cannot be so refuted.

Part Two

Solipsism and Our Knowledge of Other Minds

1 Introduction

We have talked about the existence of material things and our knowledge of their existence. We have concentrated on some of the difficulties that lie at the source of the inclination to deny (i) the existence of material things and (ii) the possibility of our having any knowledge of it.

I have also touched on the inclination to think of these difficulties as academic and trivial. We have seen the sense in which they are indeed 'academic', though this does not mean that there is anything trivial about them. In the last chapter of the previous essay I have tried to indicate something of their depth.

In this second part of the book we shall study parallel questions about the nature and existence of the mind and of our knowledge of it.

The first thing that strikes us here is the peculiar *intangibility* of the mind. Whether we speak of the mind, the soul, consciousness, thinking or feeling, the moment we try to focus on any of these it slips between our fingers. Remember St. Augustine: 'What then is time? If no one asks me, I know: if I wish to explain it to one that asks, I know not' (*Confessions* Bk. xi: xiv).

In a sense 'material thing' is a philosopher's concept and it is meant to cover a variety of things – tables and chairs, smoke, the wind, rainbows, shadows and mirror images. Except for the first two examples, these are not what would normally come to one's mind if one were asked to think of a material thing. I confined myself to such examples as tables and chairs, sticks and stones. These seem to be among the most *concrete* and *tangible* things we can think of – in contrast with time and the soul. Still we faced and combated the tendency to think that we cannot *perceive directly* even these things, that is see and touch them without an intermediary.

In the case of what is mental, a so-called state of consciousness, a similar tendency splits into two. We are inclined to say that we cannot have any kind of direct acquaintance with someone else's state of mind, whereas we can have direct acquaintance with our own mental states: so direct, indeed, that it is impossible we should err. Here then our sceptical question 'Can we have knowledge of another person's mind – of his thoughts and feelings?' will have a counterpart: 'Can we ever communicate our thoughts and feelings to other people? Can we ever escape the solitude and privacy in which we live?'

Some of those who asked the former question took a line which in some ways parallels the line which Berkeley took in opposition to the sceptic who doubts the possibility of our knowing whether or not material things exist. He had said that material things are nothing over and above our sense impressions, so that when we have certain sense impressions we perceive directly such things as tables and chairs and, therefore, know that material things exist. The difficulty with this view was that in equating material objects with a different category of things, namely sense impressions, Berkeley denied, or had to go through elaborate contortions to avoid denying, what is of the very essence of a material thing, namely its so-called independent existence.

Now the philosopher who wishes to avoid scepticism with regard to our knowledge of other people's minds often takes a line parallel to the one Berkeley took. He says that minds are nothing over and above people's behaviour. This has equally unpalatable consequences. Thus a voice within us whispers: 'Berkeley equated matter with what he called "ideas" and found it very difficult to preserve what is of the essence of such things as tables and chairs, in contrast with sensations and mental images, namely their independent existence. The behaviourist insofar as he reduces mind to behaviour equally denies something that is of the very essence of mind, namely its privacy.' This objection embodies serious confusions, as we shall see, but there is nevertheless something right about it.

The voice within us raises a second objection: 'If mind is

nothing but behaviour, then it would seem that there is no categorial difference between human beings, animals and machines; only quantitative differences. So if a machine could imitate or reproduce human behaviour in its performance we would have to grant that it had intelligence, even that it was capable of thought and perhaps feeling. Yet surely this cannot be.' Here we have one upshot of behaviouristic thinking which we should like to resist. It lies diametrically opposed to another idea, once equally popular, namely the idea of the soul as a substance.

I want to begin by examining some of the confusions behind these opposing philosophical conceptions of a human being.

2 Reality of the Soul: Human Life and Behaviour

It is sometimes said that a human being has a soul, whereas animals and lifeless things do not. The distinction made is of significance probably for most religions.[1] Although it sets man apart and places him in a unique category, it should not be taken to imply that there is no difference between what is alive and has sentience, apart from man, and what is lifeless and unconscious. This was Descartes' error. For he ran together several distinctions and equated the soul with consciousness.

It is very difficult not to think of the soul as a substance – 'something subtle like air or fire or aether (as Descartes puts it) mingled among the grosser parts of the body'. Those who denied its existence have very often done so just because they thought of it as a substance and could not find any evidence for its existence – in J. B. Watson's words: 'No one has ever touched the soul, or seen one in a test tube, or has in any way come into a relationship with it as he has with the other objects of his daily experience.'[2]

Wittgenstein opposed this picture. He pointed out the

[1] We are not here concerned to appreciate the religious import of this distinction, but something that lies at the basis of the possibility of those distinctions, bound up with the notion of the soul, that are important in religions – such distinctions, for instance, as the one between a man who has lost his soul and one who has found it. For a discussion of these further questions see my paper 'Wittgenstein on the Soul', Parts Two and Three, *Understanding Wittgenstein*, ed. Prof. Godfrey Vesey. The present chapter is more or less identical with Part One of that paper.

[2] J. B. Watson and W. McDougall, *The Battle of Behaviourism*, Psyche Miniatures General Series, p. 13

respects in which it shackles our understanding and he helped to liberate us from its influence. I mean that he helped us to appreciate what the existence of the soul amounts to without thinking of it as a substance: 'The human body is the best picture of the human soul' he wrote in *Philosophical Investigations* (p. 178). And again: 'If one sees the behaviour of a living thing one sees its soul' (*Inv.* sec. 357).

Part of what is being said here is that we can see what state of soul a man is in, whether for instance he is joyful or depressed, hopeful or in despair, in his behaviour.[3] He is also saying that the reality of the soul, in other words the *possibility* of joy and sorrow, love, grief, hope and despair, depends on the life and behaviour of those who are capable of these things. In short, the reality of the soul can be seen in human behaviour.

But this is not like seeing a man's anger or distress in his words, face and deeds. For when on a given occasion what a man says or does convinces me that he is angry, or that he has been hurt or offended, the possibility remains that I may be wrong. Whereas there is no question for me whether he has a soul – unless this means whether he has lost his soul and stopped caring about the depravity into which he has sunk. My point is that the very conception I take of him when I talk of what he *says* and *does*, when I use the personal pronoun in referring to him, when I address him in the way I do, precludes the possibility of giving sense to the words 'He has no soul'. But if that has no sense, then neither do the words 'He has a soul'.

Thus if under ordinary circumstances I were to point to someone and say that he has a soul it would not be clear what I was saying. Am I drawing attention to something you are likely to forget? Could you be under some misapprehension which I might wish to correct? (See *Inv.* p. 178 – 'He isn't an automaton.') Contrast with: 'He has feelings, you know' – said to someone who is treating him callously. The point remains that in the absense of such special circumstances I might be *trying* to say something, even though what I come up with does not make sense as it stands. For I might be a philosopher fighting against those who wish to deny the existence of the soul.

What is in question is not so much a belief I have about this

[3] For a discussion of this part of what Wittgenstein is saying here see Chapter Eight below.

person in particular, or about human beings in general, as a conception within the framework of which I may hold different beliefs – for instance, that my friend is in pain:

> 'I believe that he is suffering.' Do I also *believe* that he isn't an automaton? (*Inv.* p. 178)

Compare with:

> I have a telephone conversation with New York. My friend tells me that his young trees have buds of such and such a kind. I am now convinced that his tree is . . . Am I also convinced that the earth exists? (*On Certainty*, sec. 208)

Wittgenstein would say that the latter proposition belongs to my frame of reference: What could stand upright if that were to fall? Could I, for instance, have a telephone conversation with a friend in New York?

Similarly, if I believe that he is suffering then I am necessarily taking a certain conception of what is before me. We do not have a second belief here that is open to doubt or question. Of course, during a visit to Mme. Tussaud's I may doubt, for a moment, whether what seems to be an attendant is really an attendant and not one of the wax figures to be found there. And my friend may whisper: 'I believe he is one of the attendants.' My doubt, short-lived as it is, has a specific basis: Is he a live human being or only a wax imitation? Suppose that it moves and begins to talk. This will clear my doubt. I see that he is one of the attendants, a live human being. This discovery changes my whole attitude to what is before me. If a moment ago I had thought of it as a wax figure then I could not have intelligibly supposed that he might be hungry or bored. There would have been no logical room for me to hold this belief.

It could, of course, be said that first I *believed* one thing, namely that what is before me is a wax figure, and that soon after I came to *believe* something else, namely that all the time I was looking at one of the attendants. But this is different from the case where I first *believe* that he is in pain and then come to see that he was pretending. In the former case Wittgenstein speaks of 'attitude':

> Our attitude to what is alive and to what is dead, is not the same. (*Inv.* sec. 284)

My attitude towards him is an attitude towards a soul. I am not of the *opinion* that he has a soul (*Inv.* p. 178)

Having this attitude means reacting to people in certain ways – for instance, resenting what they say, being insulted, hurt, angered or irritated by their words and deeds, being grateful for what they do, pitying them, feeling embarrassed in their presence, and so on. This attitude, these reactions are a pretty basic feature of the life we live. Without them it is hard to think what human life would be like and whether we would be human at all. They form part of the framework in which we attribute various emotions, intentions, plans and aspirations to human beings, hold them responsible for what they do, praise, blame, criticise, try and punish them. These 'language-games', as Wittgenstein would call them – thanking, cursing, greeting, praising, judging, etc. – are based on these matter-of-course reactions which constitute our 'attitude towards a soul'. Wittgenstein speaks of them as a 'special chapter of human behaviour' (*Z.* sec. 542). He says that they are a proto-type of a way of thinking (*Z.* sec. 541) and that the language-games in question may be regarded as extentions of this mode of response (*Z.* sec. 545). My relation to what I react in these ways is part of my concept of a human being (*Z.* sec. 543). Thus to think, for instance, that 'we tend someone else because by analogy with our own case we believe that he is experiencing pain too' is 'putting the cart before the horse' (*Z.* sec. 542). The horse is our natural reaction to someone who has hurt himself and is crying; and the mistake of putting the cart before the horse lies in the sceptic's idea that unless such a reaction is based on reason and can be justified it is irrational. Wittgenstein would say that if that stands in need of justification then none of our beliefs and conjectures about our friends and acquaintances can be justified.[4]

We see that there is no direct way of stating or affirming the reality of the human soul. The words 'Men have souls, whereas animals and lifeless things don't' do not express a truth we can be ignorant of unless we are insane. If we know what is being contrasted in these words, if we have the concept of a human being, then we do not need these words, and if we do not

---

[4] For a discussion of this question see Chapter Eight, Part Three, sec. A below – 'Behavioural and Verbal Criteria'.

understand the contrast in question, such words cannot possibly help us.[5] Certainly they do not say something that can be established by investigation, by a closer scrutiny of men; animals and lifeless things. They are meant to bring into focus a whole dimension of our life and speech to which it is difficult for us to conceive an alternative we can make sense of. What is at issue is the difference between the terms in which we think and talk of human beings, make sense of human behaviour, and those in which we talk about and study animal behaviour and also different types of physical phenomena. Of course there are no sharp lines between men and animals, and between what is alive and what is not. Certainly there is an overlap between human and animal behaviour, the extent of which varies from one animal to another. Still much with which we are familiar in human life has no place at all in animal life: 'One can imagine an animal angry, frightened, unhappy, happy, startled. But hopeful? And why not?' (*Inv.* p. 174).

II

Why can we not intelligibly say of a dog or an infant that it is hopeful? Or of a stone that it is in pain? (*Inv.* sec. 283). Why can we not say that a computer calculates? Wittgenstein asked this last question in the course of his considerations of the formalist view of mathematics (*Remarks* IV, sec. 2).

A computer can reel out unimpeachable answers to the questions we feed into it. It may be tempting to think that here is exemplified the kind of competence that makes us speak of thought and intelligence in a mathematician. If the mathematician differs from the computer in *other* respects why should that undermine the similarity in their mathematical performance? Certainly if a man or a child writes down the answer to a mathematical problem this, *in itself*, does not prove that he has intelligence. To think of him as having mathematical ability we want him to be able to solve *other* math-

[5] A similar point was made about 'having the concept of a material thing', namely that if we have this concept, if we understand what the difference between a reflection on the wall and an after-image amounts to, then we do not need a proof of the existence of material things. If, on the other hand, we do not yet know this difference, as infants-in-arms do not, then no proof or explanation is going to get us to recognise it. See Part One, Chapters Two and Three above.

ematical problems. Whether or not his present performance exhibits ability and intelligence depends on what he does on *other* occasions. But when we call a man who solves a wide range of difficult mathematical problems intelligent, we take it for granted that the symbols, formulae and simple operations he uses have meaning for him, that he understands them. We cannot take this for granted in the case of the computer. Merely responding to the problems fed into it with the correct answer does not show that the computer understands what it prints. If it understands the symbols in question, if their combinations mean anything to it, it must be able to use them, it must be able to count, for instance, to measure, to compare. But if it is to count, it must be able to point to or look at the objects it counts. Supposing it had a metal rod that shot out from its side and it turned in the direction of the objects it was meant to count. For this to be pointing it would have to point to things in various *other* situations and follow it up in the appropriate ways. It would have to respond to people pointing to things and places in ways that would show that it understood them. There would have to be occasions in which there is some point in pointing to things for its benefit. Holding the arm horizontal with the index finger straight is pointing *only* in the traffic of human life. What is true of the activity of calculating, then, is equally true of counting, measuring and pointing: each requires the complex surroundings of human life.

In short, if the computer is to calculate it would have to have something like the human body, with arms, face, eyes, and enter into various activities in which the symbols and formulae it prints play a role. It is their role in these many activities, in shopping, measuring, accounting, engineering, that gives them the sense they have. Without this role mathematics would be little more than 'a wall-paper pattern'. A person who cannot use mathematical symbols in their civil roles does not understand them. If a man responded to mathematical questions with the quickness of a computer and always came up with the correct answer, if he could carry out complicated formal transitions, work out involved mathematical proofs, but were 'otherwise perfectly imbecile' then he would be 'a human calculating machine' (*Remarks* IV, sec. 3). No more. A person who produces such answers, whether in words, writing or print, is performing an activity in which thought and intelligence are displayed *only* if he lives a life in which this activity has point and has a bearing on other things he does, *only* if he has other interests – interests independent of producing these answers. In the absence of such a life even a being who is alive is not a human being. At best he is a human offspring. And the activity we imagine him to carry on, in analogy with the computer, is not what it is in a life which gives it the kind of connections calculating has in our life.

Philosophers had been so preoccupied with trying to find something covert behind the overt activity, that when they came to recognise that they had been wrong they jumped to the conclusion that if a machine imitates a mathematician overtly it must be calculating, since the sequences in time, actual and possible, are what adds up to the intelligent activity of calculating. I have argued that without the wider surroundings of a human life they cannot do so. For these surroundings and the kind of connections the sequences in question have in those surroundings are logically relevant to what kind of activity they constitute. What it makes sense to say about them depends on their surroundings. As Wittgenstein would put it: If there is anything behind the calculations which human beings carry out, anything over and above my utterance of a formula when I have a flash of understanding, it is these circumstances and connections (*Inv.* sec. 154).

It is these which the behaviourist neglects, just as the formalist neglects the civil life of mathematical symbols and formulae. Hence Wittgenstein characterised formalism as the 'behaviourism of mathematics'.

What is true of calculating is certainly true of speaking, hoping, grieving, pretending and rejoicing. Rush Rhees once said that if a creature speaks and can understand you then it is the kind of creature that can be insulted by what you say, that can laugh at your jokes, and which can cry too. It must be capable of lying, pretence and deception. 'Otherwise I say things into it because I want to get certain information out. I do not take it for granted that it *understands*, in the sense in which I assume this of a human being when I am talking to him.' That he gives me 'prosaic information' in words that belong to a language I understand does not in itself show that he is speaking, or that he understands my questions. What do the words he utters mean *to him*? Indeed, what *could* they mean, if he has no interest himself in the kind of information he gives, if he doesn't carry out any investigations and obtain results that play a role in *his* life, results that make a difference to what he does in various situations, if he does not care to obtain correct results, show regard for the truth, if he is indifferent to whether or not others lie to him, if he has no feelings for those with whom he speaks or for anything else?

If he is *saying* anything to me in words which convey some information which I can use, though he is indifferent to what I do with it, there must be other occasions when he cares what he tells people. And if there are such occasions then he is a being with desires, fears, hopes and interests, and the words he utters now have a role in connection with these or are related to other words which do. There must be other contexts in which he expects things of people and responds to their demands on him, contexts in which he enters into relation with people in conversation. His saying something to me on this occasion, his understanding my questions, cannot be divorced from such numerous occasions where words play a role in *his* life and where he responds to other people's utterances – with laughter, pity, sorrow, anger, irritation, indignation, gratitude. If he is giving me some information now in words that *he* understands, he must be the kind of being who can himself ask questions, entertain doubts, and who has something to say. If he is not just repeating words parrot-wise he must live a life in which there is a place for concern, joy, anger, sorrow, fun, danger, desire and interests, to which the words he utters now have a relation, directly or indirectly through other words.

On the other hand, the kind of life in which these things are possible is unimaginable apart from language; he could not have grown into that kind of life if he did not speak a language, if he did not live with people who do. That is, the language we speak makes our lives what they are; it makes us the kind of beings we are. This is the point behind Wittgenstein's question whether we can imagine a dog or an unweaned infant hopeful or in despair (*Inv.* p. 174). He answers that only those who have mastered the use of language can hope or know despair. How can anything that a suckling does be an expression of hope? How can the smile of an unweaned infant be pretence? (*Inv.* sec.

249) The surroundings that are necessary for anything he does to amount to an expression of hope are not yet present. In the surroundings of the infant's life there is no room for the distinction between a genuine expression of feeling and a feigned one: 'A child has much to learn before it can pretend' (*Inv.* p. 229), or before he can conceal his feelings.[6] Pretending too, like grief and hope, are 'special patterns in the weave of our lives' (*Inv.* pp. 174, 229). These phenomena are modes of the kind of life we live with language (p. 174).

We see that one cannot make sense of what it is to speak, to make an inference, to calculate, if one leaves out the kind of life that surrounds people's utterances, the activities in the weave of which inferences are made and calculations carried out. Equally, one cannot make sense of what it is to form intentions, keep resolutions, fall a prey to emotions, hope, grieve, rejoice and despair, if one does not consider the kind of surroundings in which these things take place. These phenomena of human life are logically intertwined in the sense that the possibility of any one of them presupposes much of the rest. For if it is to be possible for a creature to hope or feel remorse, to deliberate before acting or to carry out a calculation, he must live the kind of life in which he exhibits a wide range of affective reactions in particular situations, a life which he lives with others like him who share these reactions and with whom he comes into contact in the various activities of such a life.

It is in this dimension that what makes us the kind of creatures we are is to be found; not in some additional substance or medium in which certain activities which we find difficult to examine go on. We have no clear idea of what such a substance would be like, and neither is it possible that we should – given the way we separate it from every activity in which we enter as embodied beings. But if the soul is not such a substance or medium, this is not to say that it is unreal.

---

[6] See Chapter Eight, Part Two, sec. C below – 'Concealing one's feelings'.

The theory that the self is the only thing that can be known to exist.

3 Solipsism

I

The Cartesian Idea of the Soul as a Substance In the last chapter we have seen that this idea is largely rooted in the attempt to grasp the reality of the soul in separation from what underlies the possibility of human joy and suffering, love, hope and despair, kindness and cruelty, good and evil. It arises when language is 'like an engine idling'.

This is not, however, always true where people have talked of the body and the soul as two different substances. When, for instance, Socrates in the *Phaedo* speaks of a purification which 'consists in separating the soul as much as possible from the body' he speaks in terms of an imagery in which the soul and the body figure as two different substances. Yet there is nothing incoherent in this idea of the soul which belongs to a language that has a long and respectable ancestry and to which Plato has contributed in the way he has *used* that language to deepen the kind of understanding possible within its framework. The Platonic picture of the soul, as opposed to the Cartesian, is not a *philosopher's* picture. For it belongs to a language which men have used for centuries in sizing up their lives and sifting their moral reactions to it. If we wish to understand what it means to speak of the soul we must turn to *this* language.[1]

The Platonic picture of the soul as a substance is rooted in such a language. Its content and significance can only be found in the way this language is used. Thus we can compare Plato's idea of the soul as a substance with other *religious pictures* – the

[1] See Dilman, 'Wittgenstein on the Soul', Parts Two and Three, in *Understanding Wittgenstein*, ed. Prof. Godfrey Vesey.

way in which people are taught to think about the world and their own life in terms of certain images and stories. These pictures are as old as the forms of language in which they are embedded and are, I suppose, inseparable from those forms of speech and thought. There is also the language of poetry, poetic traditions in which certain reflections and perceptions find expression in terms of *similes* and *imagery* from which they are, by and large, inseparable.

If I mention these, it is because I want to contrast one kind of philosopher's picture with them – *not* the sort exemplified in Wittgenstein's remark which compares the philosopher to a fly in a fly-bottle (*Inv.* sec. 309). One may call this a poetic simile. Wittgenstein's philosophical remarks are strewn with them. No, I am thinking of the kind of picture which arises when language is 'like an engine idling' – another simile which Wittgenstein uses (*Inv.* secs. 88, 132) – and which holds the philosopher captive (*Inv.* sec. 115). The Cartesian picture of the soul as a substance is such a picture.

With pictures embedded in religious thought and language it is not the philosopher's business to oppose them – any more than it is his business to find fault with language (*Inv.* sec. 124). The use of these pictures is as much part of the phenomenon of human life as the use of words and sentences. On the other hand, what I called *philosophers'* pictures[2] shackle our understanding and prevent us from getting a proper grasp of those matters which concern us when we do philosophy. So we have to free ourselves from the spell they cast on our thinking.

Now for the Cartesian picture of the soul as substance. We have seen that it is rooted in the attempt to grasp the reality of the soul in separation from what underlies the possibility of much that belongs to human life. It is this *separation* that makes

[2] E.g. Picture of the soul as 'something subtle like air, fire or aether, mingled among the grosser parts of the body' (Descartes); of thinking and remembering as processes which take place in some peculiarly intangible medium, the psychical sphere; of the unconscious mind as the submerged part of an iceberg (Freud); of a sense-datum 'as a sort of barrier which gets between us and the physical object', as an indispensable intermediary through which we enter into perceptual contact with the world; of human beings as enclosed in their consciousness as in a slender outline that prevents them from ever touching anything outside themselves (Proust); of the meanings of general words as an essence we distil from our varied perceptions as we might distil alcohol from different alcoholic drinks, etc.

any kind of communication between people problematic and inevitably leads to solipsism.[3] It will be well to remember that traditionally philosophers have spoken of substance where they wanted to talk of a category of things that exist on their own, no matter what else exists, comes into being, is altered or destroyed. As we shall see the incoherence of the idea of the soul as a substance *is* the incoherence of solipsism.

Thus those tendencies in our thinking, which Descartes pursued to their logical extreme, influence our thinking as follows: when we think of what it is to be in a certain state of soul and we call to mind such examples as pride, remorse, fear, dismay or anguish, we easily imagine that what we mean by these things can be explained to someone who doesn't understand our words without any mention of the kind of situation in which we normally speak of them. That is we think that we can explain what we mean by 'pride', 'fear' or 'remorse', without referring to the kind of thing that people feel proud or afraid of or remorseful about, and what kind of thoughts and beliefs they have about these.[4] For instance, I may feel proud of a sailing boat because I have built it and it sails well, or because I have won a race in it, or because it has made possible for the sailing club to which I belong to come out top in this year's regattas. We all know this, but we either forget it or regard it as irrelevant when we ask ourselves 'What is pride?'. So we try to catch ourselves feeling pride in the hope of discerning what goes on within us at such moments. The idea is that what goes on then is the same as what goes on at other times when we feel pride – whether we feel proud of our children, our city, our literary achievements, and so on. What goes on 'within our breast' or 'in our consciousness' – *that* constitutes the essence of pride, what we mean by 'feeling proud'. So the way we normally give expression to such a feeling, the situations in which we do so, our thoughts at such times, the terms in which we think of these situations – these are thought to form no part of what we mean or understand by 'pride'. A reference to any of these things is seen as only an external and, therefore, inessential aid to explaining the

[3] See Chapter Four below.

[4] I should add – 'explain at least to ourselves'. For, as we shall see, this leads us to think that we cannot explain what we mean by such words to other people, and we cannot be sure that they mean the same thing by these words.

differences between pride and any other emotion or attitude. For these are different 'modes of consciousness' – as it were different patterns of ripples on the spiritual stream. They are to be known by contemplating the patterns themselves, not their different 'effects' on the physical banks of the river. We become cognisant of them by means of introspection. Consequently, we think of a state of soul as something with which only the person who is in that state has direct contact. It is these that both Descartes and William James thought of as constituting the *data* of psychology.

The idea is that a man can be in a state of soul irrespective of the circumstances in which he is; what went on before and what will follow the time in which he is in that state being logically irrelevant to his being in it. Thus dissociating from our concepts of joy, anguish, pride, hope and fear much that in discourse is tied up with the use of the words for them we come to think of a state of soul as something that has nothing to do with anything physical – the circumstances of the man in that state, the bodily, facial and behavioural expressions he gives to it. This is the idea of *states of a substance*, perhaps conceived in analogy with the different physical states of water. Wittgenstein talks of this dissociation as 'the abrogation of the normal language-game' (*Inv.* sec. 288). We shall see how it leads to the idea of a 'language which describes my inner experiences and which only I, myself, can understand' (*Inv.* sec. 256).

II

Solipsism and Scepticism The idea is that a state of soul is *private* to the person who is in that state and that its identity is logically inseparable from the person's identity. It seems that the first person pronoun 'I' is inseparable from any description of a person's mental states or experiences. So if I think of what is meant by 'pain', for instance, it seems that I can only think of what I feel when I feel pain. One is inclined to say 'I find it difficult to think or conceive of a pain which I do not feel – very much as I may find it difficult to think of the past as having reality.' 'A pain that I do not feel is not real pain.' 'A pain that I felt yesterday is not real.' 'Only the experience of the present moment is real.' This idea finds expression in the words:

'Pain is what I feel when I am in pain.'

Or:

> 'When anything is seen, *really* seen, it is always I who see it.
> For what seeing is I can only know from seeing myself; I have
> only learnt the word 'seeing' to mean what *I* do.' (See *B.B.*,
> pp. 60–1.)

One is inclined to think that one learns what seeing is or what
the word 'pain' means *from one's own case*. This is an inevitable
outcome of the dissociation I spoke of earlier.

A. 'Only my experiences, my thoughts, my pains are real.'
   (*B.B.*, p. 58)

   'That there should be thinking or pain other than my own
   is unintelligible.'

   'I cannot understand the idea of pain, or any other experience, separated from me, the feeling subject. A pain
   that someone else feels is not real pain. Only my pain is
   real.'

This is what the solipsist is inclined to say.
   Contrast with another thing we may be inclined to say:

B. 'I understand only what I mean by "pain". What someone else means by "pain" I cannot understand. I do not
   know what the word "pain" means in connection with
   another person. For all I know other people may mean
   nothing when they speak of "pain". For all I know they
   may never feel pain. For all I know I may be the only conscious, sentient being in existence.'

This is what the solipsistic sceptic says.
   A. and B. are related; these two inclinations have a common
source. They are both solipsistic positions in the way they put
the subject or 'I' in the centre – the centre of the world in the
first case, the centre of knowledge in the second. In the first case
it is reality or the world that is circumscribed by the 'I':

A. 'The world is my world', as Wittgenstein puts it in the
   Tractatus (5. 641).

In the second case it is knowledge that is thus circumscribed:

B. 'I can only know what I experience.'

So the solipsist denies the reality of other people's experiences, and the solipsistic sceptic denies the possibility of knowing it. The relation between A. and B. may be compared with the relation between the denial of the existence of physical objects (which Moore tried to combat in his 'Proof of an External World') and the denial of our knowledge of it.

A'. 'Material things don't exist.'

'Material things are not anything over and above our sense impressions; they do not have a reality over and above that of our sense impressions.'

'The notion of such a reality involves a contradiction.'

B'. 'We cannot know the existence of material things.'

'We cannot have knowledge of a reality outside or beyond our sense impressions.'

'Such knowledge involves a contradiction.'

We have seen why Berkeley, for instance, thought that the idea of a physical reality independent of our sense impressions is self-contradictory. We have seen, further, that here it is not the idea of sense impressions which is at fault as such, but the idea that we can only perceive directly sense impressions, so that we can only get beyond them by some kind of inference.

A'. If we think of a physical reality as something we can at best know indirectly and so by inference, then indeed such an idea does involve a contradiction.

B'. If we can know what we call physical objects at best indirectly, then indeed we cannot be said to know them at all. Our idea of what we call 'knowledge of physical objects' involves a contradiction.

Notice the assumption common to A' and B':

If we can know the existence of physical objects at all we can only do so *indirectly*.

In both A' and B' sense impressions are thought of as coming between us and physical objects – in our perceptions.

If now you ask: How are these sense impressions identified?

you will find in yourself the inclination to answer the question
as follows:

'They cannot be identified apart from the percepient-
subject. My sense impressions are mine and your sense impressions are yours. Two people can never have or see the
same sense impressions.'[5]   *Private to I*

Thus it is not merely sense impressions that seem to come between us and the physical objects we look at and reach for, but
through them the 'I' of the percepient – when he says 'I see a
chair'. Hence we are inclined to say:

'When anything is seen, *really* seen, [and not merely inferred]
it is always I who see it.' (*B.B.*, p. 60)

Previously we couldn't think of perception without sense impressions or sense-data. We discussed some of the main problems here in Part One of this book. There I pointed the way out of
this predicament. We now see that if we are caught up in such a
predicament we have even less space to breathe in than we realised. For if we can allow ourselves to slip back into it we shall see
that it now seems that we cannot think of perception without
bringing in ourselves: 'When anything is *really* seen, it is always
I who see it.'

III

What the Solipsist wants to say The solipsist says: 'Only my pains,
my experiences are real. That there should be thinking or pain
other than my own is unintelligible.' 'Only I feel real pain.'
'Only I really see or hear.'

Just as the philosopher's 'Material things aren't real; only
sense data are real' or 'Material things don't exist' at first
sounded like 'It looks like water in the distance, but it's only a
mirage', the solipsist's 'Only I really see' sounds like what you
might expect a man who sees to say if he found himself in the
country of the blind. His 'only I feel pain' sounds like 'all the
others are only pretending, or they have been given local anaes-
thetics'.

We have seen that this is not what the philosopher in the first
case, e.g. Berkeley, meant or wanted to say. We have seen that

[5] This is discussed at length in Chapters Six and Seven below.

he is concerned with a 'philosophical' conception of matter, one that threatens to close in on him, as well as others who, for one reason or other, come to reflect on what it means to speak about physical things and on how 'in the last analysis' we can be said to know them. He finds fault with it on logical grounds and so wants to reject it: 'The idea of matter involves a contradiction.' We have seen that there really is something to be rejected here, but that it needs to be disentangled from something not to be tampered with. Otherwise we shall be unable to reject it without also rejecting what needs keeping. What we need to reject is the idea of matter as something that can be known by inductive inference only. That idea does really involve a contradiction. What needs keeping is what philosophers have tried to put into words when they spoke of the continued and independent existence of material things – the difference in grammar between a physical object and a sense impression, between a reflection and an after-image. But if we are to be able to reject the former without denying the latter, we have to see that if matter exists independently of our perceiving it it does not follow that we can at best have inductive reasons for what we say about material things.[6]

Similarly with the solipsist. If he says 'Only I really see' he is not speaking like the man in the country of the blind.

The converse of 'Only I really see' is 'When anything is really seen, it is always I who see it.' Wittgenstein asks: 'Always who?' Queer enough, he says, if I were the solipsist I would not mean 'always Ludwig Wittgenstein' (*B.B.*, p. 61).

What he claims to be really seen is his visual field and its contents. He thinks of it as something he cannot show to anyone else: 'You cannot see the contents of my visual field.' ('You cannot feel the pain I feel.')

So when he says 'Only I really see', he is saying something like: 'Only I see what you cannot see without being me.'

But this is not incompatible with: 'Only you see what anyone other than you cannot see without being you.'

If this is what the solipsist is content to rest with, then when he says 'Only I really see' he means 'Only I see what you cannot see without being me.' By 'only I' he does not mean 'only L.W.'. For in the second sentence for 'I' we can substitute any name we

[6] See Chapters Eleven and Twelve in Part One above.

like, including the second person pronoun:

'Only Jones sees what you cannot see without being Jones.'

'Only you see what I or anyone other than you cannot see without being you.'

However the solipsist is drawn into saying something stronger than this. I said that what he claims to be really seen is something which no one else can see without being the person who sees. Does he go further and equate 'the person who sees' with 'I'? I think that he is not himself clear on this point and is pulled in two directions.

On the one hand, as Wittgenstein points out, he is not using the word 'I' in such a way that it would be all right to replace it by his name. In other words, when he uses the word 'I' he means 'whoever is speaking' or 'the person who sees', and *not* this particular person, say L.W., as opposed to that one, say Jones. If so, you would not expect him to object if anyone else says what he says – that is if someone else says 'Only I really see'. In *that* case what he is saying would be the following:

'It is impossible that anyone other than me should see, really see, what I see. And it is equally impossible that I should see, really see, what anyone other than me sees.'

But I think that this is only a half-way house on the way to solipsism and has about it a symmetry which is not to be found in solipsism proper. The response of the solipsist to the above statement would be:

'"What anyone other than me sees, really sees" what does that mean? Is that something I understand? Can I intelligibly talk about it?'

What he would say, therefore, is:

'It is impossible that anyone other than me should see, really see, at all.'

The previous statement was: 'It is impossible that anyone other than me should see, really see, what I see.' And this allowed its converse: 'It is impossible that I should see, really see, what anyone other than me sees.' But the solipsist is inclined to take his criterion of *seeing* from 'what I see'. So what anyone other than me sees' doesn't make sense to him. Hence his statement:

'That there should be seeing other than my own is unintelligible.'

Why does he take his criterion of seeing, really seeing, from 'what I see'? Because of his idea that he has learnt what 'seeing' means from his own case. So, for the solipsist, understanding the idea of someone else seeing is tantamount to understanding the notion of the existence of a sight which is both seen by him and not seen by him; and this is really unintelligible – it involves a contradiction. As Wittgenstein puts it in the *Investigations*:

> If one has to imagine someone else's pain [or sense impressions] on the model of one's own [as the solipsist tries to do], this is none too easy a thing to do: for I have to imagine pain which I *do not feel* [or sense impressions which I do not have or see] on the model of the pain which I *do feel* [or sense impressions which I do have or see]. (sec. 302)

That is why he says:

> A pain which I do not feel – that is not real pain. There is no real pain, or any other feeling, that I do not feel. A sight that I do not see – that is no real sight. There is no real seeing other than my own.

IV

Solipsism and the First Person We see that the solipsist wants to focus on something which no one can see without being him, no one can feel without being him, something the very identity of which involves the identity of the subject. He wants to say that only *that* can be really seen, really felt: 'What is *really* seen is only what *I* can see.' That is when he speaks of 'really seeing' he means 'what only I can do', and when he speaks of 'what is really seen' he means 'what only I see'. So when he says, 'Only I really see' he is confusing us and himself with too many specifications – since by 'really see' he *means* 'what only I can do'. In other words, either 'I' is redundant or 'really' is redundant. A sentence that uses both words uses one word too many. Wittgenstein apparently made this point in a lecture:

If only you can have real toothache, there is no sense in saying 'Only I can have real toothache'. Either you don't need 'I' or you don't need 'real'. Your notation makes too many specifications. You had much better say 'There is toothache' and give the locality and the description. That is what you are trying to say. . . 'Only I have real toothache' either has a common sense meaning, or, if it is a grammatical (philosophical) proposition, it is meant to be a statement of a rule; it wishes to say, 'I should like to put, instead of the notation "I have real toothache", "There is real toothache".' Thus the rule does not allow 'Only I have real toothache' to be said. But the philosopher is apt to say the thing which his own rule has just forbidden him to say. . . What the solipsist wants is not a notation in which the ego has a monopoly, but one in which the ego vanishes. (From Miss Alice Ambrose's notes, quoted by her in 'Ludwig Wittgenstein: A Portrait', *Ludwig Wittgenstein, Philosophy and Language*, eds. A. Ambrose and Morris Lazerowitz, p. 19.)

What would it be for 'Only I have real toothache' to have 'a common sense meaning'? I imagine that Wittgenstein is thinking of such statements as:

'Only I have real pearls, real talent.'

'Only I really feel pain; all the others are anaesthetized. Or they are pretending.'

'In the country of the blind I am the only person who sees.'

In these statements (i) what is real is contrasted with what is false, or mediocre, or sham. (ii) The person who is said to possess real pearls or talent, or to have feeling or sight, is contrasted with others who do not possess or have these things. (iii) These two contrasts are independent of each other.

With the solipsist's statement it is otherwise. (i) The word 'real' is not used to contrast something that I have with something else others have. (ii) The word 'I' is not used to mean 'Dilman' in contrast with Jones.

In the *Blue Book* Wittgenstein suggests that the solipsist's use of the word 'I' corresponds to an actual use of the word 'I' in our language. He says that there are two different cases in the use of the word "I" or "my" which I might call "the use as object" and "the use as subject"' (p. 66). For instance, the word 'my' is used differently in 'my arm' and in 'my pain'. I can point to or refer to an arm successfully and ask 'Whose arm is that?' And the answer may be 'Mine' or 'Dilman's', or it may be 'Yours' or 'Jones''. I cannot, however, in the same way point to or refer to pain and still leave logical room for the question 'Whose pain is that?' As Wittgenstein says:

> It is possible that, say, in an accident, I should feel pain in my arm, see a broken arm at my side, and think it is mine, when really it is my neighbour's. And I could, looking into a mirror, mistake a bump on his forehead for one on mine. On the other hand, there is no question of recognising a person when I say I have toothache. To ask, 'Are you sure that it's *you* who have pains?' would be nonsensical. (*B.B.*, p. 67)

The point is that seeing an arm is one thing while recognising it as mine is another thing. So I can see an arm and not recognise that it is mine. I can be mistaken about the owner of the arm I see. With feeling pain it is otherwise. I cannot feel a pain, say toothache, and either recognise or fail to recognise that it is mine, that it is I who feel the pain. There is no logical room for the question, 'Who feels pain?'. When I say 'I feel pain' what I say cannot be an answer to such a question. This is not to say that I cannot tell *you* who feels pain. I can. For instance, you hear a groan in a hospital ward. You ask: 'Who is in pain?' I reply: 'I am.' My point is that this is not a question that *I* can ask when I feel pain. Whereas it is a question I can ask when I see an arm: 'Whose arm do I see?' I may be surprised: 'It is my arm.' But 'Whose pain do I feel?' is not a sensible question.

One could say, perhaps, that my arm has an owner. Its owner is I, Dilman, as opposed to you, Jones. But my pain does not, in this sense, have an owner. I do not mean that, like a stray dog, it does not belong to anyone, but that the expression 'my pain' does not signify ownership. (This point will be further developed in Chapter Six below.)

Wittgenstein writes:

> When in the solipsistic way I say '*This* is what's really seen'', I point before me and it is essential that I point *visually*. If I pointed sideways or behind me – as it were, to things which I

don't see – the pointing would in this case be meaningless to me; it would not be pointing in the sense in which I wish to point. But this means that when I point before me saying 'this is what's really seen', although I make the gesture of pointing, I don't point to one thing as opposed to another.

He goes on a little further down:

> When I made my solipsist statement, I pointed, but I robbed the pointing of its sense by inseparably connecting that which points and that to which it points. . . And in this way the solipsist's 'Only this is really seen' [by 'this' meaning the visual field] reminds us of a tautology. (*B.B.*, p. 71)

It reminds us of a tautology in being empty, devoid of sense, an idle gesture, not really pointing at all. The pointer of the speedometer points to 30mph if it can point to 20mph or 40mph. But if I fasten the dial to the pointer so that they go round together, i.e. if I make it impossible for the pointer to point *away* from 30mph then I have made it impossible for it to point *to* 30mph.

So Wittgenstein speaks of 'pointing to that which in my grammar has no neighbours' and says that this is no pointing at all. We have seen that when the solipsist says 'Only I can see this' he does not mean this as opposed to that. For by 'this' he means his visual field. Yet he thinks that he is pointing to something – if only for his own benefit. But he is mistaken. For if he is really pointing to his visual field, if he is operating at that grammatical level, there is nothing else he can point to. He cannot point to someone else's visual field, since someone else's visual field and his own are not in the same space. There is no space in which my visual field and yours are to be found. In that case he is not pointing to anything; he is trying to indicate the grammatical space within which he is talking and trying to say something about that. But this cannot be done in this way. In the terminology of the *Tractatus*, it *shows* itself in the way language is used here.[7]

---

[7] The difficulty the solipsist is up against here bears some analogy to the one Moore was up against when he thought he could point out something which is not an 'external object', namely a sense-datum – not this sense-datum as opposed to that, but a sense-datum as opposed to an 'external object'. See Part One Chapter Two above.

The point in question may be put like this: My visual field has no neighbours; there is nothing outside it – it has no outside. Hence it cannot be said of it, 'This is seen', nor 'Only I see this'. If you and I were standing in front of two different windows looking onto different parts of a large field with cows grazing on it, then it would make sense for me to say 'Only I see that brown cow'. To which you could reply: 'And only I see that black and white one.' One could say: If my visual field has no neighbours, then it is not mine either – not what I see as opposed to Jones.

Wittgenstein likens the misapprehension the solipsist is under when he says 'Only I can see this' or 'Only this is really seen' to the mistake in thinking that the sentence 'I am here' makes sense to me and is always true (*B.B.*, p. 72).

'I am always here'.

'I always see this – my visual field.'

'When anything is seen it is always I who see it.'

Contrast with:

'I am always at home in the evenings; I never go out.'

'My nose is too long and so I always see the tip of my nose wherever I look.'

'Whenever any ship comes within the range of the submarine's periscope it is always I who see it. For the rest of the crew are dead.'

Now when the solipsist says, 'Whenever anything is really seen, *this* is seen – my visual field, something which only I can see', he either succeeds in saying something, in which case what he says is like 'I always see the tip of my nose – wherever I look' and, therefore, plainly false, incredible, or he is *trying* to make a grammatical point but does not succeed in saying anything. In the *Tractatus* Wittgenstein says that what the solipsist is trying to say is true or correct, though the words he comes up with are nonsensical (5.62). But if we do not wish to say that he is even *trying* to make a grammatical point, we have to admit at least that certain grammatical features of our language are distorted or caricatured in his words. We have to try to see now what these are more fully. I have hinted at one such central feature when I said that if my visual field has no neighbours then it has no owner either. What is in question is the grammar of such first person expressions as 'I see', 'I am in pain' in anybody's mouth in contrast with the grammar of their third person counterparts.

Contrast:

'I have toothache' and 'He has toothache'

with

'I am five feet tall' and 'He is five feet tall'

or

'I am the winner of the race' and 'He is the winner of the race'.

Wittgenstein was clearly thinking of the former pair when he spoke of 'that which in my grammar has no neighbours'. He was clearly thinking of the contrast between the former and the latter two pairs of sentences when he spoke of two different cases in the use of the personal pronouns. About the first expression in the former pair, namely 'I have toothache' or 'I am in pain' he writes in the *Investigations*:

> In saying this I don't name any person. Just as I don't name anyone when I *groan* with pain. Though someone else sees who is in pain from the groaning. (sec. 404)

A discussion of what is involved here and how it enters into the difficulties which the solipsist and the solipsistic sceptic find insurmountable is the subject of the following four chapters.

4 'A Language which only I Can Understand'

The solipsist says: 'Only my pains are real. That there should be pain other than my own is unintelligible.' In other words, he wants to say that 'I feel pain' is perfectly intelligible to the person who says this, but 'He feels pain' is not.

Why does he say this? And *can* he say it and make sense?

Let me briefly sketch out, once more, the line of thought that culminates in the solipsist's statement.

He thinks: (1) I mean by 'pain' (and I take *pain* as one example among many) something that I can only point to for myself – *this*: fixing my attention on my consciousness when, for instance, I touch a hot plate.

In other words, each person learns what it is to feel pain by directing his attention to the right kind of thing *within himself*. Since he can observe it only within himself – for in others he can at best observe manifestations that are external to it – he can only learn what pain is *from his own case*. His interaction with other people cannot form part of this learning, or play a part in it.

(2) But what does another person mean by this word 'pain'? He cannot tell me; he cannot point to what he means for my benefit. Hence I cannot be sure that he means *the same* as I mean by 'pain', or even that he means anything at all. In short, I cannot understand what another person means by 'pain'.

Similarly, he cannot understand what I mean by 'pain' – not that I can know whether he understands it or not. I cannot *show* him what I feel when I say I am in pain, and I cannot *tell* him what I mean. I cannot describe to him what pain is like when I feel it.

(3) More than this, I cannot even understand what it would be for him to mean anything by the word 'pain', nor what it would mean for me to say 'He feels pain'. For 'He feels pain' can only mean 'He feels what I feel when I feel pain'. But how can *he* feel what *I* feel? To feel that he would have to be me; and that is plainly absurd.

In other words, from 'Only I understand what *I* mean by "pain"' he moves to 'Only I understand what "pain" means'. Behind this step is the assumption that '"Pain" means what *I* feel'.

(4) From this it is a small step to 'Only *my* pains are real'. Only my pains are real, for they are what give meaning to the word 'pain'.

What has happened here? Clearly the solipsist, in common with Descartes and Locke, thinks that his conception of pain involves no reference to human behaviour and reactions. This is his starting point, and this is where he has begun to go wrong. It is this that makes him think of pain as a 'private object', something with which only I am acquainted.

This starting assumption is an assumption both (i) about our notion of a mental state, and also (ii) about the relation between language and reality. It drives a wedge between something it calls 'internal' and something it calls 'external'. Thus we have 'inner experiences' and these have 'outer' manifestations, and there are no ties between the concepts of the language in which we talk about the former and the circumstances in which it is used – including the human behaviour which surrounds this use. In this way a wedge is driven between the inner and the outer by dissociating from such concepts as pain and anger much that in discourse is tied up with the use of the words for them. Here, as I said, we have confusions both about our notion of mind or mental states and about our ideas of sense and intelligibility – the latter in that there is a failure to recognise that the way concepts such as pain, fear, anger – or any other concept – enter our lives has anything to do with what our words for these concepts mean. In other words, the *meaning* of words and sentences is thought of as something that is independent of the roles these play in our lives, and so independent of the kind of lives we live.

Wittgenstein argues that if we start with this assumption

certain absurd consequences are inevitable and that, therefore, the Cartesian assumption is at fault and must be rejected. His argument, briefly, is as follows:

If one thinks that the idea of injury and of how people react to it does not in any way enter into our understanding of what it means to feel pain, if indeed one learns what the word 'pain' means from one's own case, then how can one be sure that each time one thinks 'I am in pain' one means the same thing, identifies the object named correctly?

This is the difficulty one avoids facing. One thinks that each time one directs one's attention inward and picks out an item of consciousness one recognises to be similar to the one originally called 'pain', one is justified before oneself (*Inv.* sec. 289).

Wittgenstein is not satisfied and asks: How can one be sure that one hasn't made a mistake? That one has identified the item correctly? That is the same, i.e. similar to the one which one called 'pain' before?

The only answer possible is: I can remember well what I called 'pain' before, and I can compare in my imagination what is present to my consciousness on this occasion with what I remember.

To this Wittgenstein has a devastating retort: But how can you know that your memory is not deceiving you? How can you be sure that you have compared the two things correctly, that you have carried out the right comparison?

His point is that given the framework of one's original assumption one has not allowed for the possibility of distinguishing between genuine and apparent memories. Since there is no possibility of distinguishing between reality and appearance here, there is no sense in saying that what one compares one's present experience with is really what one called 'pain' before. Nor can one speak of being justified before oneself.

By the same token one has not allowed for the possibility of distinguishing between the objects of comparison really being the same and their only appearing to be so. One is inclined to insist: 'But they are the same; I ought to know.' Unfortunately, this has no more force than: 'They *seem* to be the same to me.' As Wittgenstein puts it: 'Whatever is going to seem right to me is right. And that only means that here we can't talk about "right"' (*Inv.* sec. 258). He means that we can't talk about 'right' here, given our original assumption.

This means that if other people cannot tell me that I am using the word 'pain' correctly, if they can play no part in my learning what the word 'pain' means, then neither can I tell myself that I am using the word correctly. If it is to be possible for me to be justified before myself, it must be possible for me to be justified before others as well.

Wittgenstein's discussion of whether one can understand something (e.g. 'I feel pain') which cannot be said in a language that other people understand, or can learn to understand, whether one can attach any sense to the words 'red' or 'pain' independently of the language we all speak and understand, is part of his discussion of the relation between words and behaviour, language and life. We are inclined to ignore this relation (as, for instance, Descartes and Locke did) in the case of colour words and also such words as 'pain' and 'anger'. Wittgenstein shows that we are then inevitably faced with difficulties that are insurmountable. He combats, in the way I have sketched, the tendency to think that each person acquires such concepts as pain from his own case, and that it is possible that what the word 'pain' means to one person is different from what it means to another – whether or not this is so being something which neither he nor anyone else can tell. He shows that the idea of a word or sentence which only one person can understand is an incoherent one. For if we dissociate from such concepts as pain much that in discourse is tied up with the use of the words for them, then each person's use of the word will be governed by his memory and impressions, and there will be nothing outside and independent of these to which he can appeal. That is the only possible criterion of his using the word correctly on a particular occasion will be that it *seems* so to him. In other words, whatever seems to him to be the correct application of the word will *be* the correct one. So there will be nothing to guarantee that he is using the word consistently. This means that we cannot speak of correctness or consistency here at all. But where we cannot do so, neither can we speak of *meaning.*

We see that Wittgenstein opposes the inclination to think that what a word means can be given apart from the situations in which the word plays a role. The primitive idea that a word has meaning by its attachment to an object makes us think that it is the object which secures the consistency with which it is used. As Wittgenstein puts it in *Zettel*: 'One may ask, "How do I manage always to use a word correctly – i.e. significantly?" and one may be tempted to answer, "The fact that I mean something – the thing I mean, prevents me from talking nonsense"' (sec. 297). Whereas the truth (he argues) is the reverse: it is the consistency with which a word is uttered that enables it to attach to or signify anything at all. If we think of words as labels we shall forget the enormous amount of stage setting in the language that is presupposed when we successfully attach a word to anything – that is when we are able to attach it to the same thing on different occasions.

This is what the solipsist fails to appreciate right at the start. He thinks of pain as something which he cannot show to other people, though he can point to it himself, inwardly, for his own benefit. He thinks of it as a private object – like some rare diamond locked up in a bank vault which only I can enter. He thinks of it as existing in his consciousness 'in a seclusion in comparison with which any physical seclusion is an exhibition to public view' (*Inv.* p. 222). He construes the logic of such words as 'I am in pain' in a way which makes it impossible for other people to understand these words when he utters them. In doing so, we have seen, he makes the idea that these words could be used consistently by him unintelligible. This is enough to show that he has misconstrued their logic.

Why? Because we can and do talk intelligibly about our sensations and understand each other. If so, then a 'private object' to which each person is supposed to make a reference when he says 'I am in pain' cannot be part of the intercourse that goes on between us in these connections. This is what Wittgenstein points out in *Philosophical Investigations*, sec. 293:

Suppose everyone had a box with something in it: we call it a 'beetle'. No one can look into anyone else's box and everyone says he knows what a beetle is only by looking at *his* beetle.

This is just what the solipsist has supposed; it is how *he* has construed our talk about sensations.

But suppose [nevertheless] the word 'beetle' had a use in these people's language? – If so, it would not be used as the name of a thing. The thing in the box has no place in the language-game at all.

In other words, *if* when I say 'I am in pain' I mean that I have something in my consciousness which may, for all I know, be different from what you have in your consciousness when you say that you are in pain, then 'what each of us has in his consciousness and whether or not it is the same' plays no part in the language-game into which these words enter. It is an idle wheel in the mechanism of language. If it plays no part, then it cannot form part of the meaning of these words. It follows that we must have misconstrued the grammar of our words for sensations:

> If we construe the grammar of the expression of sensation on the model of 'object and designation' the object drops out of consideration as irrelevant.

In other words, what the solipsist takes to give meaning to our words for sensations, to the word 'pain' for instance, namely something to which only he can point to, i.e. a 'private object', cannot be relevant to what makes these words meaningful.

So we have to look elsewhere, in a different direction, if we wish to understand how these words come to have meaning for us. We have to look at the actions and reactions into which our utterances of these words are woven. These are not external to the form of communication that goes on in our lives when we use these words (*Inv.* sec. 7). When we see that they are not external to the forms of communication in question we shall also appreciate the kind of conceptual tie there is between our mental life and our behaviour. I shall return to this question in Chapter Eight below.

Summary We saw how the solipsist comes to think that he can intelligibly attribute pain, hope, fear and thoughts only to himself. We next saw that if one cannot say of others that they sometimes feel pain, then one cannot intelligibly say this of oneself either: 'If as a matter of logic you exclude other people's having something, it loses its sense to say that you have it' (*Inv.* sec. 398). The solipsist is inclined to say that he cannot understand or make sense of the sentence '*He* feels pain'. In that case, Wittgenstein argues, neither can he make sense of the sentence '*I* feel pain'. In other words, the thought that 'Only my pains are real' involves an *incoherence* which Wittgenstein brings out. As Malcolm puts it:

> Some philosophers before Wittgenstein may have seen the solipsistic result of starting from 'one's own case'. But I believe that he is the first one to have shown how that starting point destroys itself. ('Knowledge of Other Minds', *K.C.*, p. 137)

We have seen that the move towards solipsism involves the driving of a logical wedge between oneself and other people. This comes from serious misunderstandings – primarily those involved in separating what we understand by such words as 'pain' from the surroundings of human life and behaviour in which they have meaning. It leads to insurmountable difficulties. In other words, the solipsist is led to drive a wedge between himself and other people because of the way he separates something which he calls 'internal' from something he calls 'external'. When our so-called 'inner life' is thus separated from the common, public life in the weave of which our language has sense, it disintegrates into units between which there can be no interchange. The solipsist thus finds himself forced to favour 'a notation in which the ego has a monopoly'.

Nevertheless behind the inclination to drive such a wedge there is also something which we ought not to reject. It is the grammatical asymmetry between such first person expressions as 'I am in pain' in anybody's mouth and their third person counterparts. We shall consider what this amounts to in Chapter Seven below.

5 Myself and other People

Earlier I had urged that if we wish to get away from the Cartesian idea of the soul as a substance we have to turn our attention to what underlies the possibility of human joy and suffering, love, hope and despair. The idea of the soul as a substance is largely rooted in the attempt to grasp its reality in separation from all this. Next we saw how this separation leads to solipsism, to the questioning of whether it is possible for me to make sense of any reality outside my so-called 'inner experiences', or to communicate with anyone other than myself and, conversely, to understand what others may be experiencing or what they tell me. One is then tempted to ask the question Wittgenstein puts into the mouth of his alter-ego:

> Can't I imagine that the people around me are automata, lack consciousness, even though they behave in the same way as usual? (*Inv.* sec. 420)

Descartes' answer is that I can. What I cannot imagine is that *I* might lack consciousness – for to imagine this or anything else is for me to have consciousness: 'I think, therefore I am.'

Compare Descartes' affirmative answer to Wittgenstein's question with Berkeley's words:

> It is possible we might be affected with all the ideas we have now, though no bodies existed without, resembling them. (*Principles*, sec. 18)

For Berkeley this shows that 'matter' or 'corporeal substance' is an 'empty name'.[1] He thinks so because he believes that the

[1] He says, 'that which philosophers call matter', but he is sorely tempted to speak for the 'vulgar notion' as well. On this point he oscillates.

existence of matter can be denied without thereby any 'damage done to the rest of mankind, who, I dare say, will never miss it' (sec. 35).

> I can imagine that there is no material world, though I have exactly the same sensations that I always have.

Descartes thinks he can do the same with 'mental substance' or 'consciousness', except for the residue of his own consciousness:

> I can imagine that the people around me are automata, lack consciousness, even though they behave in the same way as usual.

In other words:

> It is at least possible that I might be the only conscious, sentient and intelligent being in existence.

But is this possible? Have we got here an intelligible supposition?

Can I suppose that the people around me lack consciousness without transforming them so radically that they are no longer people? We discussed this question earlier in Chapter Two above: 'I am not of the opinion that he has a soul' or that he is sentient. But can I suppose this without transforming my own consciousness so radically that I can no longer say what I am trying to say: 'I am'? The idea that I can do so rests on the presupposition that I can know or at least *think* all that I am capable of thinking in a social vacuum, that it rests on nothing in the way of established traditions, that it requires no conformity with public standards. If the view of human thought and understanding on which what the sceptical solipsist says rests is incoherent, then so is what he claims.

Consider such familiar activities as counting or using a word to name or describe something. A little thought will show that if I mean anything by the word 'green', for instance, then I must mean the same thing each time I say 'This is green'. But if each time I look at a leaf and say 'This is green' I could not know that it was the same colour, then neither could I know that I had kept the meaning of the word 'green' constant. Of course I can know this – I can know whether the leaves on the tree in my garden to-day are the same colour as they were yesterday, or whether the curtains I hung up at the beginning of the summer have faded. I may remember them as being a darker green than they are now. The possibility of my knowing this is inseparable from the possibility of its seeming so to me when in fact it isn't so. I mean that if I can know this then it is possible for me to be mistaken. Thus I may remember them as being a darker green than they are now, think that the curtains have faded, when this is not the case and it is my memory that is at fault. If this could be the case, as clearly it can be, then I can have evidence independent of my memory, and also regard certain memory claims as beyond question. I can, for instance, ask my wife or the shopkeeper who ordered the material for me, or I can compare the curtains with the rest of the roll in the warehouse. Even here I can be mistaken, which presupposes that others may have better eyes or can correct me by the use of instruments. But if none of these things bear on the question whether what I see now is the same colour as I saw before, then my saying that it is the same means no more than that it *seems* so to me. There is nothing, in that case, to guarantee that I am using the word 'green' consistently.

That is if the word has any meaning and so *can* be used consistently, then my judgement that what I now see is the same colour as what I called 'green' on other occasions must be open to the correction of other people. What they have to say on this matter must be relevant to what I say. Otherwise *whatever* I say is green will be what I call 'green', and this means that my word 'green' is devoid of meaning. What they have to say is relevant to my judgement now because we speak the same language, mean the same thing by the word 'green'. This, in turn, means that we agree on numerous occasions in what we call 'green'. If we did not thus agree on many occasions, my wife or the shopkeeper could not correct me on this occasion. In other words, the possibility of my using words consistently rests on a practice in which there is general agreement between the judgements and reactions of those who take part in it. This is just as true of the comparisons I may carry out to establish that what I say is green is the same colour as what I called 'green' on other occasions. For it raises the question whether what I do in carrying out this comparison now is the same as what I did on other occasions when I was comparing colours – in other words, whether I was consistent in what I did. The expression 'the same' as it occurs in my judgement 'It is the same colour as what I called "green" on other occasions' must itself be used consistently by me. And this possibility equally rests on the practice with colour words in which people agree on a great many occasions.

Put it like this: 'This is green' implies that this is the same colour as what I called 'green' in the past. This judgement presupposes that on this and on those other occasions I use the word 'green' in the same way. Unless I can be said to do so, the claim that this is the same colour as what I called 'green' in the past is empty. In other words, if my utterance 'This is green' has sense, then it makes sense to say that what I do on this occasion in using the word 'green' is the same as what I do on other occasions when I use this word correctly – i.e. that I am using the word 'green' in the same way on these different occasions. We are at first inclined to say: 'That is because what I see on these different occasions is the same colour.' But we have seen that this begs the question. For I can judge what I see on these different occasions to be the same colour because I speak the language. It is the kind of consistency with which I use colour words that gives content to my judgement that these things are the same colour. That identity judgement presupposes that these words can be and are used consistently, and so it cannot be made to carry the burden of determing their consistent use.

'I go on in the same way, use the word "green" consistently, because I can see that the different things I call green are the same colour. It is what I see that enables me to use the word consistently.' Obviously if I were blind I could not use the word 'green' consistently – unless I could rely on someone else's eyes, or some kind of instrument. But having sight alone does not give me what we want. As Wittgenstein puts it: 'Do not believe that you have the concept of colour within you because you look at a coloured object – however you look' (Z. sec. 332). What you see cannot itself determine what you are going to call by the same name on a future occasion. That depends, one wants to say, on what you mean by 'green'.

But how does it depend on that? What is it that determines what you mean by the word? 'This' we are inclined to say – pointing to a leaf. But that on its own tells you nothing about what you are going to call 'green' next, nothing about how the word is to be used on new occasions, in different circumstances. As Wittgenstein puts it: 'An ostensive definition can be variously interpreted in *every* case' (*Inv.* sec. 28). It does tell you what to call 'green' on other occasions 'only together with a particular training' (sec. 6). That is only where you have already learnt to go on in certain ways as a matter of course. The point is that this is something you must learn. You cannot derive it from the *meaning* of the word 'green', since that is determined by how the word is actually used.

You could say that the meaning of the word lies in its use – and that means its successive applications. Obviously only certain applications must be correct: if I were to utter the word 'green' whenever I felt like it, then it would mean nothing. One could say that the word's use is governed by a rule and what the word means is to be found in and, therefore, given by the rule. But this does not mean that we can formulate a rule for every word we understand. Nor do we learn most words by being given rules or definitions. Where we are given rules, or are taught by rules, we must already be in a position to understand them; and we can only be brought to such a position by means of examples. There is a point at which examples are indispensable. In an elementary arithmetic lesson, for example, the teacher can only show the pupil the right continuation of various series in examples. He cannot yet use any expression of the law of these series. Later it may be possible for the pupil to learn to develop new series by means of rules. It is the same with words and definitions. Once one is off the ground, so to speak, rules and definitions may come into the teaching, though they need not do so even then. But they cannot take us off the ground. As Wittgenstein puts it:

> At this level the expression of the rule is explained by the value [i.e. what is the correct thing to say or write down here and here and here], not the value by the rule. For just where one says 'But don't you *see* . . .?' the rule is no use, it is what is explained, not what does the explaining. (*Z.* secs. 301–2)

This is where Wittgenstein speaks of *training*: we simply learn to do what we are told as in a drill – without question. We learn if in the end we can grasp what we are meant to do without reason or explanation, if the examples in which this is exhibited speak to us directly.

If Wittgenstein stressed the importance of acquiring skills and habits in the learning of language that is because he was thinking of the learning of what underlies the possibility of asking questions and understanding explanations. He never thought that the learning of language could be confined to this. If he emphasised the importance of rules in connection with the use of words that is because he wanted to bring into prominence the way in which the distinction between using words correctly and incorrectly underlies the possibility of using them to say something. Because he wanted to show that apart from a consistent use of words there can be no meaning.

'If I mean anything by the word "green" that is because there is a regular use of this word that I comply with.' We could say that I use the word in accordance with a rule – in other words, the successive applications I make of the word are consistent. But what does this mean? What does it take for this to be possible? What does it take for the judgement that what I do with the word on different occasions is the same to make sense?

Wittgenstein imagines we are teaching someone for the first time to develop numerical series – for instance '2, 4, 6, 8 . . .' 'Let us suppose [he writes] we have done exercises and given him tests up to 1000.'

> Now we get the pupil to continue a series (say + 2) beyond 1000 – and he writes 1000, 1004, 1008, 1012.
> We say to him: 'Look what you've done!' – He doesn't understand. We say: 'You were meant to add *two*: look how you began the series!' – He answers: 'Yes, isn't it right? I thought that was how I was *meant* to do it.' – Or suppose he pointed to the series and said: 'But I went on in the same way.' – It would now be no use to say: 'But can't you see . . .?' – and repeat the old examples and explanations. – In such a case we might say, perhaps: It comes natural to this person to understand our order with our explanation as *we* should understand the order: 'Add 2 up to 1000, 4 up to 2000, 6 up to

3000 and so on'. (*Inv.* sec. 185)

We have tried to teach this pupil by means of examples and exercises how to go on adding 2, and also how he is to understand '+ 2' or the order 'add 2'. His performance up to 1000 shows that we have been successful. But beyond 1000 he goes on in a different way from what we call the correct way of going on. We say: 'This is not the way "+ 2" was meant. What you did up to this point is not the same as, or is inconsistent with, what you did before.' In short, what we say is: (i) What you do now does not accord with the law of the series – "+ 2". (ii) What you do now is not the same as what you did before. He, on the other hand, insists earnestly, (i) that '1000, 1004, 1008, 1012 . . .' does accord with or satisfy '+ 2', and (ii) that it is consistent with '0, 2, 4, 6, 8 . . .' – or, in short, that '1000, 1004, 1008, 1012 . . .' does accord with '+ 2' as this is satisfied by '0, 2, 4, 6, 8 . . .'

Surely, whether he is right or not depends on how '+ 2' is meant. It is not impossible, in fact it is very easy, to find an interpretation of '+ 2' on which (i) '1000, 1004, 1008, 1012 . . .' does satisfy '+ 2', and so (ii) one on which the way of going on that is exemplified by '1000, 1004, 1008, 1012 . . .' is the same as the one exemplified by '0, 2, 4, 6 . . .' – or, in short, an interpretation on which both '0, 2, 4, 6 . . .' and '1000, 1004, 1008, 1012 . . .' satisfy it. There is nothing impossible or internally inconsistent about such an interpretation; it is simply different from what *we* mean by '+ 2'. On this interpretation both '0, 2, 4, 6 . . .' and '1000, 1004, 1008, 1012 . . .' satisfy the same serial rule, and that means that what the pupil does after 1000 *is* the same as what he does before. So when he says 'But I went on in the same way' he is not confused as one of us would be who made a mistake in an inference or calculation and failed to see it.

We want to say, and rightly: 'If he is adding 2 when he writes down "0, 2, 4, 6 . . .", as *we* understand the expression "+ 2", then when he writes down "1000, 1004, 1008, 1012 . . ." he is not doing the same thing.' But notice the provise: '*if* he is adding 2 in the same sense that *we* understand "+ 2"'. If this is true of him, then he is inconsistent. If, on the other hand, it is left open or undetermined, then we *cannot* say that he is inconsistent in what he does. And if we cannot say this, then neither can we say that he is consistent.

He does say it himself. Presumably he has intelligently talked of consistency in other contexts. But, as we have seen, if his claim means more than 'I think I am consistent in what I do' or 'It seems to me that I am' then we, or at any rate someone else, has to be able to appreciate this.

Let me return to our proviso – 'if he is adding 2 in the sense that *we* understand "+ 2". But what would show that this is true of him? What would show that he understands "+ 2" as we understand it – as his teacher meant this expression? The answer is: His subsequent performance. We took what he wrote down up to 1000 to show or even establish that he understood how his teacher meant '+ 2'. And with good reason. For most of us, or most of our children, when we or they have been brought to go that far carry on in the way we were expecting this pupil to go on. Given the kind of instruction he has received it comes natural to us to go on in a certain way. In this we are, most of us, alike. We agree in the way we proceed as a matter of course when we have received a certain kind of instruction. But there is nothing in the instruction itself, in the gestures, examples and illustrations, to rule out of court a different way of going on. If we do not go on in the way that Wittgenstein's pupil does, if we agree in our reactions to the instruction we receive, this is just a brute fact about us. It is not because of our regard for logic that we agree at this stage or level; but rather it is because we agree here that logic can come to mean anything to us. This kind of matter-of-course agreement between people is absolutely fundamental to the possibility of logic and its playing a role in our life, it is absolutely fundamental to the intelligible use of words of logical appraisal – such as 'consistent' and 'valid'.

To return to Wittgenstein's pupil. There is nothing in the way he has gone on so far ('0, 2, 4, 6 . . . up to 1000') which *in itself* makes the way he goes on after 1000 incompatible with it. When we call it 'incompatible', the kind of agreement in how we go on as a matter of course as a result of the instructions we receive lies in the background and is taken for granted. But the peculiarity of Wittgenstein's pupil is that he does not share our matter-of-course reactions and propensities; and so the teaching stops at that point: 'It would now be no use to say: "But can't you see . . .?" – and repeat the old examples and explanations.'

Wittgenstein had said that 'an ostensive definition can be variously interpreted in *every* case' (*Inv.* sec. 28). It achieves its purpose 'only together with a particular training' (sec. 6). The success of the training depends on our natural responses. But unless there is agreement at this level our gestures can have no significance and cannot amount to pointing. This is true of rules and also of examples. One could ask: How does the rule or example tell me what I am to do next? If it is to tell me this, then I must know what constitutes accord or conflict with it. But the rule *itself* cannot tell me this, for (as Wittgenstein puts it) 'every course of action can be made out to accord with the rule' (*Inv.* sec. 201). What gives the rule a specific meaning, what determines what is to constitute accord and conflict with it, is what people following it actually do in particular cases. And, again, unless there is agreement in what they do, there can be neither accord nor conflict with a rule, no procedure that can be characterised as methodical, no foothold for the notions of consistency and inconsistency. As Wittgenstein puts it: 'A person goes by a sign-post only insofar as there exists a regular use of sign-posts, a custom' (*Inv.* sec. 198). And a regular use presupposes a background of agreement in our natural responses. *(habitual)*

Imagine that away – as the solipsist must do – and you can no longer speak of consistency or of methodical procedure. But if that is destroyed, then so is the intelligibility of everything which the solipsist is inclined to think and say. In this way the idea that I may be the only conscious, sentient being in existence collapses. I might have been the only sentient being in existence. But if I were, I could not *think* this, and I would have been radically different from what I am – certainly not a being capable of thought and reasoning.

You could say that the *thought* that I may be the only sentient being in existence is incoherent, or even that it involves a contradiction in that it denies the very thing that is presupposed by its intelligibility.

Summary   I began with the question Wittgenstein puts into the mouth of his alter-ego: 'Can't I imagine that the people around me are automata, lack consciousness, even though they behave in the same way as usual?' My answer to this question has been

Then we are committed, by our very use of language, to saying that solipsism can neither be intelligibly stated or refuted?

two-fold: (i) If I imagine them as behaving in the same way as usual then I have not imagined them as automata; on the contrary, I have imagined them as ordinary human beings, like myself. So I cannot imagine them *both* as automata *and* as behaving in the same way as usual. The thought that I am supposed to entertain involves a contradiction. We discussed this earlier when we considered where the difference lies between human beings and automata – i.e. in Chapter Two above. (ii) We have now seen that I cannot imagine them as automata, if that entails imagining that I am, or may be, the only sentient, intelligent being in existence. The thought that I am supposed to entertain involves a contradiction, even if we leave out the part about their behaving in the same way as usual. The first of these contradictions springs from misunderstandings concerning the kind of relation there is between mental life and human behaviour, while the second springs from misunderstandings concerning the kind of relation there is between myself and other people. We shall explore these further in what follows.

6 Privacy and the First Person Pronoun

'We often look at things and compare our observations. But the sense impressions I get are mine and mine alone. You and I may look at the same things, but each of us gets his own sense impressions. It is inconceivable that I should get your sense impressions or that you should get mine, and in that sense inconceivable that we should see the same things. At best we hope that what each of us sees in this sense are very like each other. But it is possible that they may not be. The colour impressions we get from a drop of blood or a pillar box, for instance, may not be the same. Worse still we may never know that they are not the same. For although we use the same word 'red' in talking about it we may not attach the same meaning to that word though we think we do. In other words, our calling the colour of blood 'red', our using the same word for it, is no guarantee that we see it alike. So we cannot know what things look, feel and sound like to others. Each person can know this only in his own case. And the same goes for every kind of experience – sensations, feelings, mental images, desires, and the rest.'

In short:

1. 'I cannot have or feel your sensations and sense impressions. They are inaccessible to me as mine are to you.'

2. 'I cannot understand what you mean by "red", "pain" or "fear". The language in which you use such words is unintelligible to me, as the language in which I use them is bound to be unintelligible to you.'

We have considered the second of these two ideas. I now turn to the first. They are two sides of the same coin.

The idea that I want to consider in this chapter is that the pain that I feel when, for instance, I burn my hand, belongs to me, is mine and mine alone. You cannot feel it, although when you burn your hand you may feel something very similar. Even then, this is at best a conjecture, for we cannot compare our respective sensations: 'I can compare what I feel now with what I felt earlier, since I can remember what I felt then. But I cannot compare what I feel with what you feel. For to do that I would have to feel what you feel, and that is plainly impossible.'

Two assumptions have been made here which need examining: (i) That to feel pain is to be acquainted with something. (ii) That what one feels cannot be identified apart from oneself.

Given these assumptions it becomes hard to resist (a) scepticism about one's knowledge of other people's thoughts and feelings and, at an extreme, (b) sceptical solipsism. Under (a) I am thinking of the philosophical doubt as to whether one can know *what* other people think and feel, and under (b) the doubt as to whether one can know *that* they think and feel at all. One doubt leads to the other: If I think that I cannot ever know what others think and feel, I am bound to ask: Can I know that they think and feel at all? 'For all I know they may be automata.'

We have seen that this is not an intelligible supposition and that, therefore, I cannot be said to *know* that the 'walking and talking figures around me' have thoughts and feelings or consciousness. As I put it earlier: When on a given occasion what a man says and does convinces me that he is angry, the possibility remains that I may be wrong. But there is no question for me whether he has a soul or consciousness: 'I am not of the *opinion* that he has a soul.' On the other hand, if we can meet the sceptic under (a) then we shall be able to say, 'We can *know* what other people think and feel, even if there are occasions when we do not.' This will still leave us with the question '*How* do we know this when we know it?' I try to answer this last question in Chapter Eight below.

It is not too difficult to see how the above assumptions lead to scepticism. The steps in our thinking that lead to the sceptical conclusion may be set out as follows:

(1) Anyone who has a sensation, sense impression, desire or intention knows that he has it. He knows it by direct acquaintance. The sensation or desire is presented to him directly, in his consciousness.

(2) There is no other way of knowing the existence of these things.

(3) Therefore, if another person is to know what sensation or impression I have, he must feel that same sensation, have the self-same impression.

(4) But surely this is impossible. How can anyone feel another person's sensations, have another person's sense impressions, experience another person's emotions and desires?

(5) It follows that no one can know what sensations or desires another person has; one can only know what one is feeling or wishing oneself.

I

Let us begin by considering the first of the above assumptions. 'One who has a sensation inevitably knows that he has it.' One is trying to say that if one has a sensation, if one feels pain for instance, one cannot think or believe that one is not feeling pain. One cannot be ignorant of or mistaken about what one is feeling. Whereas, in contrast, one may have a handkerchief in one's pocket or a bad tooth in one's mouth and not know it. In other words, one wishes to remark on a *grammatical* peculiarity of first person sensation statements like 'I have toothache' which distinguishes them from such statements as 'I have a bad tooth'. What one wants to remark on is that one cannot be mistaken about whether or not one is in pain and that it makes no sense for one to be uncertain about this – except where what one feels is somewhere between pain and pleasure.

From this, however, we should not conclude that when one is in pain one always knows it. For where one can be said to know something it must be possible for one not to know it, to be mistaken. It is because there is this possibility that one can use the verb 'know' informatively. Since here there is not this possibility, normally, 'I know that I have toothache' does not mean anything more than 'I have toothache'. It does not add anything to 'I have toothache'. It is otherwise with 'I have a bad tooth', since I could have a bad tooth and not know it, or think that I have one when I don't. Hence 'I know I have a bad tooth' not only says that there is a bad tooth in my mouth but also that I had my teeth examined. It is the same with 'I have a handker- chief in my pocket'. My wife puts a handkerchief in the pocket of the suit I am going to wear. Later on in the day when I need a handkerchief she tells me that there is one in my pocket. I reply, 'I know there is'. This is informative, for she thought I did not know. Thanks to my words she knows otherwise.

'Somebody else may be uncertain about whether or not I am in pain, but I cannot be.' If we misconstrue this grammatical remark as 'I always know when I am in pain', it can suggest that with regard to my own sensations I have a way of knowing which is fool-proof – as perhaps Orpheus had a way of knowing whether or not Euridice lied to him which was fool-proof. We shall then want to answer the question: 'What makes it fool- proof?' And we shall be tempted to say: 'We are directly ac- quainted with our sensations, they are presented to us in our consciousness. Whereas it is only the outer manifestations of other people's sensations that we detect – as we might see the shadow of something which is out of sight.'

This idea that I have a special way of knowing what I feel goes with the idea of feeling as a form of direct acquaintance. But what sort of thing am I normally said to be directly ac- quainted with? I may be said to have had direct acquaintance with the texture of some unusual material, the sound of a rare musical instrument, or the look of a blood corpuscle. The point is that I have actually felt, heard or seen these things in contrast with most other people who may have heard them mentioned or described, or who may have read about them. The best answer to 'How do you know what a blood corpuscle looks like?' is 'I have seen one under the microscope.'

'How do you know that there is one there? How do you know what it is like?' 'I can see it. I can feel it.' Here the verbs 'see' and 'feel' are used to report *perceptions*. Thus in reply to the question, 'How do you know that the first letter of the word before you is an F?' the blind man may say, 'I know it because I can feel it'. What he feels is the shape of the letter before him written in Braille. He comes to know it or gets ac- quainted with it by running his finger alongside the protru- sions and indentations. And that means that there is something for him to get acquainted with, something which has the shape of the letter F before he has come to recognise it by touch.

Where the verb 'feel' is used to report a perception it must be possible to logically separate what I say I feel from my feeling. Thus I can feel a spider in the palm of my open hand and I can say that I know there is a spider there because I can feel it. Here it is obviously possible for there to be a spider in the palm of my hand while I am unaware of its existence. The existence of the spider is logically independent of my feeling it in the palm of my hand. It can be identified independently of what I feel. Where these logical conditions do not obtain the verb 'feel' cannot be made to carry the burden of perception. So 'I know I am in pain because I feel it' has whatever plausibility it has through its mistaken assimilation to 'I know there is someone behind me because I can feel him breathing down my neck'. (Descartes would have said: When I feel pain what I feel is not anything distinct from my consciousness. But in that case 'consciousness' here cannot mean 'knowledge' or 'acquaintance'. Therefore it is a mistake to construe 'I feel pain' as 'I am acquainted with something – something that is at once a mode and object of consciousness'.) /

'But the verb "feel" here does report a perception, one that is infallible just because the perception and its object are one – as does the verb "see" used in connection with an after-image.' It is true, of course, that an after-image is something that one sees with one's eyes. When one is questioned about one's after-image it is correct to describe what one sometimes does in answering such questions as 'scrutinising the image more closely'. This is in some ways like scrutinising more closely an object before one's eyes. But we must notice how it differs from the latter. In scrutinising an object before one's eyes one may do various things: one may move closer to the object, look at it from another angle, switch the light on, and even use a magnifying glass. If one did anything like this when questioned about an after-image one sees it would show that one did not understand what one was being asked.

Scrutinising one's after-image is attending to its features to take them in better. In some ways this is like attending to a pattern before one's eyes and clearly in view in order to make out what it adds up to. In neither case is one trying to bring into focus a feature that is not clearly in view. One is not trying to see something unseen or only half-seen, but working out how what is already seen compares with or matches familiar visual patterns. Thus one may have to count the sides of one's after-image or try to make out whether its colour is nearer pink than puce. Certainly this involves using one's eyes. But it is more like thinking about what one sees than observing it more closely. If it brings about a change in one's apprehension or consciousness which can be distinguished from the image itself, this is more a change in one's understanding or thought than in one's seeing. The after-image has no reality distinct from or over and above one's seeing, as a patch on the wall which one is looking at has. For that reason when one speaks of *seeing* an after-image one is not reporting a perception.

Seeing an after-image doesn't tell me what it is like – seeing it is the same thing as having it. Where seeing something can tell me what it is like, this is something other people can tell me too. Otherwise whatever, on the basis of what I see, I tell myself is so will be so. There will be no difference between 'I see it so' and 'It is so'. But where there is no such difference what I see is no basis for 'It is so'. It is a mistake to think that here my seeing gives me a basis for anything, that it tells me what my after-image is like, that I have a way of knowing this, that the report I give you about my after-images is based on observation.

'But does that mean that here anything I say goes? Does it mean that I cannot lie about my after-images?' No. My report is not arrived at by observation, it is not derived from something which I see but you don't. But it is not arbitrary. I do not say whatever I wish as when I make up a story. As we have seen, it makes sense to speak of scrutinising one's after-image, attending to it. In a given instance I may well do so, choose what I say very carefully, and even sometimes retract what I said as not fitting and so correct myself: 'I now realise that what I said does not describe the image well.' But, as I argued, 'I now realise' here is not like 'I have at last been able to see the cracks in the paint-work'. It is more like: 'I now see (or realise) that the lines I have been looking at for the last five minutes make up an interesting pattern.'

But there is an important difference. What takes the place of the lines which I now see to make up such a pattern is the after-image, and *that* is not something I can be said to have observed. I am not trying to describe some object which I see on the basis of what my eyes tell me. What I describe is what I see in the sense of a visual phenomenon, and the visual phenomenon does not inform me of anything. Still I can describe it correctly or incorrectly because the words I use in doing so, such words as 'red', 'dark', 'triangular', have an application to the things which I and others observe. They have the same meaning when I describe my after-images, the meaning which I learnt in learning to describe the things I see and touch. But when these words are used to describe after-images, the truth of my reports is not determined in the same way as the truth of reports about what I observe.

II

If I am looking at something and observing it, then if I am distracted or interrupted, I can look at the same thing again. But does it make sense to speak of seeing the same image again later, at a different time, in contrast to one very similar? Is there logical room for such a distinction here? And if other people cannot tell me what the after-image I see is like, when I haven't told them first, if they cannot contradict me in what I tell them, does this mean that there is something to be seen which they cannot see, though I can? No. It means rather that since my *seeing* of an after-image constitutes the image's *being*, reality or existence, it cannot *tell* me what the image is like. The idea that we have something here which only one person has access to is, therefore, confused. As Wittgenstein would say: I cannot be said to observe my after-images, to learn what they are like by looking at them. I *have* them (*Inv.* sec. 246).

'But other people cannot have my after-images or see them. They are private to me: only I can see them.' We are inclined to say: 'Even if A and B see an after-image at the same time, in the same place on the wall, and their descriptions agree, still they cannot be seeing the same after-image. Each of them can only see his own after-image.' There is something right here and also something wrong. Can we disentangle these from one another?

The picture in terms of which we are thinking here is something like the following. A and B are locked up in two separate rooms. Each room contains a television set, each tuned to the same programme. At a given time A and B will see images exactly alike on their respective screens. The images each sees are exactly alike but numerically distinct.

How do we know that they are numerically distinct? Because they are images on different screens. From A's and B's descriptions of what they saw on the television at a given time we cannot deduce whether or not they watched the programme on the same set. Nor can you deduce from two photographs which in every way look alike whether they are snapshots of the same person or of identical twins.

'From the fact that A's and B's descriptions of the television images they saw agree we cannot deduce whether there are one or two sets of images described. But if they were describing the after-image they saw we would have to conclude that there were two images, even though their descriptions agreed.' But we are able to do so, if you can call that 'deducing', only because here 'there are two images' means no more than 'there are two descriptions' or 'there are two people giving these descriptions'. As Malcolm puts it:

> If from the fact that A has an after-image and B also has one we 'conclude' that 'at least two after-images exist', this would only be a bizarre way of saying that each of two people sees an after-image. (*K.C.*, p. 77)

The point in question can be put like this: A produces a photograph from his pocket and says, 'This is the girl I have been courting'. B looks worried. He produces an identical snapshot from his wallet and says: 'In that case we have been courting the same girl.' A smiles: 'We've only been courting identical twins, not the same girl.' This reply is informative because there are two distinct alternatives here, one of which it denies. Where there is no room for such a distinction, 'there are two similar images' is not informative. In contrast with A's reply in the example of the identical twins, it denies nothing and so says nothing that we did not know at the outset, namely that 'each of two people sees an after-image'.

So 'two people cannot see the same after-image, even if their reports agree in every respect' cannot mean what we take it to mean, namely that they must be seeing different or numerically distinct images. Nevertheless it helps to draw attention to what is a grammatical point, namely that here there is no room for distinguishing between exact similarity and numerical identity. In other words, when A's and B's reports agree, there is no further question: Are they describing the same thing or two similar things? If you insist on asking such a question, what *more* do you want to know in addition to what you already know? You may say that there is no such further question because we know the answer to it, namely that there are two images and not one. But I ask again: Does this mean anything more than 'there are two people each of whom sees an after-image'?

You may reply: 'If they were talking about the same thing, then if they gave different descriptions we would have to say that at least one of them is mistaken. But we don't say this. It follows that they are talking about different things. So if they agree in what they say this only shows that they are talking about similar things – but two things, not one.'

It is true that where A and B are talking about an after-image each sees, if their descriptions do not agree we do not say that one of them must be wrong. If they were talking about a television image we would have to say: Either one of them is mistaken or they are talking about two different images. If neither of them is mistaken, then they must be talking about two different images. This is the proper conclusion to draw in the case of descriptions of television images. But it doesn't follow that it is equally the proper conclusion in the case of descriptions of after-images. To think so is to assume that descriptions of television images and descriptions of after-images have the same logic. But this is a mistake.

One logical peculiarity which distinguishes the latter from the former is this. If I see an after-image and describe it, then no one can say, with finality, on the basis of what they see, that I am wrong or mistaken. But do not reply: 'That is only because they cannot see what I see when what I see is an after-image.' There is no reason why we do not count after-image reports by different people as contradicting each other when they do not agree. That we do not do so is a feature of the language-game in question and it does not stand in need of an explanation. If you think it calls for an explanation, if you think of after-images as things that you observe, you will find it difficult to avoid the reply: 'We do not count different people's reports as contradicting each other when they do not agree *because* they are about different things. They are bound to be about different things *because* none can see what the other sees.' As Wittgenstein puts it:

> The great difficulty here is not to represent the matter as if there were something one *couldn't* do. As if there really were an object, from which I derive its description, but I were unable to show it to anyone. (*Inv.* sec. 374)

III

I have argued that in the remark that two people can never see the very same after-image truth and falsity intermingle. The truth here is that we do not count reports by different people about their after-images as contradicting each other when they do not agree, or as supporting each other when they do. The falsehood is that this could only mean that their after-images are always different or numerically distinct. I argued that this conclusion is unwarranted and makes no sense here anyway. For what is 'different' or 'numerically distinct' being contrasted with in this context? The only opposite of 'different' here is 'exactly similar', and that is the sense in which we use 'same' when we say 'He sees the same after-image that I see'.

'But two people cannot both see the same after-image and give conflicting descriptions.' This only means that since it makes no sense to suppose that either of them could be mistaken (except within narrow limits) the conflict between their descriptions is our *criterion* of their seeing different after-images. If their descriptions agreed, we would say that they saw the same after-image.

In a paper entitled 'Knowing and Acknowledging'[1] Professor Stanley Cavell disagrees. Here, he insists, 'same' does not mean 'descriptively the same', and it is a mistake to think that it is impossible to distinguish between 'qualitative similarity' and 'numerical identity'. He refers to Malcolm's argument that there is *no sense* of 'same' in which two people cannot have the same sensation or see the same after-image, as there is no sense

---

[1] *Must We Mean What We Say?* Scribner's, new York 1969.

of 'same' in which two different surfaces cannot be the same colour: 'It is one of the most truistic of truisms that the very same shade of colour can be in many places at the same time.' This is what Malcolm says.[2]

Cavell thinks that the case of sensations and after-images is different from that of colours. He says: 'I do not find that I am a bit tempted to think that there is some sense of "same colour" such that the colour of one object *cannot* be the same as the colour of another.' 'But I *can* answer the question whether my headache is numerically identical with his. The answer is, Of course not!' (p. 244).

Now obviously there are differences between the case of colours and the case of sensations and after-images – and I do not think that Malcolm meant to deny this. For instance I could say: 'I had two bad headaches to-day, one in the morning and one in the afternoon, and they were very similar.' But no one would say: 'There are four colours in this room, one on each wall, but they are exactly similar.' This way of talking is intelligible in the case of headaches because it makes sense to ask '*when* did you have a headache?' and because pains are identified in part with reference to their location. So if my head aches and my back aches two aches are in question. And by the same token if my head aches and your head aches there are again two aches. The point in question is one that a philosopher may try to indicate by saying that pains and after-images are particulars, whereas colours – like gaits, builds and habits – are universals.[3]

Cavell's assertion that it makes perfectly good sense to say 'I cannot have the same pain as you – numerically the same pain' turns partly[4] on this point, namely that the location of a pain is one of our criteria of its identity. But if this is the case, then if I

[2] 'The Privacy of Experience', *Epistemology: New Essays in the Theory of Knowledge,* ed. A. Stroll, p. 141.

[3] There are differences between the case of after-images and that of sensations which I shall not consider as they do not affect the point at issue. I am thinking of the differences connected with their locality – the spot that hurts, the place where the after-image is seen – and with the importance of their locality to their individuation.

[4] I say 'partly' because, as we shall see, there is a deeper point at issue, namely the connection between the identity of a sensation and the person who gives expression to or conceals it.

could feel pain in some region of your body and feel it at the same time as you, we should say that I was feeling your pain, or at least that we felt numerically the same pain. Some people will admit this and I can see nothing wrong with it. But in that case the remark we are considering means no more than 'As things are, two people cannot have or feel the very same sensation'. While this is all right, it is not interesting: something in the inclination which leads to solipsism has gone through our net.

Let us, therefore, consider the inclination to resist the above answer. I imagine my nerves to be connected to the nerves of another person in such a way that while we go about our separate businesses in life and react to its particular tribulations in our own ways, if this man touches a hot plate and burns his hand I feel pain, at the same time that he does, and on the same spot, namely his hand. Is this an example of two people feeling the very same pain? Many people will still be inclined to say 'No'. 'I feel a pain in his hand; but the pain I feel is still mine – not his. Still I feel my pain and he feels his.'

What, then, does one feel this example fails to incorporate? What more does one want which is missing here? One wants not only that I should feel pain in his hand when he says it hurts, but also that I should feel the pain *as his*. In other words, I must feel a pain and recognise it as his – as I might feel a hand on my arm and recognise her touch, or see a car and recognise that it belongs to him – recognise it as his car. The presupposition is that normally when I feel a sensation not only am I aware of the sensation but also recognise it as mine – that this is part of what I am aware. This is bound up with an assumption we considered earlier, namely that feeling pain is a form of perception or acquaintance, the pain I feel being an object of acquaintance.

But when I feel pain do I identify something, namely what I feel, as mine? Do I both feel a pain and also recognise it as mine – as opposed to someone else's? Is that what the possessive pronoun in 'The doctor gave me an analgesic for *my* pains' signifies? If it did, then what we wish to deny should be possible; it should at least make sense for me to identify the pain I feel in his hand as his. These two possibilities go together: if it is not possible for me to identify a pain that I feel (e.g. in his hand) as not mine, then neither is it possible to identify it as mine. So the words 'even here the pain that I feel is mine; I cannot feel his pain' do not give us what we want.

We have been confused by the use of the possessive pronoun. 'My pain' means no more than 'the pain that I feel'. Someone in conversation may ask me: 'Whose pain were you talking about just now?' And the answer may be 'Mine', meaning 'the pain that I feel'. Whereas if someone asked: 'Whose house were you talking about, or pointing to, just now?', it would be no answer to say: 'The house that I see.' He might retort: 'Yes, I know that. What I want to know is whose house it is you see?' 'I was talking about the pain that I feel.' Here the retort, 'Yes, I know that. I want to know whose pain that is' would be nonsense. We have misconstrued the use of the possessive pronoun with sensations. It does not signify ownership.[5]

'I know that "my pain" means "the pain that I feel". When I said, "One cannot feel someone else's pain, one can only feel one's own pain" I meant "Someone's feeling a pain necessarily makes it his".' But what is this meant to convey? It seems to suggest something like the following: 'It has been decreed that the clothes a man wears are his, however he may have obtained them. And if someone else puts them on they become his. Here someone's wearing the clothes he wears necessarily makes them his.' But this will not do. For here although the clothes that I wear are necessarily mine, they may nevertheless be the same clothes that were his yesterday. No wonder, since ownership, however defined or determined, is transferrable; and what is owned by me need not be anyone's property. It can exist without belonging to anyone, and it can be identified apart from an owner.

If 'my pain' means no more than 'the pain that I feel', then 'I feel a pain and it is mine' doesn't say anything more than 'I feel a pain'. It is equally redundant in the case of 'I feel a pain in his hand'. If, as we were tempted, we add 'yet it is still mine – even here I do not feel someone else's pain', these words do not really say anything, though they may give us the impression of doing so.

'Even here I still feel my pain.' If these words had sense, then so should 'I feel his pain'. But the familiar sense of 'I feel his

[5] See Chapter Three, pp. 137–40 above.

pain' does not give us the contrast needed. For, in that sense, the opposite of 'I feel his pain' is 'I feel a pain qualitatively different from the one he feels – it is not acute, not in the corresponding place of my body, not part of the same complex, e.g. nausea, faintness, etc.'. If 'I feel my pain' made sense and so could be deduced from 'I do not feel his pain', then 'his pain' should mean 'a pain numerically identical with the pain he feels'. This brings us back to where we started.

I argued that if we can imagine circumstances in which we are willing to speak of two people feeling the self-same pain then our original remark means no more than '*As things are* two people cannot feel the very same pain'. But in that case we have by-passed the philosophical difficulty which interests us, and we have also managed to overlook the logical peculiarities of talk about sensations which that remark forces to our attention.

In the imaginary case of two people whose nerves are connected the inclination to say 'Here two people feel the very same pain' is not interesting. That is not to say that there is anything wrong in using these words here, in reserving them for only this kind of case. The point is that these words are felt to be appropriate here because this case constitutes an example which fails to meet *some* of our ordinary criteria for speaking of two distinct pains – as in 'I had two aches to-day, one in my head and one in my back'. This is what lies behind the inclination to use them: 'Two locations, two pains. One location, therefore one pain. Hence two people and only one pain.' Nevertheless if we say this we shall be suppressing a feeling that all is not well, a voice within us which wants to express some reservation. If we do not suppress it, 'if we let the conflicting voices here speak their fill',[6] we shall find that the fact that we have two people moaning and groaning, or one moaning while the other tries to smile bravely, militates against the inclination to speak of 'one pain'.

If I have argued that the inclination to speak of 'two pains' here comes from confusion, I did not wish to suggest that there is nothing in it. On the contrary, I believe that there is something sound in this inclination, namely a recognition that there is a conceptual link between pain and the person who gives expression to it. If you said, 'There is one pain here, and two people feeling it', this would be different from saying, 'There is

---

[6] Wisdom, *Philosophy and Psycho-Analysis*, p. 108.

one rough surface here, and two people feeling it'. For in the latter case what is felt, namely the rough surface, exists independently of anyone feeling it. Whereas the pain felt has no such independent existence. It is possible for one of the two people in my example to be given a spinal anaesthetic so that when he touches the hot plate he feels no pain, though the other one still does. But it isn't as if he *fails* to feel what is there to be felt, the pain the other man feels in his hand. It isn't as if there is a pain there to which he, but not his friend, has become 'unperceptive'. No. If A says that he feels no pain and he is not lying or joking and knows what he is speaking about, then that is an end of the matter. There is no question as to whether there might still not be a pain which he does not recognise. The fact that B feels pain in A's hand makes no difference to this. A has the final say where his own sensations are concerned. This is the truth in our idea that a pain is indissolubly linked to the person who feels it, so that where there are two people who give expression to pain there must be two pains even if there is only one painful spot. We shall consider what it amounts to in the following chapter.

Thus the person I have criticised for saying that even the two people whose nerves are connected cannot be said to feel numerically the same pain has something to be said in his favour, and Cavell is right to oppose the philosopher who makes short of what he says. For it is true that one cannot have another person's sensation *in the sense that* one can have his coat or watch, that one cannot see his after-images *in the sense that* one can see the view he sees from his window. But this is a matter of what it *means* to have or feel a sensation, to see an after-image. Yet the person who registers this truth in what he says, nevertheless fails to recognise it and speaks as if there is no difference between what it means to have a sensation or feel pain and what it means to have a coat or to feel the roughness of its material. This is precisely what misleads him into thinking that a man cannot show his feelings to anyone, that there is a limit to what he can tell or share with other people, and that consequently we are all doomed to live our lives in solitude.

Cavell is right in thinking that it will not do to say that in my example A and B feel the same pain and that is the end of the matter. But Malcolm is equally right on another point: Given that A's and B's nerves are appropriately connected, that both say they feel pain and point to the same place, namely A's hand, as the place where they feel it, there is no *further* question about whether there is really only one pain or two.

I did *not* argue that in this example there is *one* pain, that A and B feel the *same* pain. Nor yet that there are *two* pains, that A and B feel similar though *distinct* sensations. My point was that here there is no established use of 'same', or rather no obvious way of going on with our ordinary use of 'same' as applied to sensations. The reason why consideration of such an example can be illuminating is that the strain or conflict we feel with regard to what we are to say here, in this special case, helps us to face those very undercurrents of thought which flow in the direction of solipsism and to get clear about their content so that we are not carried along by them.

There is, of course, a perfectly good sense in which two people can be said to feel the same sensation. But to insist on this does not help us to solve our difficulties when we wish to say that two people cannot ever feel the same pain. On this point Cavell is absolutely right. On the other hand, this is not to say that we are right to think that two people can never feel the same pain – numerically speaking. I insisted that we are confused when we say this, even though there is something in what inclines us to say it, something which we ought to hold on to and appreciate for what it is. When we have faced the unexamined assumptions about the grammar of sensations and other feelings which give us the impression that we are irremediably cut off from each other, we shall find we are able to admit what we all cheerfully accept or take for granted in our nonphilosophical moments. We shall be able to do so without succumbing to the narrowness of vision and understanding, of which Cavell complains, when as philosophers we appeal to the ordinary use of words as a means of dismissing our philosophical disquietudes.

In this chapter I have tried to examine these assumptions or presuppositions and to show how they are wrong. But I insisted that this is not the end of the matter. In the next chapter I shall examine what it would be wrong to deny or reject when opposing the inclination which turns our face in the direction of solipsism.

Summary In the first part of this chapter I argued against the inclination to think that when one feels pain one is acquainted with an object of consciousness, when one sees an after-image one is perceiving something that is inseparable from one's consciousness.

In the second part of the chapter I argued that when we say that two people cannot see the same after-image or feel the same sensation we are confused if we mean that they always see different after-images, feel numerically distinct sensations. There is no clear sense of 'numerical identity' here which can be distinguished from 'exact similarity'.

In the third part of the chapter I probed this question further. I considered an imaginary example in which A and B feel pain simultaneously in the same place – A's hand. Here two opposite ways of thinking about this example may be represented as follows:

1.   A   B   2.   A   B
      | | \ /
   pain$_1$ pain$_2$ pain
      \   / |
      painful   painful
       spot   spot

I argued that both representations are equally inadequate. The first one raises the question of why the two pains cannot change owners which, I argued, comes from confusion. The second one avoids this confusion but at the cost of suggesting, wrongly, that A and B stand to the pain each feels as two men stand to the rough surface each feels.

We saw that when we insist that however similar two people's sensations they can never be identical 'since my pain is mine and your pain is yours' we misunderstand the use of the personal pronouns here. Still this is not to say that we should simply retract these words. For in them there is also the recognition of something important, namely that we cannot have another person's sensation *in the sense that* we may have his belongings, nor even *in the sense that* we may have his qualities, virtues and vices. For the identity of a pain cannot be divorced from the person who gives expression to or conceals it. This will be explored further in the following chapter.

7 Asymmetrical Logic of Mind

When the voices that Joan hears are public I can hear them too if I happen to be standing near her and I am not deaf, but when the voices she hears are *private* I cannot get close enough to her to hear what she hears. If the dagger which Macbeth sees is a physical dagger then I too can see it if I am in the same room with him and am not blind. But when it is a "dagger of the mind" then it is hopeless for me to try to see it. I have to rely on his words as I have to rely on witnesses if I want to know what has happened behind my back.

The idea is that another person's feelings and sensations are *hidden* from me in the way that what is taking place behind locked doors is hidden from those who are outside. My own feelings and sensations, on the other hand, are presented to me in my consciousness and so, as far as I am concerned, they *lie open to view*.

We have seen that this idea of sensations as 'inner objects' with which I am acquainted in consciousness or by some 'inner sense' is confused. Consequently, the idea that we are not acquainted with other people's sensations in this way is bound to be equally confused. Still this is not to say that there is no difference between the way a man is related to his own feelings and the way other people are related to them, and so no difference between the way he answers questions about his own feelings and the way other people answer these same questions. There is. But it is not like the difference between my way of answering a question 'Is the water high to-day?' when I am standing on the bank of the river and your way of answering that same question when a high wall blocks your view so that you can only see the mill wheel turning.[1]

You may have very good reason for answering that question in the affirmative. You see the mill wheel turning and reason that the water must have risen high enough to push its blades. The connection between these two things is contingent: The mill wheel may turn, driven by an electric motor, when the water is low; or the water may rise while the mill wheel, jammed as it may be, remains stationary. The step from what you see to the answer you give is an inductive step. It is a reasonable step and you are justified in taking it because on other occasions, in the past, you or at least others have seen the water hitting the blades of the wheel and turning it. Besides, even now, you can raise yourself, look over the wall, and confirm what you have inferred. That is to say the difference between us is a matter of accident; we just happen to be on different sides of the wall.

This could be fairly described by saying that we each answer the same question from different *positions*. I am better placed than you are since I can see the water. You, on the other hand, are not as well placed. Your basis for what you say is *indirect*. You do not actually see the river; you infer what you say about it from something else that you see. This is your evidence for what you claim; your answer to the question we have been both asked is thus based on evidence. But you can improve your position, stand where I stand, and see for yourself that what you said is true.

This possibility is, as it were, built into the question. For when I say 'The river is high to-day' I allow cameras, other people, my other senses, and the future to prove me mistaken. We have already seen that this is part of what it *means* to speak about a physical reality. To turn for a moment to the example of the dagger: When I say 'There's a dagger before me', if I allow cameras, other people, my other senses, and the future to prove me mistaken then I am speaking about a physical dagger. If I am using these words in such a way that nothing of this can prove me mistaken then I am speaking about a 'dagger of the mind', an hallucination, a mental image.

Now in the previous example what makes you say 'The water

[1] The example is by Wisdom – see *Other Minds*, pp. 227–35.

is high to-day' and what makes me say the same thing are not the same. But they could have been. You could have seen the river and said 'The water is high to-day' as I do when I say the same thing. In contrast, supposing that I see an after-image and say 'I see an after-image – a red triangle'. You too could, of course, see an after-image of this colour and shape. But you could not, on that basis, say 'He, Dilman, sees an after-image – a red triangle'. That is no basis in your case for what I said. You can only base your answer to the question 'What sort of after-image is Dilman seeing?' on my truthful report.

Put it like this. A and B are asked, 'Is the water high?' They both answer that it is. How does A answer this question? By looking. What does he see when he looks? The river. How does B answer this question? By looking. What does he see? The mill wheel turning. Now he climbs up the wall and he too sees the river. In this way he makes sure that the water is really high.

This time A has an after-image. Both A and B are asked to say what shape it is. A answers that it is triangular. What makes him say that it is triangular? The fact that the image *he* sees is triangular. B too answers this question correctly; he says that the image is triangular. What makes him say that it is? His hearing A say so and his having no reason to think that A may be lying.

In the first case A looked and saw the river, B looked and saw the mill wheel turning. He then scaled the wall that was blocking his view of the river and he too saw what A saw.

In the second case A looked at a triangular figure in suitable light, then he turned his gaze towards the wall and saw an after-image. He was asked to say what shape it is and he replied that it is triangular. Is there anything here in what A does that B cannot do? No. He too can look at the triangular figure, come to see an after-image, and describe what he sees. Yet if he does this he will not have answered the question that was put to him and to A. In doing what A does he describes the shape of his own after-image and not A's as he was asked to do; he answers a different question.

Yet compare what A and B have done here with what they do in the first case, after B scales the wall. There, in the first case, each looks and sees something, and each in saying what he sees provides an answer to the same question. In the second case, after B comes to see an after-image in the way that A does, each describes what he sees, *as they do in the first case*, and by doing this provide answers to different questions.

'But in the first case they see the same thing, in the second case they see numerically different things – for each sees his own after-image.' We have already seen that this means no more than that each sees the after-image he sees. 'But it is the same river that each sees, whereas it is not numerically the same after-image that each sees.' What makes you say so? The fact that if their descriptions differ we do not say that one of them must be wrong or mistaken. All right. But this means that these descriptions of what each sees do not count as answers to the same question – which is precisely what I have been arguing. In that case, to say 'This is because each sees something numerically different' does not add anything to what I said. What I said is where we have to rest.

'I cannot see Macbeth's dagger when what he sees is a dagger of the mind. I cannot hear the voices which Joan hears when the voices in question are hallucinations.' This makes it seem as if there is a wall between us which I cannot scale, that somehow I am stuck in a position that is second best, that I cannot occupy their positions. I have argued that the difference between us is not one of position. If it were, then it should at least be conceivable that I could improve my position. For a position is something that one can change with respect to what one is talking about, studying, or looking at. This means that changing it does not affect the identity of what one is inquiring into. In other words, the way one's position is specified is independent of the way the subject of one's inquiry is identified. This is what makes it possible to talk of different positions with respect to the same thing and to compare them with one another, calling some 'better' and some 'worse' positions for purposes of the inquiry.

'I cannot occupy his position, for I do not have the key to his mind.' This wrongly suggests that there is something he can do which I cannot. But we have seen that I can do exactly what he does and *vice versa*. I can look at the figure which he looked at, come to see an after-image and describe it. What I cannot do is both do what he does and in doing it answer the same question which he answers. For in doing what he does I describe *my* after-image. This is because of the way the possessive pronoun is used in this connection. That what I do here does not constitute an answer to the question I was asked is a matter of what it *means* to ask that question – a question in the asking of which the personal pronoun plays an integral part. The kind of question it is is determined by what counts as answering it and what does not.

I repeat. If I were locked up in a dungeon, I could not do some of the things someone free does. I could not, for instance, look out of his window and admire the view he admires. But in the case we are trying to get clear about there is nothing which he can do that I cannot do. It seems there is, namely 'look into his mind', 'see his after-image'. We have seen in the last chapter (i) that what *he* does cannot be described as looking into his own mind, and (ii) that in one sense it is simply not true that I cannot see his after-image, or the same after-image that he sees, and in another sense it is nonsense. Wisdom compared what we may still be tempted to insist on here with 'No man can do what another man does' which sounds like 'No man can punch like Cassius Clay'.

> Can one man do what another does? Surely he can. And yet it can't be that he can. For suppose A scratches his head. Then if B scratches his head he doesn't do what A does since it's not B's head but A's that A scratches. But if B scratches A's head then again he doesn't do what A does since A scratches his own head and B scratches someone else's. (*P.P.A.*, p. 177)

What A does can be described as (i) scratching his own head and (ii) scratching A's head. But only when A does the scratching can these two descriptions be used interchangeably. They are equivalent only when the scratcher is the same person as the man whose head is scratched. In the case of another person B they cannot be equivalent, they cannot be both descriptions of what B does – unless A and B were both distinct persons and yet had one head between them.[2]

Now compare with 'B cannot feel A's pain' – considered in

[2] I will not say that this is unimaginable. But if one were to imagine two people going about their separate businesses, though connected by invisible nerves to a head containing two separate brains, it would be interesting to consider to what extent and in what ways our notion of a person's body and head would be modified.

the last chapter. Let us imagine that A suffers from sciatica which gives him a peculiar painful twinge in the leg. Perhaps by means of drugs or hypnosis sciatica is artificially induced in B and he feels this peculiar twinge in his leg. We might say that B feels in his own leg what A feels in his leg. But, of course, 'his own leg' here means 'B's leg'. Since the pain A felt was in A's leg, this militates against saying that here B feels A's pain. So now we connect their nerves appropriately and B feels what A feels in A's leg. But this time he does not feel it in his own leg – as A does. Here what is claimed by 'B cannot feel A's pain' is exactly parallel to what is claimed in Wisdom's conundrum, namely 'No man can do what another man does'.

If, with Malcolm, we imagine Siamese twins with a common leg then we would have imagined a case where B can feel A's pain. However, we have seen that the difficulty which these words bring up goes deeper than this. It does not merely centre around the subject's body as containing the location through which the pain is individuated, but around the subject himself, a reference to whom seems indispensable to the identity of the pain. So one who says 'B cannot feel A's pain' will refuse to retract his words even in the case of the Siamese twins or the two men whose nerves have been connected in the way we imagined. He will say: 'Even here A feels the pain he (A) feels and B feels the pain he (B) feels.' But Wisdom's conundrum illuminates the fix we find ourselves in this case too.

To see this let us return to a variation of our original example in this chapter. A and B are both asked to describe (i) the figure on the black board which A sees, and later (ii) the after-image which A sees. By describing what he sees on the two occasions A satisfies both requests. B satisfies request (i) in the same way, by doing what A does, namely by describing what he, B, sees. We are imagining them to be in the same room and facing the blackboard. But he does not satisfy request (ii) if he does what A does, namely describe what he sees himself – in the same circumstances in which A does this. To satisfy request (ii) he has to do something different, namely ask A and quote him. In both cases a description is wanted of *what A sees*. In the first case, for B's description to be a description of what A sees, it is not necessary that B should give any special weight to what A says he sees. In fact, one can refer to what A sees here without mentioning A at all – i.e. as 'the figure on the blackboard'. Here what A says is on the same footing with what any other person says – provided he is as well placed, has as good eyes as A, and the relevant competence. These are conditions that can be fulfilled in the case of *anyone*. In the second case, for B's description to be a description of what A sees it is necessary that B should treat what A says he sees differently from what anyone else says. For what A says here has a *privileged status*; no one can take it lightly or ignore it completely and still be talking about what A sees – that is when what he sees is an after-image.[3]

We see that the expression 'what A sees' is used in two different ways. In one of these you cannot characterise 'what A sees' without referring to A. This lies at the source of our temptation to say that 'no one can see what A sees – when what he sees is an after-image'. The trouble is that these words falsely suggest that there is something here that A does which no one else can do – much in the way that was suggested by Wisdom's conundrum. When, however, we see through it we realise that we ought to have said that no one can say or describe what A sees, in the way that A does this, when what he sees is an after-image. For in doing this, which nothing prevents him from doing, he describes his own after-image and not A's. Just as when B scratches the head that A scratched he does not do what A has done, and when he imitates him, which he can easily do, and scratches his own head, he does not scratch A's head. Certainly he cannot both imitate A and scratch the head that A scratched. Likewise B can well imitate A when A describes the after-image he (A) sees. But he cannot both do so and in doing it describe what A sees. Doing so does not count as describing what A sees when what he sees is an after-image, as it does count as describing what A sees when what he sees is the river – provided there is nothing to block B's view of it.

[3] It is true that B can infer what A sees from what he, B, sees, when their after-image is produced from the same figure. But the hypothesis on which this inference is based – namely that two people with normal sight see the same after-image when the figure from which it is obtained is the same – is itself based on reports by people about their after-images on other occasions. And these reports themselves have the logical peculiarity in question. Further if B now *infers* in this way what kind of after-image A sees, whether he is right or wrong is still determined in the end by what A says he sees.

It is this difference between 'what A sees' (when what he sees is e.g. a physical dagger) and 'what A sees' (when what he sees is a 'dagger of the mind'), and between the ways in which the truth of reports about them is established, that is distorted in our idea that what A sees in the second case is a 'private object'. It is distorted in our idea that the difference between A here and another person B is like the difference between a man who can see something directly and one who can only see its shadow, or like the one between one who can see the river rising and one who, from behind a wall, can only see the mill wheel beginning to turn. We have seen how *unlike* each other are the differences between A and B in the two cases. In the second case A and B are not related to 'what A sees' as the man who sees the river and the one who can only see the mill wheel are related to what they are talking about when they say 'The water is high to-day'. The gist of my argument has been that the way the differences between A and B differ in the two cases adds up to a difference in what it *means* to speak of 'what A sees' in them – when what A sees is a river or dagger and when what he sees is an after-image or a 'dagger of the mind'.

The difference between A and B is not the same in the two cases. In the first case it is a difference in position and, there-fore, one that can be removed. In the second case the difference is bound up with the way in which the personal pronoun appears in both the question which A and B are asked and, consequently, in their answers to it – the way in which the per-sonal pronoun is part of the *sense* of the question and so of the answers given to it. To answer the same question A's answer must be in the first person and B's answer in the third person. This is precisely where the difference lies; it is a difference in the ways the first person answer and its third person counterpart are arrived at and confirmed. It is, therefore, a difference in grammar or logic. It is a difference which characterises all ques-tions and answers about thoughts, feelings, desires – just be-cause you cannot talk about these things without referring to a person whose thoughts or feelings they are. It is this difference, connected with the inevitability of such a reference, that is at the back of the solipsist's temptation to say 'Only I really think and feel', as well as at the back of the sceptic's claim, 'I cannot know what others think and feel, and even that they think and feel at all'. If the solipsist's and the sceptic's statements bring us to see this, to appreciate it for what it is, we shall find ourselves much less tempted to say what they say. But they can only bring us to see it if we can uncover and work through the difficulties which trouble them.[4]

---

[4] It is in this respect that Wisdom has compared philosophy to psycho-analytic therapy. There are of course important differences; but that is not to say that the comparison does not go deep.

8 Our Knowledge of other Minds: Mental Life and Human Behaviour

I

Argument from Analogy We have talked about the asymmetrical logic of statements about the mind. Wisdom says that this is a feature of them without which they would not be statements about the mind (*P.D.*, p. 99). In other words what is in question is precisely what distinguishes a mental reality from a physical one. Thus supposing that someone exclaims 'Hot!'. If he uses this word in such a way that what thermometers read, how other people look, and what they say they feel are relevant to the truth of what he says then he is using this word to speak about the weather. In other words, when our way of deciding whether or not what he says is true is *symmetrical* as between him and us then his word refers to the weather. If he so uses this word that what thermometers read, how others look, and what they say they feel is not relevant to the truth of what he says, then he is using this word to say something about what he feels. Here he has a way of answering the question 'Is that really so?' which no one else can have without being him.

He has a right to say that he feels hot which no one else can have without being him. But we too can have a right for saying that he feels hot. The sweat on his brow, the flush on his cheeks, and his words, in the given circumstances, may give us a right and also a justification for thinking that he feels hot. Obviously these are not what gives him a right to say 'I feel hot'. That is what gives him a right to say this and what gives us a right to say 'He feels hot' are not the same.

Generally, when I am questioned about my own feelings what I say is not based on observation – even when it is arrived at by reflection or introspection.[1] Whereas, even when another person's feelings are transparent to me, so that I know what he feels without reflection, what I claim he feels is based on what I have seen him do and heard him say. Now the question is: How is what I say based on his words and behaviour?

One answer is that a man's angry words and behaviour are symptoms of the anger he feels in the way that his high temperature and dizzy spells may be symptons of an inflamed appendix. This is the Cartesian answer which we have already seen to be inadequate. It presupposes that anger is an object or mode of consciousness, visible only to the angry man, and that the connection between anger and its expressions is contingent or accidental. The idea is that one first learns what anger is from one's own case. One then learns, by experience, that it is generally connected in one's own case with such-and-such modes of behaviour – its so-called outer expressions or manifestations. On meeting such modes of behaviour in other people one infers, by analogy with one's own case, that the people in question feel angry – the same as what one feels when one behaves in this way. This is the so-called argument from analogy.

Here one's knowledge of other people's feelings is assimilated to the kind of knowledge which, for instance, a watch mender has of the mechanism inside watches he has not yet opened. He has opened many watches and has seen what makes them tick. A customer brings him a watch that does not work properly. His experience with watches he has opened and examined gives him a pretty good idea of what to look for and put right in this watch. The trouble is that the situation in which we are pictured as being with regard to other people's feelings is different from the situation of the watch mender with regard to the watches he has not yet opened and examined. It is different in an important respect which rules out the possibility of the kind of inference which the watch mender is justified in making.

There is no radical difference between the watch mender's relation to the watches he has opened and his relation to those he has not yet opened. A watch he has not yet opened to-day will move from one category to the other when he opens it tomorrow and looks inside it. If he has a right to infer, for

[1] See Dilman, 'The Unconscious: A Theoretical Construct?', *The Monist*, July 1972.

instance, that the spring inside this watch must have broken, then he must have made similar inferences in the case of other watches and subsequently found out he was right. Besides it must be possible for him to find out that he is right in this case too. In the case of our supposed inferences about what other people think and feel it is otherwise. For there the possibility of finding out we were right in inferring what we did is thought to be ruled out. Perhaps the other person corroborates our inference, avows that he feels angry. But this is still supposed to be indirect evidence for what *he* knows directly, so that our original situation remains unaltered. If our situation can never be changed, as it can in the case of the watch mender when he opens a watch and looks inside, how can we be justified ever in making such an inference? How can we even have formed a conception of the kind of thing we are supposed to infer?

Here, once again, as a second measure, one resorts to the *analogy* between oneself and other people: If I suppose that someone is angry, then I am simply supposing that he feels the *same* as I have felt when I was insulted or thwarted (see *Inv.* sec. 350). But the hurdle which is largely of our own making cannot be surmounted in this way. For *if* one could and did learn what anger is from one's own case, and *if* the kind of situation which calls for anger and the way people respond to such situations when angry had nothing to do with what we understand by 'anger', then we wouldn't know what other people mean when they say they are angry. What I am supposed to mean by 'anger' in my own case would not commit me to a particular way of understanding what it means for other people to be angry – just as little as the teaching Wittgenstein imagines of 'adding 2' with numbers below 1000 commit the pupil to a particular way of understanding this operation beyond 1000 *in the absence of an established practice or custom.* One tends to think that the meaning of a word one has learned in one sort of situation can guide one in one's application of that word in different situations. But the application of a word cannot, in this way, be extracted from its meaning, since it is its actual application that determines what it means.

If you say that the word is to be used in the *same* sense in the new cases as in the old, this still does not tell us what that comes to – as again Wittgenstein's example in *Inv.* sec. 185 illustrates.

The question is: 'What does "same" mean here?' For the pupil in Wittgenstein's example thought that in continuing the series 1000, 1004, 1008, 1012 he was going on *in the same way* as before. But, as we have seen, what decides this question can only be found in the actual practice of developing such series. It is that which gives content to the identity in question and not the other way around. Therefore if you say that for someone other than yourself to feel angry means for him to feel the *same* as you, yourself, feel when you feel angry, you will not have said anything unless you told me what it means for him to feel the same as you feel. But what this means can only be gathered from our actual practice of making such judgements about other people. If I do not know how to judge other people's feelings then I do not know how to judge that they feel the same as I feel in particular situations.

When would I say that another person feels angry? 'When he feels the same as I feel when I feel angry.' This is no answer to my question. For until I know when I am to say that another person feels angry I do not know when I am to say that he feels the same as I feel when I feel angry. In other words, in the absence of some criteria for the application of such words in the case of other people the appeal to identity is an empty gesture.

To sum up. If our initial assumptions force us to the view that we cannot ever know directly what another person feels, we have to admit that we cannot know this even indirectly – i.e. that we cannot know it at all. But if we cannot ever know what another person feels, if we can never tell whether or not a claim about another person's feelings is true, we have to admit that we cannot even understand any such statement, know what it means to talk about the feelings of other people. This understanding which our initial assumptions have made impossible cannot be restored by recourse to identity.

II

Behaviourism I asked: How is what I say about another person's feelings based on his words and behaviour? I considered the Cartesian answer according to which the connection between anger and its manifestations on which I base my claim that someone feels angry is contingent or accidental. So what I say about another person's feelings has an *inductive* basis. The behaviourist denies that the connection between anger and its manifestations is contingent. He insists that 'there must be some sort of conceptual tie between the language of mental phenomena and outward circumstances and behaviour' (Malcolm, *B.P.P.*, p. 152). But he wrongly construes this as a *deductive* connection. So he suggests that 'consciousness is to its manifestations as electricity is to its manifestations' (Wisdom, *O.M.*, p. 222). His view is that what a man feels is nothing over and above the way he behaves, or at least that a certain pattern of behaviour is essential to a man's feeling this or that on any particular occasion.

This view has to its credit that it redresses some of the mistakes for which we have criticised the Cartesian view. However it commits other serious errors. First, in assimilating the logic of anger, hatred or pain to that of electricity, it denies or at least obscures the asymmetry that belongs to our mental concepts. As Wisdom puts it:

> It is senseless to talk of knowing that a thing has electricity in it [e.g. that a battery is charged] without knowing this from what we misleadingly call effects of electricity. But it is not in the same way senseless to talk of knowing that a man has anger in his heart without knowing this from the effects of anger. For the man himself does this. (*P.P.A.*, pp. 257–8)

In other words, though when we are right about what other people feel we know this from their behaviour and from what they tell us,[2] when we tell others what we feel ourselves what we tell them is not in this way based on observations of our behaviour. The behaviourist does not acknowledge this and so denies the difference between how we come to say such things as 'I am angry' and 'He is angry'. (The Cartesian philosopher at least does not deny that there is a difference, even though he misconstrues it.)

Secondly, in thinking that what we mean by anger, hatred, joy or love can be given or defined by a disjunctive listing of types of behaviour or tendencies to behave in certain ways, the behaviourist is mistaken – as we shall see. But here he has at least this advantage over the Cartesian, namely that he shows some recognition of the disastrous consequences of imagining

[2] *How* we know it is the topic of the present chapter.

that the connection between kinds of feeling and behaviour is merely accidental or contingent.

Thirdly, behaviourism is inadequate in that it does not take sufficient account of the fact that a man need not express his emotions at all. This is at least part of what Malcolm has in mind when he writes that 'people tell us things about themselves which take us by surprise, things which we should not have guessed from our knowledge of their circumstances and behaviour' (*B.P.P.*, p. 153).

We have already considered the asymmetrical logic of statements about the mind. So it is the last two defects of the behaviourist answer to our question that I want to consider now. This will involve a further consideration of the kind of *conceptual tie* there is between the language of mental phenomena and outer circumstances and behaviour, and so the sense in which human behaviour as well as what people tell us about themselves in certain circumstances constitute our *criteria* for the application of such concepts as pain and anger to them. An explanation of this is surely a discussion of the question, 'How do we know what other people feel?'.

A

The supposed essence of angry behaviour For a man to be angry it is certainly not necessary that he should behave as an angry man – that, for instance, he should clench his fists, look daggers at the person with whom he feels angry, and perhaps also want to hit him. People do not always show their emotions and sometimes they conceal them. Besides the manifestations of anger, and perhaps even more of other emotions, are widely scattered. As Malcolm puts it in the case of *remembering*: 'The word "remembering" is actually used by us to range over a diversity of events and circumstances that are not united by an essential nature of remembering' (*W.N.M.*, p. 21). This is just as true of 'anger', 'sorrow', 'joy' or 'love'. In his search for characteristic modes of consciousness the Cartesian philosopher fails to recognise this. But so does the behaviourist in the way he attempts to define or analyse what 'anger' or 'love' means. In this both may be said to be guilty of 'essence mongering'.

The behaviourist is inclined to think that for a man to be angry it is *essential* that he should behave in certain ways, ways which constitute angry behaviour – the behaviour of an angry person. But what is it to behave as an angry person? Here we can at best give examples; perhaps we can mime anger. It is a mistake, however, to think that we could exhaust the grounds in this way and that the examples stand to one another in any one relation – for instance, that they all have something in common apart from being instances of angry behaviour, or that they could be constructed in accordance with a rule or formula. Certainly most of us would recognise them as instances of the way angry people behave or tend to behave, though few of us would find it easy to say what it is about this or that instance that justifies us in talking of anger in connection with it. The important point is that it is not always one and the same thing, nor one or more different things out of a set. In Wittgenstein's words, the concept of behaving as an angry person – which is not the same as the concept of being angry – 'comprises many manifestations of life'. These phenomena are 'widely scattered' (Z. sec. 110). And it takes certain circumstances, a complicated background, before we can even have those 'manifestations of life' that would constitute an instance of angry behaviour. So the answer to the question of whether a man *must* behave in one of the ways illustrated if he is to be angry is 'No'. We could go on multiplying our examples indefinitely – and not, of course, as we may go on constructing an infinite series in mathematics.

Besides, how much in a given example belongs to 'behaviour' and how much to 'surrounding circumstances'? Is what we isolate as behaviour *enough*, and is it even *necessary*? Do we not want to know whether the man who behaves in this way was thwarted, insulted, offended, cheated, humiliated, or at least whether he thought or imagined he was? I suppose that to some extent the behaviour can be recognised as angry behaviour in separation from the circumstances; otherwise I could not mime anger. Still, in recognising it as angry behaviour do I not fill in the background in imagination? Do not even mimes on the stage, however bare the setting, *suggest* some such background, *hint* at certain circumstances – if not real at least imaginary? Even if we did not wish to commit ourselves to a generalisation on this point, we would have to admit that forms of behaviour cannot always be identified or characterised apart from circumstances. Wittgenstein mentions the case of pain-behaviour and the behaviour of sorrow and suggests that in both cases we may have nothing more than crying: 'If a child's mother leaves it alone it may cry because it is sad; if it falls down, from pain' (Z. sec. 492). This means that when we talk of pain-behaviour and the behaviour of sorrow here we mean more than crying; we give a wider description of the tears, a wider co-ordination of what goes on here, when we describe it as 'pain-behaviour' for instance. Wittgenstein says that the behaviour in these two cases can only be differentiated or described 'along with their external occasions', that the two 'belong together' (*ibid.*). They are tied together in our *concepts* of pain-behaviour and the behaviour of sorrow. This is not to deny that there may be differences in the movements and sounds of the person crying that may betray his rage, despair, grief or purely physical pain. But what betrays one of these emotions also necessarily suggests a wider background and certain thoughts which the subject may come to articulate.

We see (i) that there are no set forms of behaviour essential to anger, and (ii) that even when we have a distinctive form of behaviour which manifests anger, to see or describe it as such means placing it against a wider background and connecting it with certain thoughts in the person behaving in this way. So even in a particular case we cannot say of a form of behaviour we are able to isolate (e.g. the look he gave her, the way he snapped at her, etc.) that it is *sufficient* to the person in question being angry.

But is it even *necessary*? Could we say that a man *must* behave in one of these ways if he is angry? Could we say that he *must* be angry if he behaves in one of these ways? The behaviourist is inclined to answer both these questions in the affirmative, and he is wrong to do so. For, obviously, a man may act as if he is angry, pretend to be angry, without being angry. On the other hand, he may feel angry and yet conceal his feelings.

B

Psychological language and human behaviour But how are these possibilities – pretending to be angry when one is not and acting as if one is not angry when one is angry – compatible with there being a conceptual tie between feelings and behaviour, i.e. a connection between the concept of anger and the scattered behaviour illustrated in examples?

The connection is not deductive in that a man need not behave in any of the ways mimed or otherwise illustrated and still be angry. It is nevertheless a conceptual connection in that it is not conceivable that a man should be unable to recognise any of these instances as instances of angry behaviour and yet still know what it means to be angry. A man's knowledge or understanding of what it means to be or feel angry[3] cannot be divorced from his recognition of certain forms of behaviour as expressing anger and certain kinds of situations as calling for this kind of response. Some reference to both would have to come into an explanation of what it means to be angry. So it is equally not conceivable that a people who never exhibit the kind of behaviour with which we are familiar in people who are angry should nevertheless be angry on accasions. The Cartesian philosopher thinks that such a people can nevertheless know anger in themselves and have a concept of anger equivalent to ours. What he does is to divorce the *meanings* of words such as 'anger' from the circumstances in which they are used. He thinks that the kind of life and behaviour that surrounds their applications is external to what these words mean and has nothing to do with it. Wittgenstein showed the incoherence of such a conception of language and he opposed it in the notion of a 'language-game' he developed: 'I shall call the whole, consisting of language and the actions into which it is woven, the "language-game"' (*Inv.* sec. 7).

A man's feeling of anger can, certainly, exist apart from the kind of behaviour we have been talking about. He may really be angry and yet conceal his anger, not show it in any way. But the *use* of the word 'anger' cannot be intelligibly dissociated from the circumstances in which people behave in certain ways – are thwarted, insulted, cheated or humiliated, for instance, and react by wanting to retaliate, to hurt the other person, perhaps to strike him, get red in the face, and so on. We learn the meaning of the word 'anger' in connection with this kind of situation and this kind of behaviour. The *meaning* of the word is bound up with the situations in which we learn to use it – though there is no common essence that ties them together, not even one that can be specified disjunctively.

[3] I make no distinction throughout between *feeling* and *being* angry.

It is in this sense that our idea of the ways in which angry people behave, or tend to behave, is an *inseparable* part of what we mean or understand by 'anger', an *essential* part of our conception of anger. But from this it does not follow that one or other of these behavioural expressions is essential to a man's being angry on any particular occasion. I am making two points here as against the behaviourist: (i) That there is no common essence of anger which would allow it to be defined in the way the behaviourist thinks it must be definable. This is an error which the Cartesian philosopher shares with the behaviourist. (ii) That there is no one form of behaviour, nor even any form of behaviour, which is essential to a man's being angry on a particular occasion. For a man may really be angry and still not show it. His behaviour may in no way betray his anger – not even to a perceptive friend.

C

Concealing one's feelings People's behaviour sometimes gives us no clue about what they feel, even when we know them well. Sometimes it positively misleads us. We find out how little we knew about their feelings subsequently from what they tell us or other people. The behaviourist knows this as well as anyone else, but he attributes our ignorance in such cases to our unperceptiveness or our lack of further knowledge about the behaviour of the people concerned and its background. His idea is that given this further knowledge we should be able to *deduce* from a person's behaviour what his real feelings are. The kind of discrepancy we have between a person's behaviour and his feelings when he conceals them or when he pretends to feel differently from what he really feels is incompatible with the idea of a deductive connection to which the behaviourist is committed. So he wants to deny such discrepancies, to represent them as more apparent than real.

I should like to argue that the existence of such discrepancies is one of the facts of life that we must accept and not try to explain away. One can accept it without returning to a Cartesian view of the mind. Of course there is a *difference* between a man who is angry and one who merely acts as if he were, and a *similarity* between a man who gives expression to the anger he feels and one who conceals it from other people – even though their behaviour makes the first two men *look alike* and the last two *different*:

I.   Similarity $\left(\begin{array}{c} \text{Man who is angry} \\[6pt] \text{Man who pretends to be angry} \end{array}\right)$ Difference

Behaviour ↑

Feeling ↑

II.   Difference $\left(\begin{array}{c} \text{Man who is angry and who gives} \\ \text{expression to his anger} \\[6pt] \text{Man who is angry and who} \\ \text{conceals his anger} \end{array}\right)$ Similarity

↓

↓

Yet what makes the first two men different is *not* to be found in differences 'within them' – unless that means no more than that one of them feels angry and the other does not. Nor is the similarity between the last two men to be found in 'what goes on in them'. In both cases we have to turn to the *surrounding circumstances*. It is these which the kind of behavioural description which the behaviourist focuses on leaves out.

Wittgenstein mentions the following example which one can imagine taken out of the pages of a novel: 'He measured him with a hostile glance and said . . .' (*Inv.* sec. 652). He comments:

The reader of the narrative understands this; he has no doubt in his mind . . . It is also possible that the hostile glance and the words later prove to have been pretence.

The question is: What is it that makes the reader think it is pretence? What is involved in thinking that it is pretence? Wittgenstein answers:

The main thing he guesses at is a context. He says to himself for example: The two men who are here so hostile to one another are in reality friends, etc., etc.

It is the context which determines whether he really measured the other with a hostile glance and meant what he said to him, or was only pretending. Whether a man means his words to another or utters them in jest is not a matter of what goes on within him when he speaks these words, nor a matter of his tone of voice and the like – though, as a matter of fact, there may be differences in both respects between a person who means these words and one who does not.

It is the same with the man who gives expression to his anger and the one who conceals it. We may say of the latter: 'He did not behave as an angry man, yet he was angry.' Again it is the context which connects these cases together, not some 'inner experience'. What is it that makes us say of the man who has not given expression to his anger that he is angry? Briefly, the whole setting, the insult perhaps which preceded the occasion, the connection which this setting gives the present occasion to others where men shout, fight, and say unpleasant things to each other. It is in this connection that the conceptual tie with behaviour is to be found. In a given case there may be nothing to enable us to make the connection. After the occasion the man in question may confess that he was angry. If we have no reason to suspect that he may be lying or teasing us we may believe him. But if we do, we shall expect that the thoughts he will convey to us, if he is open, will make us see his situation, real or imaginary, as one in which it makes sense to want to hit or hurt someone, return a humiliation or lash at him in words. When I imagine a man who successfully conceals his anger it is this kind of connection that I imagine. I do so by picturing his situation in a certain way through his thoughts. That is, I understand what is in question as being the case of a man who is angry with reference to cases where anger is displayed, not concealed.

It is in this sense that instances where anger is given open expression in words and behaviour have logical precedence over those where it is concealed. The meaning of the word 'angry' brings in a reference to such cases. Thus the idea of a people who never exhibit their anger when they feel angry is an incoherent one. The behaviourist is right to criticise the Cartesian philosopher on this point. On the other hand, the behaviourist equally goes wrong when he swings to the opposite extreme and claims that whenever a man feels angry there must be something about his behaviour from which we should deduce that he is angry.

There are, I think, certain 'primitive' and 'natural' expressions of anger. Wittgenstein would say that the child learns to use the word 'anger' in the first person in connection with such reactions – e.g. crying in rage when frustrated. Adults talk to him and teach him exclamations and, later, sentences. This is an extention of the natural reactions. As the child learns to speak and grows, his world widens and encompasses an ever greater variety of situations. He learns to co-ordinate his reactions, so that they are modified according to the situation to which he responds affectively. Further, as the use of words give him a much wider scope of response the original behavioural expressions of anger take on newer forms and become more scattered – e.g. a letter written in cold anger and designed to make the person to whom it is addressed to feel small. In addition, as he learns to reflect on the situations that confront him and to anticipate other people's reactions he learns to check and control his impulses, to conceal his feelings.

Concealing one's anger is logically a more sophisticated form of behaviour than giving vent to and displaying it. Not only is this something that needs to be learnt, but it can only be learnt by someone who has learnt many other things. It requires a certain minimum of intellectual sophistication and, therefore, the kind of surroundings with which we are familiar in our life. Without the kind of life that can provide such surroundings, a man or other creature cannot be said to be angry when he displays none of the patterns of behaviour we expect from an angry person, in the way that one of us who similarly displays no anger is sometimes said to be concealing the anger he feels.

The Cartesian philosopher thinks that anger is essentially a private thing and that expressing it is something extra – a positive doing like reporting an incident which one need not have reported. I have argued that the affective response in which a man's anger finds expression comes first and that remaining silent, controlling one's impulse is a positive doing. A person is not passive when he keeps silent and conceals his anger, and he has to learn much before he can do so. The point I am making is a logical one and says nothing about what it takes in terms of the will to conceal one's feelings. This depends on the person, the feelings and the occasion. For it may cost a person much to control his affective impulses, to renounce the satisfaction of giving them expression, and to conceal his feelings. But it may equally cost him a great deal to avow or confess them – because of their intimate character, or because he feels ashamed. My

main point, though, has been this: that the conceptual tie between the language of emotions and the behavioural expressions of emotions does not preclude the possibility of
having an emotion and not expressing it, or conversely, of pretending to have it when one is indifferent or unmoved or feels
the opposite.

D

Emotions and their outer circumstances As against the behaviourist
we want to say that anger or joy is something *over and above*
angry or joyful behaviour. But this does not mean that joy is
something additional to or behind the joyful behaviour, something with which only the joyful person is acquainted. If joy
cannot be identified with or reduced to joyful behaviour, this
does not mean that it is something interior, intangible, hidden
from everyone else, something that cannot be further anato-
mised – as William James might have put it.

Take an example which was once put to me, in a different
connection, by Dr. David Pole: a man reading an account of
war atrocities and feeling a thrill of excitement. He was thinking in terms of a rather unfortunate dichotomy: episode *versus*
disposition. Surely a thrill of excitement is an 'episode' he
suggested. He might have added: 'it has quite a special content'. He was thinking of a thrill down the spine – a bodily feeling or, perhaps, sensation. He thought of this as constituting
the *content* of the experience and contrasted it with a special pattern of behaviour. His point was that the thrill of excitement is
something over and above any such behaviour.

This, however, is confused. What we call 'content' here in-
cludes various things, but above all the man's thoughts. As for
the bodily feeling in question, it is only in certain circumstances
or connections that it is a thrill of excitement. In particular circumstances we may call it an *expression* of the excitement the
man feels. But it is *not necessary* that he should have it for him to
feel a thrill of excitement. Is the bodily, sensuous experience
itself describable as a 'thrill' or 'quiver' apart from certain circumstances? To some extent – yes. For it can be connected with
what occurs at other times in circumstances in which it does
amount to a thrill of excitement. So we may speak of it as a
'thrill' irrespective of the present circumstances. It could be a

thrill or quiver without being a thrill of pleasure or excitemend.

Is the thrill of excitement 'a pattern of behaviour'? Dr. Pole rightly wanted to say that it was not. Is it 'a disposition to behave in certain ways'? Again he said, No. Is it not then 'an episode'? You can call it that: after all it is something the man felt at the time he read the story. ('But don't you feel grief *now*?' *Inv.* p. 174.) On the other hand, it cannot be identified with the thrill or quiver he felt running down his spine, the bodily feeling. *Nothing* that went on at the time, no such episode, can amount to what he felt at the time, namely the sadistic feelings, the thrill of excitement, apart from particular circumstances and connections – the texture of the man's life, his thoughts on this occasion which he may be able to articulate later, links and bridges with other incidents in his life: all of these giving the particular occasion a physiognomy which connects it with occasions in other men's lives where they find pleasure in cruelty. I repeat: nothing that took place at the time can in itself amount to a thrill of excitement. In *that* sense the thrill is *not* an episode – as a stabbing pain or flash of lightning is. The before and the after, the man's thoughts, bear on its identity. Thus contrast an attack of anxiety with an attack of indigestion; a pang of remorse with a tug of pain. It is this contrast which the distinction between an episode and a disposition disguises or obscures. For an attack of anxiety, as opposed to a man's vanity or generosity, like an attack of indigestion is an episode and not a disposition.

I said that joy is something over and above joyful behaviour, and equally that a thrill of excitement is something over and above a thrill or quiver felt running down one's spine. Both are *expressions* of emotion.[4] But in what sense is joy something over and above joyful behaviour? In what sense is joyful behaviour an expression of joy? In the sense that 'a young woman's joyous exclamations, movements, smiles, would not be manifestations of joy [as Malcolm puts it] if they occurred in quite different circumstances. Instead they could belong to a bitter parody of joy; or they could be symptoms of madness' (*W.N.M.*, p. 17). The word 'joy', Malcolm says, 'is not used to stand for some constel-

---

[4] There are differences here with which I am not now concerned. I have touched on *some* of these in an early paper, 'An Examination of Sartre's Theory of Emotions', *Ratio* December 1963.

lation of behavioural responses. There is no grouping of gestures, movements, utterances, such that we can say: *That* is
what joy is.'

Let me quote from *Zettel*:

> 'But I do have a real *feeling* of joy!' Yes, when you are glad
> you really are glad. And of course joy is not joyful behav-
> iour . . .
> 'But "joy" surely designates an inward thing.' No. 'Joy'
> designates nothing at all. Neither any inward nor any out-
> ward thing. (sec. 487)

The joy she felt is *not* a *further* occurrence to her joyous exclamations, movements, smiles. It is not a quiver down her spine,
nor a flutter in her heart. Of course, she *feels* joy, and feels it *now*,
and what she feels is not her behaviour. But neither is it a flutter
in her heart, or anything like it, though she may feel a flutter in
her heart. The joy she feels is just as much over and above the
flutter she feels as it is over and above her movements, exclamations, smiles. If there is anything behind, further to, over and
above these it is the *particular circumstances*. It is these that make
the difference between real joy and a pretence or parody of it.
To put it tersely, there is no mental occurrence of joy *in addition
to* the words, gestures, actions and reactions, and the flutters
and quivers in which joy finds expression, although these are *not*
the joy in question.

Let me add to this what I argued in the last section, namely
that although joy is not something additional to its expressions,
something behind or alongside these, nevertheless on a particular occasion there can be joy in a man's heart without his giving
expression to it in words, gestures, movements, actions and
reactions. Thirdly, as I argued in section B, this possibility does
not make such expressions external to what we *mean* by 'joy'.
You cannot explain what joy is without giving instances of the
way it finds expression in human life, as well as of the situations
in which it does so.

III
Knowledge of Other People's Feelings We saw earlier that when we
know that another person feels angry or depressed we know this
from his behaviour and from what he tells us – whereas what we

tell others about our own feelings is not in this way based on observations of our behaviour, nor yet of something inward and
private. This led us to ask *how* we know other people's feelings
from their behaviour and from what they tell us. In other
words: How is the basis of our knowledge in these cases related
to our claims about other people's feelings? To put it differently: How are their expressions of emotion related to what
they feel?

We considered two radically opposed answers which we are
inclined to give, the Cartesian and the behaviourist answers,
and found them both to be defective. According to the first of
these the manifestations of an emotion are related to the emotion in the way that the symptoms of an inflamed appendix are
related to the inflamation of the appendix inside a person. We
saw that this involves difficulties which are insurmountable.
According to the second answer the manifestations of an emotion are related to the emotion in the way that what justifies us
in thinking that a battery is charged is related to the charge. But
if a battery is charged, when we connect it to a galvanometer or
voltmeter in good working order we necessarily get a positive
reading, since getting such a reading, and the like, is what we
mean by the battery being charged. In contrast, we have seen
that a man may be angry and in no way express his anger. We
have also seen that while it is senseless to talk of *anyone's* knowing that a battery is charged without knowing this from galvanometer readings, and the like, it is not senseless to talk of
anyone's knowing that Joan is angry without knowing this from
what Joan says and does and the way she looks. For when Joan
herself tells us she is angry what she tells us is not based on her
behaviour and facial expressions.

If, then, both these answers have to be rejected, we are still
left with the question: *How* do we know what other people feel?
What we have already seen about the relation between an emotion on the one hand and its manifestations and surroundings
on the other, already gives us a clue to the answer of this question. This is now what I wish to follow up.

A

Behavioural and Verbal Criteria In an earlier chapter I quoted
Wittgenstein's remark that 'our attitude to what is alive and to

what is dead is not the same' (*Inv.* sec. 284). I explained then that having this attitude means reacting to people in certain ways as a matter of course and without question – for instance, resenting something they tell us, being insulted, hurt, angered or irritated by their words and deeds, being grateful for what they do, pitying them, feeling embarrassed in their presence, and so on. Take the example of tending someone who has hurt himself. Wittgenstein says that here there is no reasoning from his behaviour to the belief that he is in pain. My conviction that he is in pain shows itself in my deeds, in my reaction; and my conviction, reactions, and deeds are not reasoned. Such unreasoned reactions lie at the basis of the kind of reasoning which I am going to consider in the following section. Thus in *On Certainty* Wittgenstein quotes Goethe's words from *Faust*:

> . . . and write with confidence
> In the beginning was the deed.

In *Zettel* his comment on the idea that 'we tend someone else because by analogy with our own case we believe that he is experiencing pain too' is that this is 'putting the cart before the horse' (sec. 542). As I said, the horse is our natural reaction to someone who has hurt himself and is crying, and the mistake of putting the cart before the horse lies in the sceptic's idea that unless such a reaction is based on reason and can be justified it is irrational. Wittgenstein would say that if *that* stands in need of justification then none of our beliefs and conjectures about our friends and acquaintances can be justified. If there is a justification *here*, then there is no justification at all.

In the *Investigations* he takes the same example:

> A doctor asks: 'How is he feeling?' The nurse says: 'He is groaning.' A report on his behaviour. But need there be any question for them whether the groaning is really genuine, is really the expression of anything? (p. 179)

Wittgenstein's answer is No. His point is that unless there are a great many such occasions on which we react to people's behaviour in these ways, naturally, as a matter of course, and agree in our reactions, we could not even wonder what other people think and feel. He would say that if there is a making sure *here*, on these occasions, then there is no making sure at all. (These

are the occasions about which when questioned by the philosophical sceptic, 'But, if you are *certain*, isn't it that you are shutting your eyes in the face of doubt?', he replies, 'They are shut'—
Inv. p. 224.)

Further than this, there are also occasions where it is not at
all obvious or clear what people feel. If we want to know, and
considerations of tact, etc., do not stand in our way, we ask
them. As Malcolm says: 'The testimony that people give us
about their intentions, plans, hopes, worries, thoughts and feelings, is by far the most important source of information we have
about them' (*B.P.P.*, p. 153). His point is that just as in the previous example where the nurse says 'He is groaning' the
patient's behaviour in the circumstances described (e.g. he is a
patient in hospital, perhaps he has a tumour or he has been
knocked down by a car) is the doctor's *criterion* of the patient's
being in pain, similarly such first person utterances as 'I
intended to keep my appointment' or 'Now I am annoyed' are
often our *criterion* of what the person in question intended or
feels. Malcolm says: 'We use this testimony as a new criterion
of what he is feeling and thinking, over and above and even in
conflict with the behavioural criteria' (p. 153).

This does not mean that we can never question this testimony. For surely we can have reason in a particular case for
thinking or suspecting that the person giving it is insincere or
self-deceived. But if we have grounds for doubting a person's
testimony about his intentions or feelings in a particular case,
there must be many cases where we have no such grounds and
even where we would find a doubt unintelligible.

The possibility of reflecting on another person's situation,
words and behaviour with a view to forming a judgement about
his feelings, hopes, motives, intentions and character presupposes that there are circumstances where we are prepared to
take other people's testimony at face value and not meet it with
doubt or suspicion — just as if we can, in special circumstances,
wonder if our senses are deceiving us there must be a great
many occasions where we would regard a doubt as unintelligible: 'If there is a making sure *here* [on the latter occasions] then
there is no making sure at all.' If I am in doubt, in a particular
case, as to whether my senses are deceiving me, whether what I
see is an illusion or hallucination, then I try to look at what

seems to be before me from a different angle, perhaps alter the conditions of light, and if I think I may be seeing an hallucination I try to touch what I see. Thus my sense perceptions can turn out to be deceptive in one situation because I regard them as reliable in other situations.[5] It is the same with the testimony other people give us about themselves. If, in one way or another, this testimony can be deceptive in one situation, or even in a whole series of situations, this is because there are circumstances in which we regard them as reliable and beyond question.

There are, then, circumstances in which we regard other people's testimony about themselves as beyond question, circumstances in which we take their behaviour to express or reveal their feelings. These are circumstances in which other people become *transparent* to us and we mention or illustrate such circumstances if we try to explain what it *means* to feel this way or that. The kind of behaviour, in those circumstances, belongs to our *conception* of those feelings – hence the *conceptual tie* of which I spoke earlier. We now see that the kind of behaviour, scattered as it may be from one case to another, in the right circumstances constitutes part of our *criteria* of what other people desire, feel, intend, and so on. This is not surprising since, as we saw earlier, criteria for a word's application are a matter of what the word means: The way the inflamed appendix looks is at least part of what is meant by its being in a state of inflammation. Similarly, in the way an angry man behaves, when he does not check or conceal his anger and gives way to it, we shall find an instance of what we mean by being angry – or, at least, of what is involved in our meaning. So when, in particular circumstances, we recognise a man's behaviour to be of this kind we know that he is angry. Here we are not making an inference to something that lies behind the behaviour.

In the case of the appendix removed by an operation I said: 'Here on the basis of the way the appendix looks the doctor may say that the patient has an inflamed appendix. But this is not an inference. The inflammation of the appendix is not something over and above what the doctor sees here.' In the case of the other person's anger and his angry behaviour we noticed at least two important differences, namely (i) that the behaviour is

[5] See Part One, Chapter Ten above.

at least partly subject to the person's will and that he can control it with a view to concealing his anger,[6] and (ii) that unlike
us he does not have to observe how he behaves and looks in
order to tell us that he feels angry. Thus while the right description of the way the patient's appendix looks does entail the description of it as inflamed, no description of his behaviour
entails that he is in pain. There is no general description or set
of descriptions from which such conclusions follow deductively.
As we have seen, a further reason for this is (iii) that a person's
behaviour cannot be described in separation from the particular circumstances in which he is, as well as the way he, himself,
sees those circumstances and the thoughts he has about them.[7]

B

Scope for reasoning and reflection Although, as I have argued, there
are circumstances in which we see people's feelings *directly* in
their behaviour and take their testimony about themselves at
face value, this is not always so. There are circumstances in
which we would be deceived if we took a friend's behaviour and
actions at face value, if we trusted what an acquaintance tells us
about himself. We may have grounds for suspecting that he
may be acting, that he is not sincere, or even that he is deceiving
himself. We may have reasons for thinking that we would go
wrong if we took his words and behaviour at face value – though
we may not be able to put our reasons into words or articulate
the grounds for our suspicion. In these circumstances we shall
have to reflect on his words and behaviour now, as well as on
other occasions, and we shall also want to talk with him – not

[6] There are interesting questions about the sense in which emotions can
hold a man captive, dominate his consciousness, influence and sometimes
cloud his judgement, though they may also at times open up a new vista for
him. There is much conceptual work that needs to be done here which I am
putting aside in this book.

[7] Obviously there are important differences between the way we know
what a man thinks and the way we know what he feels – though these are
intermingled and cannot be wholly separated. These are bound up with the
differences between the relation of thoughts to human behaviour and the relation of emotions to human behaviour. In this book I limit myself to simple
and common instances of sensations and emotions. The reason for this is that
my interest centres around the general outline of certain problems rather than
the various details surrounding them.

merely to observe him. But it is only in these special cases or occasions that we need to reflect – though by 'special' I do not mean rare or uncommon. These are cases or occasions where we have grounds for suspecting insincerity, duplicity and self-deception, or at least mistrust, caution or reserve.

So our question 'How do we know what other people think and feel?' has to be reworded and broken into two questions; (i) Where we suspect that another person is not sincere, has something to hide, has ulterior motives, puts on an act, or wears a mask, how can we be sure that we are right? (ii) If we are fairly certain about this, how do we find out what he is hiding, what he really feels? If we decide that we were mistaken about this person, then our second question becomes redundant. On the other hand, if we become convinced that his expressions of feeling are not genuine, then the substantiation of our suspicions merges into the process of finding out his true feelings. So in practice there is no sharp line between these two questions.

First about the first question. There is no general rule or theory which sets out when we can trust someone's self testimony, in what circumstances what a man says about himself can be taken at face value. We have already seen that talk of *criteria* carries no such suggestion. If a person's self testimony is my criterion of what he feels it must be spoken in certain circumstances, uttered in a special tone of voice, etc. These, at least to some extent, vary from one person to another, and their significance has to be gathered over a certain period of contact with the person. This is one reason why it is so difficult to generalise, or why generalisations are of little worth here. As Professor Anscombe puts it: 'There is a point at which only what the man himself says is a sign; and here there is room for much dispute and fine diagnosis of his genuineness' (*Intention*, p. 44). The reasoning to which such diagnoses are responsible is neither inductive, nor deductive, though it may contain both inductive and deductive steps. What is more: 'There is in general no complete agreement over the question whether an expression of feeling is genuine or not' (*Inv.* p. 227). This lack of complete agreement (Wittgenstein argues) characterises our knowledge of human beings – i.e. it belongs to the logic of our knowledge of each other. But although there is no complete agreement here,[8] there is nevertheless some agreement. If there were no agreement, there could be no knowledge either – no knowledge of human beings.

I argued that the question 'What does he really feel?', which we ask only in special cases, incorporates two questions, though in practice these merge into one another. I also suggested that the form of reasoning or reflection which it calls for is neither inductive, nor deductive, though it may contain both kinds of step, and that it does not always lead to a conclusive answer. This does not justify scepticism – for, as Wittgenstein puts it, 'there are those whose judgement is "better" and those whose judgement is "worse"' (*Inv.* p. 227). I want to add now that if our question is to be answered by reflecting on the words, behaviour and circumstances of the man in question, sometimes taking these over a long stretch of time, the way in which it is answered must include talking with him.

Answering such a question does not merely consist of reflecting on complex patterns that stretch in time. For what we are reflecting on is a human being, one who is capable of lying and deception, as well as trust and sincerity. What we are confronted with is a foreign will capable of responding to us. So although we have to reflect, certainly, we also need to ask questions, respond, talk and listen – we need to make contact with a will independent of ourselves. To some extent at least we have to enter into a relationship with the other person, to come to know him as a person. To do so is not just a matter of assessment. It involves the give and take of a personal relation, so that if I know a person I can, for instance, ask him something or ask something of him. At any rate, if I want to know what he really thinks and feels about his wife, friend, or the painting on his wall, and I listen, he will be talking to *me*, responding to my questions and remarks, reacting to my attitude towards him. What I am like and the character of my interest is not irrelevant to what he chooses to tell me and even to what he is able to express.

I am not saying that you can only know another person's thoughts, feelings and desires if you enter into a relationship with him. On the contrary, I started by pointing out that there

[8] As there is among mathematicians over whether a calculation is correct or not.

is a great variety of occasions where this is not so. But where you are uncertain and you want to know, you cannot pursue your questions as an observer or a complete stranger.

We have a variety of cases here, but I think that roughly they can be divided into two classes – though there is no sharp boundary between them. On the one hand we have people who are reserved or insincere, who want to keep their feelings to themselves, are mistrustful of others and who cannot or will not open up – a whole range of cases. On the other hand we have people who are false or self-deceived. In both cases what impresses us is that what the person we come into contact with thinks and feels is not apparent, not manifest, but hidden, and so not easily accessible. We may have a suspicion of what he thinks and feels on specific occasions, we may even snatch a glimpse of what lies behind the appearances. But in either case we have to rely on his good will or other motives, if his feelings are to become manifest, to be given direct expression in his words and behaviour. Or we may hope that we shall catch him off his guard – as when the malingerer forgets to limp or in panic starts to run.

My main point is that to know another person's mind, when he is not transparent, is to penetrate behind the moving surface of a living person – a surface of words, gestures, postures, attitudes and behaviour. To know what these add up to we need to reflect. This involves making comparisons, groping for connections, discerning patterns, noticing repetitions, following leads, sifting out genuine from false clues. This reasoning is neither inductive, nor deductive, and more like the kind of reasoning we carry out when we are trying to assess character, read a poem, apportion blame in a complex situation when we are not ignorant about the sequence of events that led up to it. To penetrate behind this surface is not to infer what lies behind it, but (i) to discern its sense or significance, to make out its features and what they add up to, and (ii) to make contact with an alien will. When that surface, the words, behaviour, postures, expressions, pauses, form a barrier or façade, what we are up against is another person's *will*. Without its ultimate consent or ratification, or without its breaking up or letting go, the judgements in which our reflections issue can at best be tentative. This is part of the asymmetrical logic of the mind we have examined earlier. So in our reflections we attach special weight to the other person's testimony about himself, even though we do not exempt it from questioning and criticism. When we judge that we can take it at face value, when the person we talk to consents to be frank, open and direct, then the surface in question becomes transparent. It is no longer a barrier or façade, so that there is nothing that we need to get behind – contrary to what philosophers have often thought.

It is important to see that what I have called 'the moving surface of a living person' is not necessarily a barrier or façade. Though it can be a barrier, it need not be so. It can be transparent. When it is so we can be said to have *direct* knowledge of another person's mind.

Thus the obstacle to knowledge of another person's mind is not a logical gap which no reasoning can bridge, but the other person's unwillingness, reserve, mistrust or insincerity. Sometimes the person himself finds it difficult, even impossible, to overcome his fears, mistrust, reluctance, and those habits of response which keep his own feelings at bay. Here often our success in coming to know him will depend on our success in helping him to come to know himself. But this opens up a new sphere of philosophical questions which I cannot pursue here.

Summary   We saw that the way I answer questions about another person's feelings differ from the way I answer questions about my own. Part of this difference is that my judgements about other people's feelings are based on their behaviour and self testimony or avowals, whereas this is not true of my own testimonies, nor even of my reflective judgements about myself. But *how* are my judgements about other people's feelings based on their behaviour and self testimonies?

In Part One of this chapter I considered briefly the Cartesian answer – the argument from analogy. I was brief since I had considered various facets of it earlier. In Part Two I considered the behaviourist answer. We had already seen it to be defective in one respect, namely in that it denies or obscures the asymmetry we considered in the previous two chapters – the asymmetry with which the solipsist is in close contact. Here I concentrated on two other defects: (i) the behaviourist's idea that mental phenomena can be *defined* in terms of behaviour, and (ii) his idea that the connection between statements about mental phenomena and descriptions of behaviour is *deductive*.

A criticism of the behaviourist on these two points helped me to consider the sense in which there is a *conceptual tie* between the language of mental phenomena and human behaviour and its surrounding circumstances, and so the sense in which, in particular circumstances, what people say and do are our *criteria* of what they feel. It is in the context of these questions that in Part Two, sections A to D, I considered the relation between emotions and human behaviour. I argued that the relation is not contingent, so that our claims about other people are not arrived at or supported by inductive reasoning. It is not necessary either so that, for instance, a person may pretend to have feelings he does not have or conceal what he really feels. How is this compatible with there being a conceptual tie between the language of mental phenomena and behaviour and its surroundings? This is the question I discussed in Part Two, section C of this chapter.

Part Two of this chapter was a necessary preparation to the positive part of my answer to the question I raised at the beginning of the chapter, namely '*How* do we know what other people feel *from* their words and behaviour?'. I developed the positive part of my answer to this question in Part Three. Briefly, my answer was that in a great many cases other people's feelings are transparent to me so that I know what they feel *directly* and without inference or reflection. If this is not at once apparent I can find out by asking them. On a great many occasions what they tell me will convey their feelings to me directly – section A. In section B I considered how we find out when this is not so, and how we can distinguish between cases where people are open and transparent and cases where they are opaque – where they conceal their feelings or wear a mask. My main points here were (i) that the kind of reasoning in question is neither inductive, nor deductive, but more the kind of reasoning we use in trying to assess the character of complicated patterns that are difficult to grasp, (ii) that it is not generally conclusive, (iii) that ultimately it waits upon the direct confirmation to be found when the other person becomes transparent, and (iv) that since what keeps me from having direct knowledge is the other person's will, coming to know what he really feels is bound to involve talking with him, responding to him and eliciting his response.

The real obstacle to knowledge of another person's feelings and thoughts is his unwillingness to let me near him, perhaps his unfriendliness and suspicion, his reluctance to let me see him as he really is. This may be his response to my clumsiness, selfishness, hostility or plain unperceptiveness, it may be rooted in some misunderstanding between us, or it may be his response to the world as he sees it, a vision influenced by his moral convictions, and sometimes dominated by his anxieties, fears and fantasies.

Given that the logical difficulties which lead to philosophical scepticism here are the product of conceptual confusion and can be surmounted, this is not to say that there are not real difficulties, sometimes insuperable, which are part of the very texture of human life.[9]

[9] See, for instance, Proust.

9 Conclusion: Cartesianism and Behaviourism

In the second part of the book we have considered the notion of mind and the kind of knowledge we have of its states. That is we have been concerned with the mind primarily from the standpoint of our knowledge of it rather than from the standpoint of human actions. But, of course, these two areas of philosophical investigation – that is those questions about our knowledge and understanding of ourselves and others and those about our relation to the intentions we form, the decisions we take and the actions we perform, as well as the kinds of reason we have for the things we do, in short questions about the will and human movements and actions – cannot in the end be completely separated. The questions that arise in these two connections run into each other in all sorts of surprising ways.

Thus we have already seen how much when we are genuinely in doubt about another person's attitudes, feelings and designs what we are up against is his will. It is not only to his own feelings that a person is related differently from the way in which he is related to those of other people. This, we have seen, is right at the centre of solipsism. But this asymmetry, that is reflected in our use of personal pronouns in connection with 'mental states', is one that we have to come to terms with in relation to questions about the will and human actions. It is certainly reflected in the way we talk about reasons for what we do. Hence the contrast between what we mean by reasons for what we believe and reasons for what we do.

You can say that a man's relation to what he expects to see and his relation to what he intends to do are different. If he has reason to expect an explosion now, then anyone who has the reason he has will also have the same expectation. On the other hand, what is a reason for him in the decisions he makes or the resolutions he forms need not be a reason for another person in the decisions he has to make – even when he appreciates the weight which this reason carries for the other person. We have here a whole field of interesting questions that merge on the one side with those that are at the centre of solipsism and on the other side open up into ethics. Obviously it would take another book to explore them.

Another area of questions which I have not explored centre around the notion of self-knowledge and the way self-knowledge can be obstructed by the person's own will. These are questions that have to be considered by one who wishes to appreciate Freud's contribution to psychology.

The questions I did discuss in both parts of the book are related and run parallel a good deal of the way. They part company precisely where the difficulties raised by the solipsist appear on the scene. The philosopher who is troubled by our 'knowledge of the material world' finds it difficult to understand how we can bridge the gap between 'the private world of our sense-data' and 'the public world of material things'. It seems to him that if we can have any knowledge of the latter it is bound to be *indirect* knowledge. The philosopher who is troubled by 'our knowledge of the mind' finds his difficulties confined to our knowledge of other people. It seems to him that if we can have any knowledge of other people's minds it must be differently acquired from our knowledge of ourselves. He is inclined to think of the difference very much as the first philosopher thinks of the difference between 'our knowledge of perceptual sense-data' and 'our knowledge of material things'. He is strongly inclined to hold that our knowledge of our own mind is *direct* and *immediate*, whereas our knowledge of other people's minds is *indirect* and *inferential*. This is one of the central doctrines of the Cartesian view of the mind.

Where the philosopher troubled by 'our knowledge of the material world' is concerned we have seen that while it does make sense to talk of sense-data, there is something seriously wrong with the idea that whenever we look at or touch anything what we immediately perceive are always and necessarily sense-data. There is something seriously wrong with the idea that we derive our notion of material things from the sense-data we have, that the latter notion is logically more primitive than the former. We have seen that when we can appreciate what is wrong with these ideas we shall no longer be forced to say that our knowledge of material things is always and necessarily indirect. In this way the problem about bridging the inferential gap between the claims we make about physical things on particular occasions and our basis for such claims will vanish. We shall not only have been freed from the temptation to scepticism here, but also come to appreciate what it means to talk about knowledge, reasons and evidence in connection with physical things.

The sceptic about our knowledge of material things is impressed by a difference in grammar between discourse about chairs, tables, smoke, shadows, reflections and mirror images on the one hand and discourse about hallucinations, mental images, after images and 'sense-data' on the other hand, though he is confused about the complicated relations between these two large and mixed areas of speech. Likewise the Cartesian philosopher is rightly impressed by a difference in our ways of answering questions about our own minds and questions about other people's minds, though equally he is confused about what this difference amounts to. I have tried to show that if one can appreciate what this difference comes to one will recognise that what we have here is not a contrast between *direct* and *indirect knowledge* at all. This will help us to see, as in the case of the difficulties raised by the first philosopher, that there are numerous occasions when other people's minds are transparent to us and where there is no inferential gap between our bases for what we claim about them and these claims.

No inferential gap that needs closing. This we discussed in the last chapter of this part of the book when we considered the relation between human behaviour and mental life, and the sense in which, in certain circumstances, other people's behaviour and the testimony they give us about their minds constitute our *criteria* of what they think and feel.

Still just as how things stand in the material world may not be apparent on some occasions and we may be positively deceived, likewise other people may at times become opaque to us. Here too, as in the former case, it may be that the conditions are unfavourable to our having a better view or apprehension of their thoughts and feelings, intentions, designs and desires. But it is often the people themselves who refuse to reveal themselves to us, who remain reserved, hide their feelings, and even positively deceive us by lying, acting and pretending. This is, of course, an enormous difference between what it is we seek to have better knowledge and understanding of in the two cases. There could be no more obvious as well as momentous difference between persons and things which affects the form which our inquiries take in the two cases, and so the character of the knowledge we seek. Therefore, where we are concerned with the logic of our knowledge of other people's minds it is important to recognise that we have to do with creatures that speak a language, who can tell us things about themselves, as well as lie to us, and so creatures who may wish to be frank with us or who may resent our demands and expectations. Thus what we are faced with here is something active and not merely inert or passive as with matter, a will with which we may be in conflict or harmony insofar as as we want contact with it, knowledge and understanding.

We have seen something of the relative merits and demerits of both Cartesianism and behaviourism in their search for a better understanding of the conceptual issues that centre around the logic of our knowledge of mind. We have seen how each reminds us of something important which the other ignores, though doing so in a misleading way. The Cartesian philosopher will not let us forget that there is a difference between the way we answer questions about our own minds and the way we answer similar questions about other people. He puts this, roughly, by saying that my basis for saying 'I have toothache' and my basis for saying 'He has toothache' are not the same. In this way, however misleadingly, he draws attention to what I called 'the asymmetrical logic of mind'. On the other hand, he misunderstands this difference and comes to think that what is relevant to the truth of statements about sensations and emotions is something that occurs in a person's consciousness, something with which only he can have direct acquaintance. We have seen how *both* the idea of something inevitably hidden from everyone except the person who feels the sensation or emotion *and* the idea of something going on at the time he feels angry or jealous are misleading. The behaviourist is equally tempted by the latter idea, even if he takes a different view of what it is that goes on at these times. Still what he takes to be 'going on' here is a little nearer the mark insofar as it enables him to consider the circumstances in which the emotions in question are felt. This helps him to avoid some of the pitfalls of Cartesianism. It enables him to appreciate a little better than the Cartesian philosopher the kind of connection there is between an emotion or intention and its so-called object.

Here one should remind oneself of the considerations that led Wittgenstein to insist that a 'language-game' is not merely the utterance of words and sentences but also the behaviour, actions and reactions with which the utterances are interwoven. These considerations apply equally to what may be called 'the life of the mind' – the forming of intentions and resolutions, the criticism and abandonment of them, the feeling of emotions for things and people, the attempts to come to grips with them, and so on. We saw in Part Two, Chapter Two that just as one cannot make sense of what it is to speak if one leaves out the kind of life into which people's utterances enter, so too one cannot make sense of what it is to form an intention or to fall a prey to an emotion if one does not consider the circumstances of human life in which these things take place.

Both the Cartesian philosopher and the behaviourist ignore this, or fail to appreciate its significance. For they share the misconception that being frightened or angry, for instance, consists in something going on at the time a man feels frightened or angry – the Cartesian thinking of it as an 'inner state of consciousness' or 'mental process', the behaviourist thinking of it as an 'outer piece of behaviour'. As I said, while both are wrong on this point, the behaviourist is a little nearer the truth – just as in connection with the difference between 'our knowledge of ourselves' and 'our knowledge of other people' it is the Cartesian who is nearer the truth. In connection with the former point Wittgenstein repudiates *both* philosophies of mind:

A move in chess doesn't consist simply in moving a piece in such-and-such a way on the board – nor yet in one's thoughts and feelings as one makes the move: but in the circumstances

that we call 'playing a game of chess', 'solving a chess problem', and so on. (*Inv.* sec. 33)

Wittgenstein compares the questions 'But don't you feel grief
now?' and 'But aren't you playing chess *now*?' Obviously he
doesn't deny that someone may be feeling grief now or playing
chess now. The question is: What does each consist of? His answer is: Not of anything that goes on now. Nothing that is going
on now can amount to either grief or a game of chess apart from
the whole setting in which it takes place. That is why Wittgenstein contrasts 'For a second he felt violent pain' with 'For a
second he felt deep grief' (*Inv.* p. 174). His point is that the latter
doesn't make sense. Nothing that a man feels for only a second
can be grief. As he puts it: '"Grief" describes a pattern which
recurs, with different variations, in the weave of our life' (p.
174). This is not true of pain. Many animals feel pain. Pain, we
can say, does not require the complex background of human
life, though *naming* pain, talking about pain does.

It is the latter point which the Cartesian philosopher fails to
appreciate. In doing so he tends to think of the meaning of the
word 'pain' as something private – 'Only I understand what I
mean by "pain"'. He tends to think too that what I feel when I
feel pain is something which only I can know: 'Two people
cannot feel the very same pain.' We have examined what there
is to be said both for and against this. When the Cartesian
philosopher insists that a person's feelings are *private* he shows
recognition of at least three important points: (i) That I do not
tell you that I am angry or in pain in the way that you say this of
me. (ii) That mental states cannot be individuated without reference to their subject and so that the use of the personal pronoun is essential to our references to mental phenomena. (iii)
That I need not reveal what I feel, express or avow my feelings,
that I can conceal them from other people. Still, as we have
seen, if there were no such thing as expressing one's feelings,
there could be no such thing as concealing them. We can only
learn to conceal our feelings after we have learned to avow
them.

Pain, I said, does not require the complex background of
human life, though talking about pain does. On the other hand,
both thought and its articulation require this. We learn to think

as we learn to talk and the words in which we express our thoughts are the same words which we learned to use in talking about and describing things and matters which we are thinking of now. We could say that there are as many modes of thought as there are modes of speech. This means *grammars* within which we think and speak. Each grammar has its particular reality or identity within the kind of activities in the weave of which we use language and think. This was the point Malcolm made in connection with *remembering*:

> Memory-images are images that go with remembering and seeming to remember. These latter concepts require something more than imagery; and what could this 'more' be, if there was neither the behaviour nor the language of memory? One is tempted to supplement the imagery with feelings of 'familiarity', 'pastness', or 'fittingness', as philosophers have done. But these inventions could not turn images into memories or make them refer to the past. ('Memory and the Past', *K.C.*, pp. 197–8)

I made a similar point about *imagining* in a paper entitled 'Imagination': 'If there were not an imaginative use of language, the form of life in which such a use of language is embedded – and I am thinking of story-telling, pretending, entertaining hypotheses, and miming – then my having a mental image of X *could not* amount to my simply imagining it, as opposed to, say, my remembering, expecting or wishing to see X' (*Analysis* Jan. 1968).

While we use the word 'pain' in telling someone what we feel and while we may describe the pain we feel as e.g. 'throbbing' or 'sharp', it is otherwise with the words we use in communicating our thoughts. For the latter words do not describe any state we are in; they are not in that way reflexive. They are, one could say, the very substance of the thoughts themselves and through them we are able not just to describe our thoughts, but to think them – i.e. to think about the various things that enter our thoughts.

Thus the relation between sensations, emotions and behaviour, and the relation between thought and human action are different. There are, for instance, no natural reactions and bodily expressions of thought as there are of sensations and many emotions. But still, as I have pointed out, the possibility of thoughts does presuppose certain forms of behaviour. This is obviously relevant to the question 'How do we know other people's thoughts?'. This is important in a full discussion of our knowledge of other people's minds since a knowledge of their thoughts is integral to a knowledge of most things about them. There is obviously very much more to the questions 'How do we know other people's minds?' and 'How is what is mental related to human behaviour?' than I have considered.

I want to repeat that I have been concerned with certain central questions concerning matter, mind and our knowledge of each. But there is a great deal of ground even around the questions on which I have concentrated that I have not covered.

Bibliography

Ambrose-Lazerowitz, Alice, 'Moore's Proof of an External World', *Essays in Analysis* (Allen & Unwin, 1966)
—— 'Ludwig Wittgenstein: A Portrait', *Ludwig Wittgenstein: Philosophy and Language*, ed. Alice Ambrose and Morris Lazerowitz (Allen & Unwin, 1972)
Anscombe, G. E. M., *Intention* (Blackwell, 1957)
Austin, J. L., *Sense and Sensibilia* (Oxford, 1962)
Ayer, A. J., 'The Terminology of Sense-data', *Philosophical Essays* (London: Macmillan, 1954)
Berkeley, George, 'Principles of Human Knowledge' and 'A New Theory of Vision', *A New Theory of Vision and Other Writings* (Everyman's Library, 1950)
Cavell, Stanley, 'Knowing and Acknowledging', *Must We Mean What We Say?*, (New York: Scribner's, 1969)
Descartes, René, *Meditations on First Philosophy* (New York: Liberal Arts Press, 1960)
Dilman, İlham, *Induction and Deduction, A Study in Wittgenstein* (Blackwell, 1973)
—— 'On Wittgenstein's Last Notes (1950–51) On Certainty', *Philosophy*, April 1971
—— 'Paradoxes and Discoveries', *Wisdom: Twelve Essays*, ed. Renford Bambrough (Blackwell, 1974)
—— 'Wittgenstein on the Soul', *Understanding Wittgenstein*, ed. Godfrey Vesey (Macmillan, 1974)
—— 'The Unconscious: A Theoretical Construct?', *The Monist*, July 1972
—— 'Imagination', *Analysis*, January 1968
—— 'An Examination of Sarte's Theory of Emotions', *Ratio*,

December 1963

Dilham, İlham, and Phillips, D. Z., *Sense and Delusion* (Routledge, 1971)

Hume, David, *A Treatise of Human Nature*, ed. L. A. Selby-Bigge
(Oxford, 1967)

James, William, *Principles of Psychology*, vols. 1–2 (London: Macmillan, 1901)

Kant, Immanuel, *Critique of Pure Reason*, trans. Norman Kemp
Smith (Macmillan, 1961)

Lewis, C. I., *Mind and The World Order* (New York: Scribner's,
1929)

Locke, John, *An Essay Concerning Human Understanding*
(Everyman's Library, 1959)

Malcolm, Norman, *Knowledge and Certainty* (Prentice-Hall,
1965) – *K.C.*

—— 'Moore and Ordinary Language', *The Philosophy of G. E.
Moore*, ed. Paul A. Schilpp (New York: The Library of
Living Philosophers, 1952)

—— 'White on Moore', *Mind*, January 1960

—— *Ludwig Wittgenstein, A Memoir* (Oxford, 1967)

—— *Dreaming* (Routledge, 1959)

—— 'Behaviourism as a Philosophy of Psychology', *Behaviourism and Phenomenology*, ed. T. W. Wann (University of
Chicago Press, 1964) – *B.P.P.*

—— 'Wittgenstein on the Nature of Mind', *Studies in the Theory
of Knowledge*, ed. Nicholas Rescher, Amer. Phil. Quart.
Monograph Series, No. 4 – *W.N.M.*

—— 'The Privacy of Experience', *Epistemology: New Essays in the
Theory of Knowledge*, ed. A. Stroll (New York: Harper &
Row, 1967)

McTaggart, Ellis, *Some Dogmas of Religion* (London: Arnold,
1906)

Moore, G. E., *Philosophical Papers* (Allen & Unwin, 1963)

—— 'A Reply to my Critics', *The Philosophy of G. E. Moore*, ed.
Paul A Schilpp, (New York: The Library of Living Philosophers, 1952)

Proust, Marcel, *A La Recherche du Temps Perdu*, vols. 1–3 (N. R.
F., Bibliothèque de la Plèiade, 1954)

Russell, Bertrand, *The Problems of Philosophy* (Oxford, 1950)

Watson, J. B., and McDougall, W., *The Battle of Behaviourism*

(Psyche Miniatures, General Series No. 19, Kegan Paul, 1928)

Wisdom, John, *Other Minds* (Blackwell, 1952) – *O.M.*

—— *Philosophy and Psycho-Analysis* (Blackwell, 1964) – *P.P.A.*

—— *Paradox and Discovery* (Blackwell, 1965) – *P.D.*

Wittgenstein, Ludwig, *Tractatus Logico-Philosophicus*, trans. Pears and McGuinness (Routledge, 1961)

—— *The Blue and Brown Books* (Blackwell, 1958) – *B.B.*

—— *Zettel* (Blackwell, 1967) – *Z.*

—— *Remarks on the Foundations of Mathematics* (Blackwell, 1956)

—— *Philosophical Investigations* (Blackwell, 1963) – *Inv.*

—— *On Certainty* (Blackwell, 1969) – *Cert.*

Index